T0352410

How to Think Like an Officer

How to Think Like an Officer

Lessons in Learning and Leadership for Soldiers and Other Citizens

Reed Bonadonna

STACKPOLE
BOOKS

Guilford, Connecticut

STACKPOLE
BOOKS

Published by Stackpole Books
An imprint of The Rowman & Littlefield Publishing Group, Inc.
4501 Forbes Blvd., Ste. 200
Lanham, MD 20706
www.rowman.com

Distributed by NATIONAL BOOK NETWORK

British Library Cataloguing in Publication Information available

Library of Congress Control Number: 2020940212

Library of Congress Cataloging-in-Publication Data available

ISBN 978-0-8117-3941-2 (cloth : alk. paper)
ISBN 978-0-8117-6937-2 (electronic)

♾™ The paper used in this publication meets the minimum requirements of American National Standard for Information Sciences—Permanence of Paper for Printed Library Materials, ANSI/NISO Z39.48-1992.

For Luke and his Brothers

All things are ready if our minds be so.

—*Henry V*, IV, iii, 71

We are but warriors for the working day.
Our gayness and our gilt are all besmirch'
With rainy marching in the painful field.
There's not a piece of feather in our host—
Good argument, I hope, we will not fly—
And time hath worn us into slovenry.
But, by the mass, our hearts are in the trim.

—*Henry V*, IV, iii, 109–15

There is one right even more important than the right to send
men to their deaths: the right to think twice before you send
men to their deaths.

—Vasily Grossman, *Life and Fate*

Contents

Acknowledgments

I've got [x] years [or months] to get you thinking like an officer.

$\mathcal{I}$ would sometimes use this line talking to midshipmen during my years in the Commandant's Department at the US Merchant Marine Academy. The academy, also known as Kings Point, trains and educates officers for the merchant marine. About 25 percent of all graduates accept active-duty commissions in the armed forces. The rest are required to take a commission in some reserve component. The school is run on military lines with the students ranked as midshipmen, in uniform, and organized into units. My duties as company tactical officer and later as director of Ethics and Character Development put me into contact with the midshipmen in a variety of settings. I taught academic classes, often with a focus on leadership. I participated in the summer training of the new plebes and the military instruction of midshipmen that took place during the academic year. For several years, I was the adviser to the midshipman Honor Board, and I started an ethics club that met weekly and competed in collegiate and military ethics bowls. I sometimes told myself that the thread connecting all of these disparate activities was that I was trying to get the midshipmen to think like officers. Sometimes we would discuss what this meant. My notes and recollections from these discussions comprised the very early beginnings of this book. In a sense, the fact that my institution and all maritime colleges in the United States are run as military schools is one indication of the broad value of officer education. I would sometimes tell my students that if they wanted to blame someone for the fact that Kings Point is a military school, they might go back to Plato, who may be credited in *The Republic* with originating the idea in the West that there was something uniquely edifying about military training. All the guardians of the Platonic state first had to train and serve as auxiliaries, as soldiers and officers. This experience would give them an idea of what it means to serve, of the sharp end of policy and state decisions. It would also (for the more intelligent especially, those fit to pass on to the ranks of the guardians) introduce them to thinking and acting under stress and in matters of great and immediate importance.

I also remember an encounter I had with a member of the faculty (a good friend). She had acted in a way I thought inconsistent with her role as a servant of the academy. In frustration (and affection) I told her, as someone who had never served in uniform, that she "needed to start thinking like an officer!" So this book is also an effort to articulate why I believe that thinking like an officer may be useful to non-officers as well.

When I was speaking to students on this subject, I generally meant that I wanted them to try to think like warfighters, like tacticians and strategists. I sometimes saw in them what I thought was a lack of the killer or predatory instinct needed in a tactician, although sometimes also a lack of knowledge and respect for the laws and conventions of war, for the serious ethical and human consequences of decisions that they might be making in matter of months. I also wanted them to at least start developing a strategic sense, to realize that mere "problem-solving" might not be enough if they were solving the wrong problem, like trying to fix the palace plumbing while Rome burned. When in contact with my fellow faculty members, what I usually meant was thinking like a committed member of an organization, a kind of principled rendering unto Caesar. Finally, I would sometimes remind them of "the day." This was the day, with a big hole in the side of the ship or bad guys in the wire and no comms, when officers have to earn the better pay, bigger cabin, shiny brass, perks, and prestige of the commissioned person. How, I sometimes asked my fellow teachers and officers, do we get them ready for that day? Really, the goal of getting midshipmen to think like officers in time for graduation was at once too limited and overly ambitious, since learning to think is an activity that officers must continue all of their professional lives and even beyond. Otherwise, they will find themselves frequently incapable of meeting the diverse demands of their profession, and of fulfilling their opportunities for continued service once they assume the role of veteran. I came to realize that these opportunities and demands are too large and complex for simple rules or easy formulas, and this book is the result. The multiple cognitive challenges of warfighter, member of an organization, and crisis manager will inform this book, although, in the last chapters especially, I will not stop there.

An early inspiration was hearing Dr. Gregory Reichberg lecture on the nature of military prudence, which led me to read his published writings on the subject.[1] I had touched on the subject of officer thought in a previous book, *Soldiers and Civilization: How the Profession of Arms Thought and Fought the Modern World into Existence*, and after Reichberg and some more research, I felt ready to take on the subject more directly. *How to Think Like an Officer* is in some ways also the product of *Soldiers and Civilization*. Both books combine the descriptive and prescriptive. In *Soldiers and Civilization*, I argued that soldiers had made a broad contribution to the practice of civilization, and that they should continue to do so, rather than narrowly define their role as mere "managers of violence."[2] In that book, I also made the claim that, considered most comprehensively, the profession of arms should be thought of as a subset of the humanities. This theme of both a broad conception and contribution of the military profession is one that I will pursue in the current work. In *How to Think Like an Officer*, I write about how officers think, but also how they ought to think.

In addition to the midshipmen and faculty of Kings Point, many people have contributed to this book. The cadets, officers, and faculty of the Virginia Military Institute started my education in thinking like an officer. This was continued for many years by the thousands of Marines with whom I came into contact during my service, and by the Marine Corps as an institution with its centuries-long traditions of leadership and innovation. I should not omit the officers of the sibling services with whom I also served, since they sometimes introduced me to a broader strain of officer thought. Throughout my career as an officer, teacher, and writer, S. L. A. Marshall's classic *The Armed Forces Officer* (1950/1975) has been a source of instruction and inspiration. It remains the best book on what it means to be an officer in the service of a democracy.

Edited versions of the sections in this book on military prudence and strategy appeared on the website "The Strategy Bridge," and "War on the Rocks" published online a short article on how to think like an officer. I must thank the editors of these publications, perhaps especially Eric Murphy and Usha Sahay, respectively, for their corrections and suggestions, many of which have made it into this work. The *Marine Corps Gazette* published a review of Leo Murray's *War Games* that became the basis for my discussion of the book in my chapter on warfighting.

Some people may be put off by my switches in gender pronouns, either because they find it distracting or because they believe I am trying too hard to be trendy. I can only say that this was my solution to the matter of personal pronouns and I found it strangely liberating.

Finally, I think that being a father made me a better officer (and being an officer made me a better father), so even more than most authors I need to thank my wife and children: Sue, Luke, Devon, and Erik. I named only Luke on the dedication page because, maybe like all last children, he has sometimes felt neglected, and in case there is any merit to this feeling, I'd like to try to even the score.

Introduction

$\mathcal{A}$s I said in the acknowledgments, I used to tell my students at Kings Point that I was trying to teach them how to think like officers. Of course, I was challenged on this. "What do you mean by that exactly, sir?" This book represents an extended effort to answer that quite reasonable question. What is it to think like an armed forces officer? Is there some distinctive mental pattern of officer cognition that can be identified and improved upon? Are there best, most exemplary instances of officer thought? What are the inherent and contingent obstacles and impediments? Can civilians and other non–officers benefit from a greater understanding of how officers think, and can officers benefit from becoming more self-conscious about how they think? I will contend that thinking like an officer is *the* most defining aspect of military professionalism, more than values, character, or knowledge, and that it has been neglected in officer education. There are many books on military tactics, strategy, and leadership, but few if any treat these subjects as matters of thinking, as cognitive challenges that are distinct but also related in that they take place in the officer's mind and within the context of the military culture and profession.

CHALLENGES TO THINKING

The challenges of officer thought are great. Officers fill many roles. They lead, command, advise, and instruct. They operate at various levels, from the rarefied atmosphere of a service headquarters to a "muddy boots" assignment with a small combatant unit. Officers are expected to think clearly under extremely stressful conditions. War is a protean activity that makes enormous and

1

ever-changing cognitive demands. The officer may have to adapt to changing tactical situations and a shifting strategic context. He may have to change roles from organizer to warfighter to diplomat and back again as quickly as a harried plebe dressing for parade amid changes in the uniform. These roles may call for combinations of discipline and creativity, of belligerence and empathy. The breadth (if not always the depth) of cognitive demands that officers can be called upon to meet is perhaps unique among the professions. To attempt to think like an officer is to expand one's mind, and likely in multiple directions at once. The unpredictable nature of military operations also means that the officer, no matter how experienced or educated, must be willing to enter a realm of uncertainty, of nearly imponderable and unprecedented factors brought on by the enemy will, by the uncertain impact of technological change, and by unfamiliar histories and cultures. Officers today are learning about the unfamiliar cultures of the Middle East, with their impact on the motives and actions of combatants and others in the region. They are also absorbing the impact of new technologies, perhaps most significantly of the cybertechnology that is arguably creating a new domain of warfare as significant as those of land, sea, and sky. These cognitive challenges and the officer's way of meeting them define his professional identity more than oaths, or uniforms, or even knowledge.

Along with (and to a degree contrary to) officers' extreme focus and discipline is their need for a wide lens encompassing history, language, psychology, and culture. The military culture of discipline and obedience can be the enemy of clear thinking. History offers many examples of officers who expanded their range of capabilities through broad reading and reflection on their own. While serving as commandant of the US Army Infantry school, George C. Marshall hosted an after-hours discussion group. J. Lawton Collins (like Marshall, a future Army Chief of Staff), recalls the group addressing subjects that "ranged from geopolitics to economics, psychology, or sociology."[1] During my tour as a field historian in Iraq, I interviewed a company commander who was holding discussions with local leaders about establishing democracy in the town that was occupied by his company in the weeks following the invasion. He told me that he had been reading a biography of John Adams on the ship prior to the invasion, and that his reading had given him both inspiration and practical advice about building a new democracy.

THE PROBLEM NOW

There is evidence to suggest that the current caliber of officer thought is inadequate to the demands of the times. The failures of the armed forces to achieve policy goals over the recent past is an indication that officers have not completely mastered the intellectual demands of their profession in this century, though, to be fair, there is blame to go around for military leadership, civilian leadership, and more. In the case of Iraq, unrealistic expectations, short-sightedness, and poor planning contributed to a bloody and protracted conflict, despite the efforts of dedicated professionals like the company commander mentioned previously. Set, inflexible procedures, an emphasis on tactical solutions, and unrealistic theorizing in too many cases ruled out creative thought and solutions, compounding the failures of the civilian leadership.[2]

Concern for improvement in the caliber of officer thought is not limited to the armed forces of the United States. The British Royal Military Academy Sandhurst has been trying out different models for officer thought, adding the word "Reflective" to its model for problem-solving and thinking skills in a 2013 "Occasional Paper."[3] An article co-authored by professors at the Netherlands Defense Academy, "What Sets the Officer Apart?" calls for a redefinition of military professionalism based on thinking skills inculcated through a fusion or dialectic of the abilities of the scholar and soldier.[4]

I am making the assumption that, adequate or not, officer thought can be improved upon by a focused attention that makes use of the historical record, of contemporary events, of some venerable philosophical ideas, and of modern concepts from the cognitive sciences. Officers, as individuals and in groups, have been capable of much distinguished thinking across a wide spectrum. Despite the undeniable room for improvement among officers, being able to think like an officer would benefit many non-officers. This includes aspiring officers, noncommissioned officers and other enlisted members, and some civilians, perhaps especially (although not exclusively) those who work with military officers in the areas of defense, foreign policy, and peace operations. More than this, the breadth of cognitive demands that officers can be called upon to meet is such that few (and I will discuss those few) have been completely equal to the challenge. In addition to thinking about difficult subjects under very demanding conditions, the military profession requires learning that is unceasing and often urgent. The tragic trope of anagnorisis, of a sudden recognition of a hitherto hidden reality, may be part of the officer's experience.

One reason that the caliber of officer thought is inadequate is that the subject per se is generally neglected in military culture and education. There is little encouragement in officer education for thought to become self-conscious, and thereby subject to development. To make an analogy, the service academies used to assume that cadets were absorbing leadership abilities and ethical awareness through the example of the commissioned officers with whom they came into contact, but over the past few decades leadership and ethics have become subjects for formal instruction, discussion, and critique.

The same direct attention should be given to cognition as is now given to leadership. Without this attention, a vital component of officership is left to chance and osmosis, to a vague hope that the study of history, strategy, and other subjects will indirectly cultivate officer thought. Distinguished American combat leader and writer Glover Johns would enjoin his eager and active young subordinates to sometimes just put their feet up and think. The culture, environment, and tight schedule of military organizations can make this an elusive practice, and even time permitting, thinking is a demanding art that must be understood and practiced.

In *Soldiers and Civilization,* I traced the historical evolution of the profession of arms, its contributions, and indebtedness to the broader evolving idea and practice of civilization. I focused on those who not only bore arms but who also exercised authority and leadership: officers and proto-officers, the Greek *strategos,* Roman centurions, and medieval knights. The soldier, I said, is both the least civilized and the most civilized of persons. Warfare, the soldier's defining activity, is destructive of civilized works and attitudes. Soldiers often inhabit a lawless landscape in which force seems to be the only rule, and they run the risk of becoming what they behold. On the other hand, soldiers guard and build as well as destroy. They exercise whatever restraint exists in war. Their professed willingness to serve their societies even at the risk and sacrifice of their lives is perhaps the ultimate mark of the civilized person.

Running through this argument was the theme that the military profession should be considered a subset of the humanities. In its dependence on and contributions to language, its inevitable confrontation with questions of ethics, of community, and even of existence, the military profession both needs and nurtures the humanities. In fact, on reflection, the profession of arms represents not just a subset of the humanities, but its origins. The coming together of organized human societies, as Socrates and others have noted, is inseparable from the origins of armed conflict and of a genus of humanity who bear arms as a profession. The origins of storytelling, of questions of value, of language itself are bound up with those of organized armed conflict and a professional warrior class. Much of this narrative, discourse, and language formation has been undertaken by the soldiers themselves, to include some of the best of them, from Socrates and Aeschylus, to Tolstoy, Grant, and Eisenhower. The soldier may acquire a special knowledge that goes beyond the technical aspects of warfighting, an insight into the human heart. No wonder that the soldier, and perhaps even more often the veteran, is often a philosopher. The officer/veteran has been witness to waste and suffering, to people at their best and worst. Some may return from service isolated and embittered, their sympathies limited to their compatriot veterans, and even with feelings of anger or complicity toward those with whom they served. With greater understanding, and maybe better fortune, they can return home with a heightened sense of human solidarity, tempered by realism concerning the possible, with the moral courage to face unpleasant facts undeterred, and the willingness to take responsibility for past actions and for the shaping of the future.

In this work, although I will address the more mundane aspects of soldier and officer thought, I will steer on this compass bearing: that the officer must think in broadly humanist and far-reaching terms, often as scholar, teacher, writer, scientist, and artist. The officer must overcome institutional, environmental, and psychological impediments to clear thought, some of them particular to military organizations and the practice of warfare, while also cultivating multiple intelligences to meet the demands of military professionalism and to expand them.

Along with this, she should have a proper self-respect based on the long history of her distinguished calling and on the potential for growth and greater understanding that military service can provide. Writing of the British army of Marlborough's time, historian Stephen Saunders Webb calls it, "the greatest school of the age."[5] Although the competition among learning institutions is keener in the modern era than it was in the early eighteenth century, the armed forces remain a great school, especially if the experience of military service is approached in that spirit. The military officer must be open to instruction and critique from outside but not overly deferential to civil expertise from academe, the commercial sector, even from government. As George C. Marshall remarked to President Franklin D. Roosevelt at a meeting when one-star Marshall was Deputy Army Chief of Staff, "I am sorry, Mr. President, but I don't agree with that at all."[6]

Thinking is not all that officers do, but it is an important and neglected activity. My own experience of training future officers as a service academy director of Ethics and Character Development gave me a sense of the importance of ethics and character and also of their limitations absent cognitive abilities. Lieutenant General Harold Moore once noted that officers are expected to display good judgment, which no amount of character or even intelligence will guarantee.[7] A person's character, morals, and even emotions are to a degree dependent on the intellect. Our feelings and character shape our thinking, but thought can also provide a tool to shape character, enabling us to interpret, guide, and control our feelings, and to navigate difficult ethical matters. Teaching at an academy and enjoying a close working relationship with representatives of the other service academies also taught me that the intellectual development of future officers was left largely to the academic departments, mostly leaving aside the question of what might be distinctive about officer thought. The trainers and disciplinarians at the academies sometimes doubted the relevance of the academic instruction, and not entirely without reason, because many of the professors were reluctant, and often unequipped, to connect what they did in the classroom with the preparation of cadets to be officers. The uniformed officers were sometimes impatient and even suspicious of the academic experience and of intellectual development in general, fearing its "liberalizing" influence and tendency to promote doubt and skepticism.[8] Not all soldiers are afraid of thinking, or of too much thinking, but thinking is a demanding art that must be understood and practiced. The art of thinking requires command attention.

Because of the officer's need to engage in thought at many levels and under many difficulties (not all of them obvious), a consideration of officer thought could also be useful to the members of other professions, for whom some of the challenge and versatility involved in thinking like an officer could be very useful. In fact, the professions may learn how to think from each other. One example is *How Doctors Think* by Jerome Groopman, MD.[9] As Dr. Groopman demonstrates, a consideration of professional thought can benefit from reference to some of the recent work in cognitive science. It can also shed light on some claims and theories of cognitive scientists. Indeed, Dr. Groopman (and I) may be heading a new subfield of professionally oriented cognitive studies. This development could enable a wide spectrum of people to do their jobs better.

As I have already said, this book is intended to be both descriptive and prescriptive. Officers have exercised brilliantly clear and creative thinking, but as a group there is room for improvement. The importance of this project has been borne in me over the course of a long career. I remember a young lieutenant outside An Nasiriya, Iraq, the site of the first bitter, at times disorganized, battle of the invasion, asking me why, "after 225 years" we hadn't learned to do things better. This book arrives too late to have an impact on my own service, but I hope that it will help a rising generation of officers avoid the mistakes of their elders, those I have made, those I have witnessed and borne, and those that make more than somber the record of history and the parade of events in our own time.

DO OFFICERS THINK?

Despite some of the foregoing claims, it might be best to acknowledge early on some not-entirely-specious objections to the underlying premise of this work. Civilians, enlisted members, and some officers might well ask, "Really? You mean officers think?" Officers have variously been depicted as upper-class twits, as poseurs and mountebanks, as more physique than brain, more uniform than imagination, more doctrine than original idea. Officers are sometimes seen as directed by custom, habits, training, and orders from above rather than by thought or reason. Officers at entry level do not have the same lengthy postgraduate education as some other professional groups (like physicians and lawyers), and such advanced education as junior officers do receive is perhaps more in the nature of training than of education, and it may even have the effect of undoing some of the curiosity and creativity that they had acquired as undergraduates.[10] Philip Caputo's experience of the "trade school" pedagogy of the Marine Corps Basic School for second lieutenants may be typical in some ways.[11] There is an undeniably anti-intellectual strain in military culture, and even some intelligent officers catch this early on. It is practically a point of honor among officers to be self-deprecating about their intellectual abilities. I was found with a copy of Peter Matthiessen's *Far Tortuga* during a vehicle movement while at Officer's Candidate School, and I remember a gunnery sergeant's scorn at my reading such "weird civilian bullshit." I came to share (or at least imitate) some of the military contempt for anything smacking of the artistic or literary. Although as a junior officer I sometimes felt too busy or too tired for reading, the reading habit crept back on me after a year or two of service, as it did for some of my fellow lieutenants. We also acquired the habit of "professional reading," which the Marine Corps was just beginning to officially endorse in the 1980s, and about which I will have more to say later.

Considered historically and internationally, military officers constitute a large and very diverse group, and almost inevitably they will include examples of incompetence, stupidity, and even wickedness. A 1935 article in *Fortune* magazine captured nicely a precocious paradox in the officer persona, the author describing the army officers he met as "a queer mixture of the clergy, the college professor, and the small boy playing Indian"![12] Despite their deficiencies and peculiarities, military officers are generally held in high regard in the United States and much of the world. Their prestige and privileges along with their uniforms and ranks set them apart, and it may seem sometimes that they are above criticism, both from within and outside the armed forces. As an officer advances in rank, and given the very rank-conscious culture of the military, she comes into contact with fewer and fewer people whom she views and who view themselves as qualified to offer real criticism or register serious disagreement. Outside the military, the deference accorded to service members and to officers in particular may be excessive and harmful, as argued by James Fallows in his much-circulated article, "The Tragedy of the American Military."[13] Absence perhaps makes the deference greater. The American military concentration in a few southern and western states, its sequestration on large bases, and its frequent deployments mean that fewer Americans (and even fewer Europeans, whose military establishments are proportionately much smaller) have as a neighbor someone who is in the armed forces or is even a veteran. In the officer ranks especially, there is a tendency for certain families to send their sons and daughters into the service, while large segments of the society have seen no recent military experience.

WHAT ARE OFFICERS?

Especially given the common deficit in knowledge of the military, it might be useful to define the term "officer," to delineate the officer's historical origins, significance, and societal role. The term "officer" has a common root with the words "office" and "official." As such, it connotes a person who holds a public position, usually within a hierarchy, and involving a degree of authority. The term "officership" has been coined to encompass the condition and defining traits of being an officer.[14] Two aspects of officership are central. These are leadership and the status of the officer as a member of a profession. The theory and practice of leadership on the part of officers will be discussed at length throughout this work. The idea of officership as a profession will occupy us next.

The idea of a profession has been explicated by sociologists and other scholars over the past century. In the years after World War II, writers like Morris Janowitz and Samuel Huntington discussed the senses in which military officers were members of a profession.[15] Members of a profession are distinguished from those in other types of occupation by certain factors. They are generally the products of a combination of higher education and advanced professional education and training. They combine expertise with a humane appreciation of the nature and import of their work and are ideally motivated by an ethos of service. In return for their demonstrable expertise and professional ethos, members of a profession are granted a high degree of respect and autonomy by their societies. Although they may work within an organization, individual members of a profession are thought to possess "portable" capabilities that free them from complete reliance on a bureaucracy. Professional communities are generally permitted to set their own standards for entry and advancement. Medicine is perhaps the "poster child" of professions, with physicians in the lead. The law and lawyers occupy a somewhat disreputable place in the professional pantheon. Other members include the clergy, educators, scientists, engineers, architects, and some highly qualified business and government workers. A profession, and membership in a profession, ultimately resides in a combination of knowledge, belief, and the means used to generate and transmit them. The terms "professional" and "professionalism" are used to describe members of a profession and their conduct, but the terms may also be applied to someone whose conduct approaches or equals professional standards, even if he or she is not strictly speaking a credentialed member of profession. As noted by Pauline Shanks-Kaurin and others, a profession (and perhaps the military profession especially) is to a degree aspirational.[16] All professionals are trying to become the professionals that they profess to be. In fact, it could reasonably be argued that the member of a profession who is satisfied with his professional attainments and capabilities has lost the sense of what it really means to be a professional.

Although the theory of professionalism has been studied and explicated most often by sociologists, professionalism is at least as much a cognitive and epistemological as a sociological construct. Professionals must have the approval and even the cooperation of the larger society in order to fulfill their society role (and this approval and cooperation is perhaps uniquely vital to military officers), but prior to this acceptance a profession must establish for itself the terms of the knowledge and belief that will define it, and also how such belief and knowledge are to be instilled, inhered, and improved upon.

THE EDUCATION OF OFFICERS

Education is a major aspect of military professionalism and officer cognition. Through a highly developed system of service academies, schools, and commands the US armed forces invest huge resources of time and money on officer education. Officer education begins before commissioning, at one of the service academies, in a Reserve Officer Training Corps (ROTC) unit or at an Officer Candidate School (OCS). For commissioned officers, opportunities for formal advanced education in the form of Professional Military Education (PME) and graduate school occur at every stage of promotion. Resident PME occurs on a selective basis at the career, intermediate, and top levels. The Top Level Schools (TLS) are the various war colleges, both joint- and service-specific. Attendance at graduate school may be said to produce a number of diverse outcomes. Officers obviously acquire knowledge, some of it scientific or technical, some of it historical, philosophical, and even literary. At the PME schools they learn about warfighting, with the emphasis evolving from the tactical to the operational to the strategic levels as they move up the rank and PME hierarchy. The PME experience also helps to build relationships among promotable officers of the same grade. Civilian graduate school has the benefit of developing relations between civilian and military communities and individuals. Advanced education, whether PME or graduate school, both reinforce institutional values and hold them up for examination. Perhaps the most important (although usually implicit) function of both military PME and graduate school for officers is the degree to which they teach officers how to think, presumably with increasing knowingness, rigor, and creativity. How exactly this is taking place may be the subject of a certain amount of reflection on the part of the officer-students, their teachers, and superiors. Officers may also learn to think on their own and on the job, as they pursue personal courses of reading and writing, reflect on their own and others' mistakes and success, and participate in the local and informal officer education that is conducted at some units. Military organizations, as well as military schools are, at least ideally and professedly, "learning institutions."

In recent years, there have been several voices raised to suggest that the armed forces of the United States and other developed countries have not done enough to develop their intellectual capital. Retired officers David Petraeus, Rupert Smith, David Kilcullen, Daniel Boger, and John Nagl, all of them drawing on active service in the Middle East, have written about the need for armed forces to diversity the skills and knowledge that they can bring to bear on complex problems, to include especially those that lie in the shadowy domain between "purely" military operations and the act of nation-building, whether that domain is described as counterinsurgency, or stability operations, or peacekeeping, or by another term from the military professional vocabulary.[17] Part of the solution may be to develop a broader base of knowledge within the officer ranks and armed forces, to send more officers to graduate school and to PME. A more rigorous approach might be taken to officer education. The officer corps, as a body and as individuals, should also be encouraged to be more self-reflective about how they think, and how examples from the past and emerging modern knowledge might make them better thinkers with a diverse repertoire of diagnostic, creative, and problem-solving abilities.[18]

There is an ancient paradox to military life. When George Orwell wrote of "the essential horror of army life," he meant the dangers and deprivation of being on campaign, but others have used this phrase to describe the boredom and stultification of the soldier's existence.[19] Military organizations can be insular, tribal, and atavistic. Leaving the military is often experienced as uniquely liberating and humanizing. On the other hand, many experience military life as a special and privileged time, as a chance to do work that could be fully engaging across the spectrum of human experience, and that might be very important in the lives of others, in a historical context, and even in an ontological sense. Military service may be both a devouring and a defining experience. Both halves of this paradox may be felt most keenly by the sensitive and intelligent person, whether officer or no, but the university-educated officer with sufficient imagination may feel relief on leaving the service and yet experience an abiding sense that nothing he does afterward quite has the significance of his years in uniform.

"THE MILITARY MIND"

Most past writing on how officers think has been concerned with what is sometimes referred to as "The Military Mind." The leading example of this is undoubtedly Samuel Huntington in his groundbreaking *The Soldier and the State*.[20] Huntington and his fellow military sociologists, however, have been mainly concerned with what officers believe rather than with how they think. In this sphere, the conclusions he draws are reasonable, although it may also be said that they reflect conventional attitudes toward military officers. Officers are conservative and realistic or pessimistic about human nature and its potential for perfectibility. Their experience and reading of history tell them that humankind is too prone to violence and injustice to make likely a state of perpetual peace, especially if one considers that, given the many other forms of violence and repression, peace consists in more than the absence of war. Huntington and other sociologists are mainly concerned with the attitudes that shape an officer's role in the larger society, not with how an officer performs his or her professional role. To fill this gap, we must go beyond belief and ideology to examine patterns of thought.

In this work, I make frequent references to the thinking of a select group of officers whose professional thought was outstanding and who left behind memoirs and other accounts that trace their intellectual development and their thought processes on a number of different subjects, from the commonplace to the profound and philosophical, representing the broad range of cognition officers have learned and practiced. In this pantheon of great officer-writers, I include Ulysses S. Grant, Joseph Collins, Joseph Stilwell, Dwight D. Eisenhower, and William Slim. Towering over all is George C. Marshall. Marshall did not write memoirs of his service in World War II but of the years following for which he is famous and universally admired.[21] Fortunately, he conducted a lengthy series of interviews with historian Forrest Pogue that were recorded, so that we can hear the great man's voice as he reflects on his early life and career, service as Army Chief of Staff, Secretary of Defense, and Secretary of State. These interviews were also an important source for Pogue's four-volume biography of Marshall and the succeeding biographies that continue to appear. Marshall's combination of character and intellect, the candor and modesty of his reflections, and his interest and involvement in the education of officers and in selecting and preparing them for positions of great responsibility make him an outstanding source and subject for a work on how officers ought to think and be taught to think. His injunction to subordinates that they should not be better at feeling than at thinking has been one of my guideposts while writing this book. Our feelings are important, often acting as a kind of cryptic moral sense, but an officer is paid to think in situations in which thought is difficult and emotions may be overwhelming.[22]

In this work I also, modestly and I hope not too obtrusively, draw on my own experiences as an officer and teacher of officers and future officers. One of the reasons I entered the service was that I was fascinated by the intellectual challenges of such areas as tactics and leadership, and in teaching others I have found that this motive is far from unique. In addition to my own periods under instruction at OCS, The Basic School, Infantry Officers Course, and the reserve versions of Amphibious Warfare School and Command and Staff College, I was an instructor of midshipmen at Kings Point and in the Marine Enlisted Commissioning and Education Program, and of serving officers as adjunct faculty for the nonresident Command and Staff Course. Of course, all military service is a matter of teaching and learning, even if not at the "schoolhouse." I have kept many notebooks and a few journals, particularly of my deployment to Iraq in 2003, and these have been helpful to me in recalling how I (finally) learned to think like an officer.

"OFFICERS: MAKING SIMPLE SHIT HARD SINCE 1775"

I am aware that my focus on the officer ranks might strike some as elitist. In fact, I hope that by elucidating officer thought I will be demystifying it as well. In this I will be joining efforts to bridge what has been called "the gap": the disparity in professional education and cognition between the ranks of officers and enlisted persons, even among the most senior enlisted ranks.[23] As the t-shirt slogan above about making the simple difficult illustrates, there has often seemed to be a cognitive culture gap between officer and enlisted ranks. A debate in recent years has concerned which military members deserve the right to be considered as members of a profession. Some would deny this status to enlisted members because their ranks do not require advanced education. Others argue that senior enlisted members have more claim to professional status than do many officers, reservists, and junior, short-service officers among them. The argument for more inclusiveness can be countered by a concern that such a leveling might result in a dumbing-down of the military profession, perhaps recalling Gibbons's observation that the Romans had elevated war to an art, but then debased it to a trade. The officer corps has been democratized, but it still constitutes a distinct group, with its own credentials and culture. Passage from enlisted to officer ranks is more marked and more limited than ordinary advancement within the officer and enlisted ranks, respectively. The distinctiveness of the officer body is likely here to stay. However, this does not rule out an inclusive approach that seeks to "raise all boats." Given the relatively small size but generally ample resources of the current US armed forces, is it too much to ask that all ranks be trained and educated to occupy positions above their nominal ranks? To render complex matters simple is a worthy goal, as long as we do not oversimplify. There are hard problems to be solved, and the more minds that can be put to the task, the better for all.

One of the distinguishing features of officer thought over the centuries in effect lies outside the purely mental realm. Officers have been the masters at translating thought, or ideas, into action. For officers, thought is a prelude to action. This is both an advantage and a limitation, but if it can be transcended when necessary, the officer's "bias for action" is something that officers and non-officers alike should seek to cultivate. The self-consciousness and self-justification of mental activity is valuable, but so is the "I think therefore I do" of the officer not content with what goes on inside his own head. Officers are scholars, but generally with the purpose of becoming better officers, not better scholars. Several distinguished soldiers have been would-be academics, or men who were drawn to academic pursuits after their service. These include the elder von Moltke, Robert E. Lee, Ulysses S. Grant, and Dwight D. Eisenhower. Some of the best officers have been distinguished by a great desire to learn more than their roles strictly required, and by an impatience at the limitations of military life.

Perhaps more than other professional group officers must beware what is sometimes called the *deformation professionelle*, which is both an addiction to a certain way of thinking and the misperception that such professional lines of thought describe the entire human condition. It is a paradox that we shall return to that the most complete officer is the one who is sometimes able to lay professional thinking aside, to embrace other identities and modes of thought, and to enlarge what it means to think like an officer.

Several themes I hope will emerge throughout this book. These include the importance of considering ends as well as means, of learning as well as doing, of meaning as much as "mission accomplished," and of a concern for lives and values: leading like people matter. Military officers see people at their best and worst. They experience the heights of heroism and the depths of barbarity. They know the value of civilization because they have been at its ragged edge. Over the past few years, voices within the military have been raised decrying the erosion of the practice and idea of officership as a profession. Some officers believe that they have been relegated to the status of bureaucrats and functionaries by excessive supervision from the military chain of command and by civil authority. If these complaints have merit (and I think that they do), I contend that the professional status of the military profession is largely in the hands of the officer corps and of individual officers. Most officers are physically fit, disciplined, and committed to their mission. The greatest scope and need for improvement lies in the mental arena, and abetting such improvement is an aim of this book.

THINKING AND LEADERSHIP

I have organized this book into two main sections: "Thinking and Learning" and "Thought and Action," both divided into chapters. In the first section, I offer some thoughts and ideas about thinking. Some of these are derived from cognitive science and philosophy. I then discuss how thinking, and officer thought in particular, can be learned. I devote a chapter to the importance of reading to thinking. I next discuss some particularly military impediments to thinking. In the section on intellectual virtues, I go inside the mind of the officer to illuminate the different approaches to thinking that her profession may require. These approaches, as defined by Aristotle, are art, science, moral prudence, wisdom, and intuition. To borrow an analogy used by Ludwig Wittgenstein for language, the intellectual virtues are like a toolkit; some are more suitable for specific tasks and situations than others, some are more broadly useful, like a plumber's wrench, but all may have their uses in an uncertain future.

The second half of this book is called "Thought and Action." This is where I map out the thinking of officers with respect to the challenges that they may face. I define the main arenas or categories of officer thought as organizer, warfighter, and visionary. Under organizer I include selection, training and education, command, force structure, and doctrine. I divide warfighting into tactics, operations, and strategy. In the final chapter on the officer as visionary, I address the officer's larger societal role and higher cognitive challenges, challenges that go beyond the officer's professional province as usually defined, but which I consider no less essential, partly because they have been overlooked.

I add to the book a conclusion focusing on what civilians can learn about thinking from officers. Officer thought may be useful in a variety of group undertakings that require a combination of discipline, esprit de corps, and leadership. The officer's organizational and tactical sense are also valuable (as many former officers have learned) outside the military setting. Officers are not the only people who accomplish important missions under the pressures of time, in direct competition, and under various forms of adversity. However, their experience of these challenges is often uniquely immediate; lives are at stake, ethical implications are sharpened, events and decisions weigh heavy, and they take place in a context of history and of centuries of professional self-consciousness.

I hope that one of the benefits of this book will be to introduce the reader to many other works on the military profession and its challenges. These works in turn have bibliographies and reading lists of their own. I leave it to the reader to compile her own personal reading list based on the bibliography in this work and in others. Under required reading, I might include *The Armed Forces Officer*, either in the original 1950 or 1975 edition, still likely the greatest book on officership, the book you hold now not excepted. Another book I highly recommend is one of the last I consulted in the preparation of the current work. This is *War Games: The Psychology of Combat* by Leo Murray, a retitled version of the 2013 *Brains and Bullets*, and one of the most exciting books on tactics ever written. Among shorter works, Michael Howard's "The Use and Abuse of Military History" stands out for its conciseness and common sense.

I

THINKING AND LEARNING

*M*any philosophers have concerned themselves with questions regarding what it means to think. These ideas may seem remote to the ordinary problems that officers have to address, but they highlight the power of thinking, although perhaps also its limitations. Mere thinking cannot always make it so, although sustained thought, married to a willingness and capacity to act, can be powerful indeed and even fraught with hazard. The Western tradition of cognitive psychology probably begins with Aristotle. The clarity and rationality of his ideas will be very helpful in the coming chapter on officers and the intellectual virtues. A significant moment in the progress of self-consciousness on the matter of thinking undoubtedly occurs over two thousand years later with Rene Descartes, whose *cogito ergo sum*, "I think; therefore I am," began a philosophical debate on the ontological significance of thought that continues today. Descartes's formulation has some affinity with idealism, which may be said to begin with Bishop George Berkeley in the eighteenth century. Idealism holds that we create the world in our heads, in fact that thought, the idea (we spirits and our ideas, for Berkeley), is all that there really is. Immanuel Kant gave great philosophical importance to thought through his emphasis on reason. Not quite as much a dualist as Descartes, Kant nevertheless mapped out a separate space for the exercise of reason, one that could seem almost autonomous from the world outside. This view was soon challenged by Hegel and his followers, who gave more importance to historical and social forces than to the exercise of the individual reason. The twentieth-century philosophy of existentialism in a sense returned thought to its central philosophical position. We are not made, but we rather create ourselves and the world in our minds.

Philosopher of education John Dewey, whose *How We Think* was published in 1910 and is still in print, addressed the practical matters of clear thinking and its impediments. Unsurprisingly, Dewey is very interested in how thinking can be taught. A rationalist like Aristotle, he is a believer in rigorous, sequential critical thinking who also recognizes the many psychological, cultural, and practical obstacles to clear thought. Dewey argues for the cultivation of a state of constant questioning and dissatisfaction with conventional wisdom or easy answers. Dewey's major concern seems to be the elimination of unexamined and misleading beliefs, superstitions, and prejudices. His approach to thinking can be applied to the kinds of problems encountered by officers. Military questions often involve the need to face unpleasant facts without avoidance or denial. Also, the solutions to tactical and other warfighting questions are often hidden in a fog of enemy movements and intentions, of relative strengths and weaknesses, of the nature and larger purpose of the immediate conflict. The solutions to these problems often go far beyond a tactical playbook or the mere application of maneuvers learned and practiced in training, or even read in the pages of history. For these situations, the officer must have a restlessly inquisitive approach to command that is hungry for facts, open to the observations and suggestions of others, that is skeptical of both early impressions and fixed ideas. To quote a favorite line of Harold K. Johnson as commandant at the US Army Command and General Staff College at Fort Leavenworth, "Question the Assertion," or in George C. Marshall's often repeated question, "Why do you say that?"

Since Dewey, writers from different disciplines have written about what it is to think, and some have even placed these ideas in professional contexts. Groopman's *How Doctors Think* is an example. Officers can learn a number of important lessons from Dr. Groopman's observations about physicians, such as his discussion of the importance of language, of speech especially. Physicians and officers both spend much of their time talking and listening, but their training involves little practical instruction in either of these practices. Physicians and officers are both trained to use deliberate analytic processes, but in the clinic and field they often rely on instinctive "pattern recognition" to make decisions. Physicians may be led astray by their emotions; either affection or antipathy for a patient may lead to error. The officer may be even more beset and led astray by feelings of fear and hatred, of comradeship and loyalty. Other causes for physician misdiagnosis are reminders of sources of military error. Physicians and officers can get too wedded to rigid guidelines (sometimes referred to as heuristics), neglect the importance of language in favor of a reliance on technology, make assumptions based on a prior diagnosis, or engage in "hindsight bias," crediting themselves with greater prescience than they displayed.

William Carlos Williams was a doctor-poet whose interests went beyond diagnosis. In "The Practice" he writes,

All day long the doctor carries on this work, observing, weighing, comparing values of which neither he nor his patients may know the significance. He may be insensitive. But if in addition to actually being an accurate craftsman and a man of insight he has the added quality of—some distress of mind, a restless concern with the. . . . If he is not satisfied with mere cures, if he lacks ambition, if he is not content to. . . . If there is no content in him and likely to be none; if in other words, without wishing to force it, since that would interfere with his lifelong observation, he allows himself to be called a name! What can one think of him?

Williams's curious physician tries to peer into the mystery and motives of his patients, to see them as individual humans and as representative of humanity, as the stuff of poetry. This can be a model for the officer who desires a deeper understanding of the situations in which she finds herself, of the people around her, of her own inner self and the nature of her calling.

Another writer-physician whose work officers would do well to take in is the neurologist Oliver Sacks. Sacks's approach to medicine is literate and literary. It goes beyond diagnosis to embrace understanding and empathy. In effect Sacks was (consciously) going back to an earlier, nineteenth-century medical profession that sought to cultivate a relationship with the patient and to construct a narrative of his condition.[1] Some of this was determined in the past by the absence of diagnostic methods and technology, but even the advent of these aids does rule out a humanistic approach to medicine. The same can be said of the military profession. Technology and procedures have not reduced the officer's reliance on language and understanding. In some regard they have made words and empathy more immediate, because they are more ringed about by a bodyguard of machines and bureaucracy.

It might be said that there are two approaches to thinking about thinking. The first concerns the encouragement of good thinking, often with an emphasis on curiosity and creativity. The second is more concerned with the avoidance of error. Most writers on thought will address both goals, while usually emphasizing one or the other. In his work on *Curiosity*, Alberto Manguel explores the paths and limits of curiosity. He observes that Homer's Ulysses seeks knowledge boldly, even recklessly, resulting in the death of his shipmates and others. His curiosity is like an unquenchable addiction. Even bad (pointless, excessive, impious) curiosity can have a purpose, however. Ulysses's tale could not be so fascinating (or instructive) if it had not pushed the limits of acceptable curiosity. Dante's search for knowledge in the *Inferno* is more humble and regretful, but he is almost guiltily entranced by the scenes of the damned. For the officer, the sublime landscape of the battlespace, whether it be of earth, sea, sky, or all three, combined with the power to command enjoyed by Ulysses, may add up to a guilty knowledge of the violence and barbarism so close beneath the surface of civilization.

To think creatively and with curiosity is to let the mind go free. To avoid error is to self-consciously hold the mind in check, controlling rather than giving free rein to natural propensities. Since the doctor and the officer both wield the power of life and death, and they are often granted great authority and latitude, it may be understandable and right that their professional emphasis is on the avoidance of error, although this can lead to caution and conformity. The officer, like the scientist, the doctor, even the artist, may possess or seek out what Roger Shattuck calls "forbidden knowledge" that extends the range of the permissible, that has the potential to harm the person who has it and those around her.[2] The officer's possession of expertise in weapons of death, to include weapons of mass destruction, may strike others or even herself as unholy and impious because it can bestow god-like power, or put the officer in a relationship with death too familiar for any mortal.

Another writer on thinking is Gordon Rattray Taylor, author of the modern classic *A Natural History of the Mind*.[3] Taylor reviews the theories and empirical approaches to defining and measuring human intelligence. In the chapter "Thinking about Thinking" he attempts to understand thinking itself. In Taylor's account, while there may be a place for pure cognition, it is a rather limited one, and perhaps reserved to "clever idiots" who are capable of complex mathematical calculations or other specialized mental functions, but whose range of understanding is often below average, and sometimes far below. Thinking is influenced by the emotions, by beliefs, by motivation, even by feelings of connectedness to others, because such feelings can fuel the ability to group together data, to discern patterns and their relations to concepts. For the officer, this links feeling of esprit de corps to problem-solving, both subjects about which I will have more to say later.

Another insight of Taylor's (actually the work of another cited by him) is the possibility for regress into "paleological" thinking. This primitive, pre-rational thought may lie close to the surface in the minds of even disciplined combatants, in addition to being responsible for the feelings of individual and group antipathy that cause and prolong wars. Indeed, the officer may sometimes feel herself to be the rational servant of atavistic impulses, or even as someone who unleashes irrational, uncontrollable forces in the service of a putatively rationally conceived state policy. Here we find the paradox of Clausewitz's remarkable trinity of passion, reason, and chance, represented for him by the people, the government, and the army. Perhaps she may also be reminded of the verse from Aldous Huxley's *Ape and Essence*,

Surely it's obvious.
Doesn't every schoolboy know it?
Ends are ape-chosen; only the means are man's.
Papio's procurer, bursar to baboons,
Reason comes running, eager to ratify;
Comes a catch-fart, with philosophy, truckling to
tyrants;
Comes, a pimp for Prussia, With Hegel's Patent
History;
Comes with Medicine to administer the Ape-King's
aphrodisiac;
Comes, Rhyming and with Rhetoric, to write his
orations;
Comes with Calculus to aim his rockets
Accurately at the orphanage across the ocean;
Comes, having aimed, with incense to impetrate
Our Lady devoutly for a direct hit.[4]

• 1 •

Learning to Think

$\mathscr{L}$earning how to think like an officer is a process that ought to begin very early and continue throughout a career and beyond. Former officers may be in a better position to explore, expand, and share their own thinking than those still serving, given their greater time and freedom for reflection, even for testing limits in the manner of Ulysses. Most young people who set their sights on becoming officers have been inspired by stories of officers and other military leaders of the past. Along with the inspiration often comes the desire to emulate, to act, and therefore to think like their exemplars. My own interest in military service was strongly fueled by reading. Biographies of generals George S. Patton and Lewis B. "Chesty" Puller that I read in high school cemented my desire to attend the Virginia Military Institute (VMI) and enter the Marine Corps. At VMI, I caught the prevailing idolatry of George C. Marshall, and I would (and sometimes still do) often ask myself, "What would George C. Marshall do?" in a sense trying to understand Marshall's thought patterns and to recreate them.

In this section, I will address several different ways in which the capacity for officer-like thought can be cultivated. The topics include formal education and instruction, reading, reflection and writing, and mentoring. The section on reading includes discussions of several different genres. Combined with the other enablers of the capacity for thought, broad reading can both enhance and expand competence, helping the officer to avoid the trap of narrow competence, of limited concerns and sympathies.

FORMAL EDUCATION

The shortcomings of much officer education have been alluded to in the introduction. PME can encourage "groupthink." It is generally better at imparting information than at developing critical thinking skills. "Professionalism" can come to be equated with a "playbook" mentality, or even worse with the mere mastery of technical jargon.[1] Thomas Ricks and Timothy Challans are two contemporary writers who have been extremely critical of military education in the United States. Ricks targets the neglect of strategy in favor of the lower levels of warfare. Challans finds much military education shallow and insular, the cadets at West Point being offered a smorgasbord of facts, with little chance for selection or reflection. Both are critical of what they perceive as a lack of rigor and a generally anti-intellectual bias.[2] In the following pages and in the chapter on the officer as organizer, I will suggest some solutions to this bias and to the limitations of PME.

The periods of formal military education in an officer's career are at least presumptively the times when she is most involved in self-consciously improving her ability to think. Formal education may do this by increasing the officer's fund of knowledge, the raw material of thought, and by forcing her to think through and answer questions and solve the kinds of problems that she might encounter in the next stage of her career. The contact at PME with other officers can broaden the student's perspective and range of available experience, of "data," to be mined and referenced as the problems of the future arise. In a sense, the officer in a service school is acquiring the institutional knowledge of his branch and of the officer body, often to include some officers of allied nations. In one of the interviews that he conducted with historian Forrest Pogue in the 1950s, General Marshall noted the importance and influence of institutional wisdom. During a discussion of some changes that he had initiated as commander of the Infantry School at Fort Benning, Marshall had this to say:

> As I have said several times, this puts me in the embarrassing position of seeming to be the one who knew. Well, as a matter of fact, throughout all of this, I'm largely recording my reactions to the experiences of the AEF and later training the army when I was with General Pershing, and my own experiences in those schools.[3]

Marshall saw himself not so much as a person of special abilities or even knowledge, so much as the repository and conduit of much institutional knowledge. If he had a special trait (along with his great humility), it was perhaps his receptivity and retention of knowledge that was there for the taking.

Formal military education can do much. It can impart up-to-date information, focusing on the knowledge most needed at a certain stage of a military career. It can develop the corporate sense of an officer body. It can provide the time and tools for reflection that may be lacking in the busy world of warriors for the working day, in the field or in garrison, in times of war or peace. Finally, however, even the most assiduously educated officer, the graduate of service schools and even of civilian graduate school, must take responsibility for her own intellectual development. After graduating from Sandhurst, Winston Churchill undertook a program of reading and writing that he saw as an effort to learn the English language as if it were a foreign tongue. In his memoir, Joseph "Lightning Joe" Collins recalled that the West Point curriculum, although largely technical, left time for reading, so that he was able to develop a taste for literature that lasted throughout his life and that contributed to the humanity and common sense that characterized his service.[4] His knowledge of poetry often gave him an apt quotation with which to succinctly express his thoughts on a subject. In James Webb's novel of the Vietnam-era Naval Academy, *A Sense of Honor* (1981), the midshipmen are seen being turned into officers by the school's rigorous academic program and disciplined environment, but many also pursue a course of development apart from, and even in opposition to, the established curriculum and existing policies. A midshipman headed for a Marine Corps commission conducts morning runs, sometimes with a plebe in tow, along the academy seawall, developing fitness and fortitude in an unauthorized act. His mentor is a combat veteran Marine captain beset with personal problems and chafing under the sometimes petty and demeaning regime of a military academy. The captain tells the midshipman that it is part of his job as an officer to be sensitive, strong but not brutal, in a sense going against the prevailing Academy code of stoicism and rigid suppression of feelings.

One of the important aspects of formal military education is that it is a group undertaking. This is modified somewhat in the case of distance education conducted away from centers of learning like Leavenworth, Newport, or Quantico, but even distance education provides for some student interaction with instructors and other officer students. Formal military education is a form of socialization as well as of education. It can be a time for questioning, an escape from the more conformist and "just get on with it" atmosphere of an operational unit. Formal military education also gets out of the classroom. War games and staff rides are a regular part of formal military education, contributing to an officer's spatial, tactical, and historical sense.

THE SOCIAL SIDE: PEERS AND MENTORS

The highly social aspect of military life creates an atmosphere in which officers can learn how to think from one another. Although much of this interaction and instruction occurs informally and without direction, some military commands have tried to institutionalize and lend support to such practices as coaching and mentoring. Coaching and mentoring both usually involve a junior and a senior. The goal of coaching is narrower and generally focused on a single problem or capability. Mentoring aims at broader professional development. Peers may also enter into a relationship that helps to develop the ability to think of the officers involved. We are often blind to our own faults and shortcomings, and startling things happen when we listen to each other.

One of the most famous mentors in American military history was General Fox Conner. At different times in the years encompassing World War I and World War II, Conner mentored Dwight Eisenhower and George C. Marshall. Conner recognized early the capabilities of these two men, and he foresaw that their talents might be needed in a major future war. Conner and Marshall met in France while Conner was operations officer of the American Expeditionary Force (AEF) headquarters in Chaumont and Marshall was operations officer at the First Division.[5] Conner would spend one day a week at division headquarters working with Marshall. Later, Conner had Marshall transferred to AEF headquarters to assist him in the operations section. When the First American Army became operational, Conner moved Marshall down to take over as Army operations officer. Conner was worried that Pershing had taken on too much by insisting on taking command of the First Army while retaining command of the AEF, and he wanted Marshall in a key position where he could make up for times when Pershing might be distracted. Marshall derived some important lessons from the relationship with Conner: the importance of seeing the ground and not relying on reports for all information, also the value of competition, since Conner would sometimes pit officers against each other by having them work independently on plans for the same operation, eventually backing the planner and plan that seemed to him to have the most promise. Marshall would later devise ways to test officers before sending them off to command or to otherwise operate independently. The regard that the two men held for one another did not go unnoticed, and they were sometimes referred to (perhaps not without some irony and envy) as a "mutual admiration society."[6] For his part, Conner came to consider Marshall "nothing short of a genius."[7] After the war, Conner asked George Patton to recommend a junior officer to be his executive officer. Patton unhesitatingly recommended Major Dwight Eisenhower and, in the manner of the regular army at that time, after some socializing and personal appeals to old comrades in positions of authority over officer assignments, Eisenhower followed Conner to Panama and the 20th Infantry Regiment. The relationship between Conner and Eisenhower was as much of friendship as of mentorship. The two fished and rode together. Their wives were constant companions. Recognizing that Eisenhower still felt an antipathy to historical study (a result of the rote-learning methods of West Point), Conner started him on military fiction, then progressed to more difficult works.[8] Not all of their readings were military. Conner and Eisenhower read Shakespeare and Nietzsche. They studied biographies of Civil War generals to assess their decisions, and they tackled Clausewitz. Conner had Eisenhower write a daily operations order for his command, an exercise that Eisenhower would later say prepared him to craft the orders for the large organizations that he commanded in World War II. Before meeting Conner, Marshall and Eisenhower both had established reputations in the army as top performers, but Conner saw the potential for growth as well as the talent in his two subordinates. Interestingly, all three men had been average to mediocre students in their undergraduate days at West Point and VMI. Active service, advanced military education, and contact with a senior officer mentor had been required to develop latent abilities and interests. Conner seems to have had an instinct for what was missing in the education of a junior, and perhaps also in what direction his best talents might lie. Marshall went on to become the army's greatest staff officer, and Eisenhower its greatest senior commander, although neither had ever commanded tactical units in combat. Together, they formed the indispensable partnership that would organize, command, and hold together the allied coalition in World War II, while providing strategic vision and an unflagging grasp of the human dimensions of war.

One of the greatest mentoring guides was written by a soldier who had forsaken the sword. This was Ignatius Loyola, whose *Spiritual Exercises* were likely inspired while he was recovering from a wound suffered at the Siege of Pamplona in 1521. Loyola's laying aside of the sword was literal, since he placed his sword before the statue of the Virgin of Montserrat, but in a figurative sense his approach represents a fusion of the military officer and the clergyman. Even his choice of the latin title "*Exercitia spiritualia*" evokes the Roman word for army, "*exercitus*," reflecting the Roman identification of the army with ceaseless training. Loyala's guide is intended to be read by the "spiritual director," the religious mentor of the student undergoing the exercises. This regimen of meditation, contemplation, and prayer is quite demanding, especially when combined with the cloistered and ascetic surroundings in which it was meant to be conducted. Loyola emphasizes "*discretio*," an ability to distinguish the greater from the lesser course, even when the distinction might be clouded. The spiritual protege is in search of self-knowledge as much as of faith. Loyola's *Exercises* unite the dedication and self-denial required of the religious and military professional and practitioner. It may not be an exaggeration to describe his twenty-eight-day intensive program as a spiritual "boot camp" (although he allows for a more spread-out, "distance education" version!). The combination of commitment and self-knowledge seen in Loyola's exercises might also be described as the classical mold for military mentoring, and not without its secular uses today.

Not all mentoring is senior to junior. One of the most famous examples of peer mentoring in military history was that of Grant and Sherman in the American Civil War.[9] Although Grant was in command, they were contemporaries. (In fact Sherman was older.) The imperturbable Grant and the volatile Sherman retained their essential traits of character, but their ideas as well as their personalities complemented one another, and they learned from each other different approaches to command and warfighting. Although he was often uncomfortable with others, Grant welcomed the conversation of the uninhibited Sherman. Grant was known for keeping his own counsel, but perhaps due in part to his very open relationship with Sherman, his headquarters was host to a stream of senior officers whom he welcomed to share their views on operations. Grant learned from Sherman that it was not always the rebel armies that were the objective, but sometimes the confederacy itself: its productive capacity, infrastructure, confidence, and will to win. In a sense this approach was itself a logical next step to Grant's relentless, attritional, total war strategy, which Sherman had absorbed from Grant.

It is especially important that junior officers are prepared to learn from their subordinates. Many junior officers report to their first command frankly insecure and unwilling to admit any gaps in their knowledge. It might be helpful to him to address his first platoon or naval division thus—

> I have the advantage over you of having had the benefit of a lengthier education, and I'm coming from a recent course of training. You have the advantage of practical experience. You all know much more about your individual jobs in the unit than I do. If we are open to learn from each other, we are almost guaranteed of a successful tour/cruise/deployment.

My own experience includes several examples of informal learning from peers and unofficial mentors. I kept a notebook of my experiences of my first two company commanders: the good, the bad, the instructive. One man was faultlessly correct, but also forbidding and unapproachable. The other was rough of manner and even sometimes publicly insulting, but he may have been the better leader and tactician. I also remember an exercise in which my New England reserve infantry battalion was subordinated to a fighter aircraft group based in Texas. A deeper cultural divide can scarcely be imagined! But we came together to conduct the training exercise that we had been ordered to execute. The infantryman showed the aviators the outlines and limits of our earth-bound battlefield, while the aviators gave us an idea of the possibilities of movement through the air, where speed and distance take on different meanings from those on land. The cement of this mutual learning was a growing feeling of comradeship and healthy competition.

THOUGHT AND CHARACTER

The officer's most prized possession is or ought to be his character. I allude to the importance of character in other parts of this book, most particularly in the section on moral prudence. In this section, I will take on character as at least a cognitive challenge. In fact, I will suggest that the distinction between mind and character is not as sharp as is sometimes understood. Like other human capacities, character may be partly innate, or a matter of accident and outside influence, but we may also consciously think ourselves into character.

Since Aristotle, character has been thought to be based on habit. In humans, who are less guided than animals by blind instinct, and still less like inanimate objects that may assume a certain shape from use and environment, habits require the intervention of the conscious mind to acquire, apply, and adapt them. Some habits may creep up on us unawares, and we may even find ourselves one day with a character (not necessarily a bad one) that has been acquired willy-nilly, and without intention. This is the power of the environment to shape us. In fact, most military institutions aim at the development of character, and include "character building" as part of their stated mission. Character development is thought to be imparted both by exposure to the cultures of these institutions and also (more recently) by programs specifically aimed at character development and assessment. Even at the service academies, however, where character is "on the menu" (and perhaps is even force-fed), the individual as well as the institution has an important reflexive and deliberative role to play in the development of her own authentic character.

Some definitions of character will be helpful at this point. Philosopher Joel Kupperman says this: "X's character is X's normal pattern of thought and action, especially in matters related to the happiness of others and of X, and most especially in relation to moral choice."[10] In Joseph Conrad's *Heart of Darkness*, the narrator refers to character as a "deliberate belief" that goes on after mere ideals have been found wanting. Writing in *The Armed Forces Officer*, S. L. A. Marshall wrote,

> What is the main test of human character? Perhaps it is this: that a man will know how to be patient in the midst of hard circumstance, and can continue to be personally effective while living through whatever discouragements beset him and his companions. Moreover, that is what every

civilized man would want in himself during the calmer moments when he compares critically what he is inside with what he would like to be.[11]

Lord Moran, an army doctor in World War I who would go on to be Winston Churchill's personal physician, wrote about British soldiers in the trenches "moving away from . . . primitive valour, fumbling for a type of soldier whose courage was a thought-out thing." He concludes that "it is the thinking soldier who lasts in modern war."[12] Moran holds up as an example for character an aristocratic officer named Barty Tower. After Tower's death in action, Moran reflects on how the combination of thought and imagination he saw in Tower had "blossomed into character," allowing Tower to triumph over fear.

History records examples of soldiers who appear to have consciously thought their way toward character. George C. Marshall was a graduate of VMI, he had excelled as a student and instructor at army service schools, and he had the benefit (as we've seen) of some great mentoring, but his biographies and his own words give the impression that his most significant learning was on his own, and that he was his own best pupil. Thousands of officers had the benefit of similar educational experiences in the inter-war Army as did Marshall, but in only one case did these experiences add up to the World War II "Organizer of Victory." Marshall invited criticism and was engaged in constant self-critique. Having disciplined himself to be able to give lectures (and later press conferences and testimony at congressional hearings) without notes, he passed on this ability to his subordinates. The ability to think on one's feet that he found so important in an officer went along with a consistent emphasis on creativity over rote solutions. The thoughts and plans an officer expresses must come not from a sheet of paper, still less a manual. They are an expression of character and conviction, of ideas matured over time. Marshall developed in himself and in his subordinates the ability and willingness to take responsibility for their own actions and over matters of enormous difficulty and importance. He expressed his desire to find subordinates who would not ask for permission, but take action and inform Marshall afterward. (Thus anticipating the adage attributed to Rear Admiral Grace Hopper that it's sometimes easier to ask for forgiveness than permission!) One of the most impressive examples of this does not find Marshall in his role as an Army officer, but as adult friend and neighbor to a little girl. Marshall began a friendship with Rose Page Wilson when she was eight years old that lasted the rest of his life. Marshall, childless himself save for the children by a previous marriage of his second wife, and proverbially friendly and kindly toward children, offered corrections and encouragement. Wilson wrote to Marshall, "I'm a lot saner and better for having had your guidance and example to follow, I thank you for all the advice and affection and even scoldings and I thank the Lord for your sense of humor which fitted all these into a workable formula."[13] One of Marshall's most memorable lessons to Rose occurred when the young lady accused herself of being "dumb." Marshall told her that she was not dumb, but rather sometimes lazy and inattentive, and that to excuse an error by calling herself dumb was "a weak pretense," even a form of "cowardice."[14] Marshall tirelessly trained his own mind assiduously to meet the demands he might face, and he exercised enormous self-discipline in fulfilling his responsibilities, responsibilities which probably reached their height in his years as Army Chief of Staff from 1939 to 1945.

In other officer memoirs and biographies, we can see the contribution of thought to character. The officer and historian S. L. A. Marshall was an autodidact who acquired on his own the facility with words and mastery of a variety of texts and subjects that made him so successful as a field historian and writer. After his service in World War I, an unemployed and married Marshall grasped at journalism as a way out of poverty and a rudderless existence. Words became his salvation. Lacking a formal education past high school, he became his own academy, reading, building a personal library and voluminous files until he had acquired an impressive knowledge of contemporary military trends. From a feckless start, Marshall developed an enormous capacity for hard work and fortitude. He rose quickly in the Army when he returned to active duty in World War II, and by his writings built an international reputation. Marshall's masterpiece, *The Armed Forces Officer*, exemplifies the importance of reading and reflection in the development of character, and also the importance of character in intellectual development.

PERFORMANCE AND CHARACTER

> Character is that which reveals moral purpose, showing what kinds of things a man chooses or avoids.
>
> —Aristotle, *Poetics* VI, 17–19[15]

Both a literary critic and moral philosopher, in the quotation here Aristotle is speaking of dramatic, not moral character. Still, Aristotle's famous words suggest that the line between the two types of character may not be absolute. Leadership is sometimes spoken of as involving performance. This may be especially true for self-consciously stagey leaders typified by Patton, MacArthur, and Mountbatten, although it may also take more subtle forms in understated leadership performances. But what of character? Is the act of acquiring or developing character at all akin to the actor's efforts to "get into character" by understanding the motives of a character whom they are trying to depict through words and gestures? My own experience suggests that it is.

In January 2003, I embarked the amphibious ship *Bataan* bound for Kuwait and the eventual invasion of Iraq. A field historian assigned to the Marine brigade being transported to war, I dutifully conducted interviews with some of the Marines aboard my vessel. After several requests and delays, I was transported by helicopter to the flagship *Kearsarge* to do some more interviews. The operations officer of the brigade, a former classmate from The Basic School, briefed me on the plan of attack. It was being increasingly borne in on me that, yes, we were going to war. After a couple of days on the *Kearsarge*, I boarded a helicopter to return to *Bataan*. Leaving the deck of the *Kearsarge*, the helicopter made a steep bank, and I caught a quick glimpse of the choppy, gray water of the Mediterranean below. I instantly thought of Homer's "wine dark sea." It reminded me of how many ships of war had passed this way, from the original thousand ships of the *Iliad*, to later Greek galleys, Roman triremes, men of war, dreadnoughts, escort vessels, and merchantmen in convoy. The part I was about to play had long been written, I thought. After decades as a Marine, I had rehearsed this part many times. Now it was up to me to give a convincing performance. There would be other players on this stage, and I was there to support them as I could, to prompt them, to stand in sorrow or even to lie down for the final scene.

When officers read military history, biography, and memoirs especially, we are often in effect rehearsing a part, hoping that some of the character of the original will not just rub off on us, but go deep, becoming part of our own strengths and outlook until the role becomes the reality. Are we ennobled by reading about the great, or is it merely out of a sense of admiration, from afar? Again, my own experience tells me that when an officer or aspiring officer reads, he is trying to learn how to think, if not like Patton or Marshall, then at least with some of the abilities on display in the original. This likely imposes on officers an obligation (paraphrasing Michael Howard on the uses of history) to choose our examples wisely, to approach them critically, and to read widely, so as not to limit our repertoire.

Simple reading aside, there may be some point to officers practicing performance as a way to develop their cognitive and leadership capacities. Roman youths were expected to memorize and recite some of the great speeches from the civic and military past in order to equip them for the tasks of leadership. Until fairly recently, American school children would memorize and recite lines of poetry and oratory. We have perhaps lost something important with the intimate knowledge and internalization that comes of memorization and recital. Performance can do more than give us an opportunity to get inside someone else's thoughts, it can be a window to self-knowledge as well.[16]

Learning the lines of Richard III, Othello, or Hamlet, we may confront the villain in ourselves and the potential for resentment, insecurity, and jealousy to cloud our efforts at clear thinking. The famous words of Henry V before Agincourt are not only inspiring, they are the speech of someone banishing distractions—either the wishful thinking for more men and better odds, or the French herald's offer of kingly ransom for Henry—and instead focusing on the mission.

It might be argued that performative styles of leadership and the actor's calling can promote self-involvement, even amounting to narcissism. Some commanders and some actors seem to have lost the ability to see beyond the stage and footlights, admiring their own image and even lapsing into carica-ture, rather than getting into character. In his memoirs, Field Marshall Slim is critical of the extreme austerity of General Stilwell's headquarters, dress, and living arrangements, calling them as much a performance as Lord Mountbat-ten's unfailingly immaculate uniforms. (Mountbatten once said that leader-ship was an act, but one that had to come from within.) The tests of such performances are perhaps their legitimacy as expressions of character and their effectiveness as tools of command. They must for this reason be self-conscious. In the film *Patton*, a subordinate observes after a Patton tirade that he is not sure that the rest of the staff knows when Patton is acting. Patton replies that it is only important that *he* know. Eisenhower archly said that he had studied dramatics under MacArthur for five years as his subordinate, but Eisenhower's grin and affability were as much performance as MacArthur's pipe, crushed hat, and carefully faded khakis. (They were also generally more convincing. Perhaps because they came from within.) Behind the smile were Eisenhower's fierce temper and self-doubt, his always-remembered grief over the death of his first son. Eisenhower knew that a show of cheerfulness and confidence were needed to hold the coalition together and move it forward one hazard-ous enterprise after another. The effectiveness of his performance has been attested by many, not least the usually skeptical Paul Fussell, who wrote of the refreshing nature of Eisenhower's presence as an antidote to the overbearing pettiness of much army discipline.[17]

The great acting teacher Constantin Stanislavski would remind his stu-dents to "Love art in yourself and not yourself in art."[18] Performance can unlock our potential for unselfishness, even for greatness and heroism. It can also help us to think, and to think our way into character. Another insight into the conscious cultivation of character is provided by the work of poet Samuel Taylor Coleridge. In his *Biographia Literaria*, Coleridge identifies what he terms a "sacred-power of self-intuition" and a "philosophic imagination" as the capacity to perceive in advance one's own capacity for development. For Coleridge, this capacity had allowed him to sustain a belief in his own poetic genius through many setbacks (which included an ill-considered enlistment in a regiment of dragoons).[19] For the officer, sometimes laboring through years of routine duties and slow promotion, the "philosophic imagination" may allow her to retain a belief in the ideals of the service, and a confidence that, given the chance, she is capable of a great contribution on the battlefield or in some other important role. The thoughtful, imaginative, and performative approach to character may also be a hedge against the developing character sliding into mere habit and dullness, taking on too many patterns and losing the interest, ability to renew and inspire which command must strive to possess.

• 2 •

Reading to Think

$\mathcal{R}$eading is an indispensable part of learning to think, furnishing and clothing the mind with the facts, images, ideas, and language that are the raw material of thought, and that sustain our inner lives and our actions in a world the complexity of which makes it often hostile to formulas and fixed ideas. Reading may put us inside the mind of another person, developing greater insight and self-awareness concerning mental processes themselves. In *The Art of Reading*, a recent book by Australian philosopher Damon Young, the author presents a brilliant, passionate, and informed argument on the many benefits of reading.[1] To cite a reviewer, Young considers reading "educational, a boon to psychological health and social connection." Reading well is also an act of character. As Young says, "Reading artfully requires a fragile poise between proclivities: thought and feeling, spontaneity and habit, deference and critique, haste and slowness, boldness and caution, commitment and detachment." Young considers how six virtues can be developed through reading: curiosity, patience, courage, pride, temperance, and justice. Reading well can be a path to virtue, to the strong but flexible character and broad cognitive abilities that officers require.

Reading is sometimes contrasted with experience, but of course reading *is* an experience. The best reading engages the reader with the mind of the writer, bringing in other texts and the reader's own experience as corollary to the words on the page before her. Good readers are thinking constantly, negotiating, and reevaluating their response and relationship to the text. English writer Thomas DeQuincy compared the mind to a palimpsest, a page erased and written over, with each successive inscription leaving its own ghostly memory and impression.[2] (Indeed, modern technology can restore the underlying texts of a palimpsest.) The things we know or believe form the background and context of what we read. For the officer, the act of reading a literal text is also preparation for the reading of a map, of terrain, of an unfolding tactical situation, for the alert interpretation of the spoken words, the faces and gestures of subordinates and superiors. Serious, concentrated reading may be an endangered activity in our distracted age. Perhaps this is why so many distinguished senior officers, to include James Mattis, James Stavridis, and Paul K. Van Riper have written and spoken recently on the benefits of reading.[3] General Rupert Smith defined victory in terms of "controlling the narrative."[4] To lead and command is to read. The officer, as Henry James said of the novelist (and perhaps most of all in the role as leader and tactician), must be someone who notices everything.

Officers read a variety of texts that enable their thinking. In this chapter on reading, I will discuss some different kinds of text typically read by officers. The list is not meant to be exhaustive. I include as categories official and semi-official documents, military history and theory, war literature, and the humanities in general. All these categories have a role in the development of an officer's ability to think. None of them, nor all of them combined, will guarantee good thinking, but reading well is surely an essential part of preparing to think.

REGULATIONS, EPHEMERA, AND THE OATH

The official publications and even the informal or ephemeral writing produced by any military organization form the quotidian background of an officer's professional reading and knowledge. From manuals to bulletin boards and webpages, the textual "buzz" of a military community is a necessary and unavoidable, although not a sufficient part of an officer's mental development. What mental purpose do these forms of writing serve? Of course, they keep the officer apprised of current events, scheduled training, guidance, and the "command philosophy" coming down from her immediate superior or higher headquarters. Reports and memoranda may give her an idea of how training and operations are progressing. The services all have formal "lessons learned" systems that attempt to capture some of the experience, the "institutional memory" of the armed forces. These different forms of writing (sometimes accompanied with pictures and diagrams) also give the officer a sense that she is an invested member of an organization. She is a part but also a moving part, and one that must work out her relationship with other members and with the whole, with the concrete reality but also with the abstraction of the military unit, the idea of it, its history, and reformulation from day to day. These prosaic forms of writing are reminders of the many details that an officer has to keep in his head in her role as trainer and tactician. Some writings are worth keeping on hand for reference. The officer has at her fingertips a great deal of information thanks to the internet and digital books, but there remains the challenge of being familiar with one's information and sources, and of selecting what is most likely to be needed. I still have the waterproofed notebook I kept as an infantry officer, stuffed with cards and clippings on land navigation, vehicle and equipment recognition, demolitions, fields of fire, calls for fire, and for aviation support. I've also kept many of the ubiquitous government-issue green notebooks that I wrote in over the years. These personal references and records certainly served a practical purpose. They were also reminders of the duties and demands of my calling, of the need to answer a call to action that might require me to react and adapt in an unexpected situation.

An obvious but still sometimes overlooked form of reading material for the officer are the foundational documents that define her obligations. Officers swear an oath to the Constitution, and they receive a large, elaborate copy of their commission with every promotion, but they don't always get around to reading these documents. The commission defines the basis and scope of an officer's authority, its grounding in the officer's "patriotism, valor, fidelity, and abilities," and that it is to be exercised "within the laws of the United States of America." If nothing else, a reading of the military commission should fill the officer with pride and a renewed sense of responsibility. The Constitutional Oath offers guidance on how and to what ends an officer's authority should be exercised. It may seem straightforward, but the military officer's relationship with the Constitution may be complex and even paradoxical. There is on the one hand considerable public agreement about the meaning of the Constitution. As Anthony Hartle, retired Army colonel and longtime English and Philosophy Department head at West Point, puts it,

> While the interpretations and applications of Constitutional law are perpetually in flux, firm ground exists for maintaining that the broad principles of constitutionalism, representative democracy, individual rights, the rule of law, and the greatest equal liberty are fixtures in our national understanding of the Constitution.[5]

On the other hand, the officer's obligation to demand military discipline and obedience, to limit, for example, certain forms of speech, to give commands, levy force, take life, and require others to risk their lives, might seem to be at odds with the broad principles of the Constitution. The oath to the Constitution might even seem inconsistent, even hypocritical. The oath is not a contradiction but a paradox, however, and a very important one. It is exactly because the officer has the potential to harm others and to violate their rights that she, even more than other public servants, requires a firm understanding and adherence to the Constitutional Oath. Only a person determined to use her authority in licit ways, consistent with the mission and with the principles of the Constitution as much as possible, even amid the violence and disorder of war and combat, is fit to undertake the authority that the commission grants. Only someone committed to the restraint of force that is consistent with human rights and the rule of law ought to be empowered to exercise the legal authority and control of lethal force that may be granted to a military officer.

The Constitutional Oath provides an essential source of restraint in war. The services appear to acknowledge the importance of the Oath by the tradition of readministering it on each occasion of reenlistment or promotion. However, the meaning of the Oath can be lost in these ceremonies, and it remains important for the officer to read and ponder Oath and Commission. How does a careful reading and understanding of these foundational documents inform an officer's service? How should they be experienced, and how should they influence her conduct as she goes about her duties? The restrained use of authority and force mentioned previously should be part of the meaning and impact of Oath and Commission. A positive respect for persons should be another. For all their enrollment in a disciplined organization and obligation to obey orders, military members are entitled to the respect accorded citizens, to be heard and to be kept informed, to understand the terms of their service and sacrifice, most of all to be subjected to risk only when necessary.[6]

Aside from the Constitution and Commission, the officer should read other important documents of American history. Some of the most important of these are the speeches that have marked the progress of American history and helped to define a nation that is always growing and changing. The American officer has an obligation to understand and to value that which she defends. Speeches like the Gettysburg Address and Lincoln's Second Inaugural Address (both on display at the Lincoln Memorial in Washington), Eisenhower's Farewell to the Nation, and Martin Luther King Jr.'s "I Have a Dream" speech have the dual purpose of acquainting a reader with important events and ideals, and of providing an education in the persuasive skills of rhetoric, that traditional staple of humanist education. Military rhetoric is a neglected but not an entirely lost art. Officers give talks ranging from off-the-cuff remarks to full-blown prepared speeches. These may be to troops before or after an exercise or deployment, to members of the civil community on a national holiday, or at a school commencement. Officers are largely self-taught orators, and it may be that officer education should treat it more as a skill to be mastered. Rhetoric is both a means of communication and an opportunity to profess and define an individual's most deeply held beliefs.

MILITARY THEORY AND HISTORY

Military theory and history play an important part in the education of officers. As an example, students of the Marine Corps Command and Staff College read sections of *Makers of Modern Strategy, The American Way of War, European Armies and the Conduct of War,* and *On War.* The services have official reading lists that lean heavily toward theory and history. How does the reading of works in these genres help an officer to think? Reading should not be thought as supplying simple, ready answers to military problems. Taken too literally or uncritically, reading can impair clear thinking. The well-read but unimaginative, pedantic officer is a stock figure of war literature (in works by Tolstoy, Mailer, and Anton Myrer, as examples), and he is not hard to find in history or in the present. Reading can promote a kind of intellectual arrogance, fueling in reaction the ever-present tendency for military cultures to lapse into anti-intellectualism, the "barrack-room philosophy" noted and deplored by philosopher George Santayana.[7] Reading can have the effect of reinforcing prejudice and other fixed ideas. George Patton's class prejudice and contempt for democracy seem to have been confirmed by much of his reading.[8] The difficulties involved in translating military theory and history into action are the basis of Jon Sumida's "The Relationship of History and Theory in *On War*: The Clausewitzian Ideal and Its Implications." For Sumida, Clausewitz's great strength and the reason for his continuing relevance is his grasp of the complexity and subtlety of military problems, so that the problem-solving process is often taking place at a level below that of language, rationality, and even consciousness.

Like so much else, the benefits of military reading are best undertaken in a spirit of open-mindedness and balance. Pursued in this way, military reading can be an enabler of clear thinking about problems of organization, warfighting, and leadership. This kind of reading is perhaps best understood as imparting a general sense, even an instinct for the dimensions and context of military problems. As argued by Olivia Garard, "the lessons from history turn out not to be particulars, but instead general properties of how to think, how we should construct our will."[9] As with other forms of reading, the feel for the human subject is all-important. A grasp of the perhaps unique space-time factor in military problems, in tactics especially, is something to be enhanced by reading, although also in training. The discipline and attentiveness required to read a battle narrative, or to follow events on a map, are related to the tactician's ability to keep in her head a rough picture of the battlespace with its most important features and ongoing events. Some histories are concerned with the structure and culture of military organizations, giving the officer-reader a feel for those that are successful and those that are dysfunctional.

Reading can also develop the instinct for leadership. Reading for leadership may be thought of as a form of habituation like any other, a developing familiarity and preference for certain types of behavior over others, for service over selfishness, for the diligent over the dilatory, for the humane over the unfeeling or mechanical.

Historian Michael Howard issues some advice on reading for officers in his much-referenced 1961 essay "The Use and Abuse of Military History." Howard suggests three approaches to military history for the officer.[10] First, history must be studied in width, that is, over a long historical period. Second, history must be pursued in depth. A soldier-student should pick a campaign and study it in detail. Third, her study must include the context, taking in "political, social, and economic factors."[11] In the spirit of this advice, I will begin this section on military history with a representative "deep dive" into a selected campaign and commander, and then broaden the focus to encompass more of history and literature.

THE DESERT GENERALS

One of my own early influences, in fact a book that helped to reawaken and confirm in adolescence my boyhood interest in becoming a soldier, was Correlli Barnett's *The Desert Generals*. I have since used this book to teach tactics and leadership. *The Desert Generals* is a study of the five officers who commanded British forces in North Africa from 1940 to 1943. My relationship with the book has spanned over four decades. I first read the book as a high school student, then as a cadet and junior officer, and as a senior officer I used it to teach officer cadets. It has worn well, and in fact my admiration has grown, even as I have come to recognize that not all of Barnett's interpretations and judgments of senior commanders (his marked preference for General Claude Auchinleck over Bernard Montgomery, for example) have gone unchallenged.[12] In fact, one of the benefits of the book has been to introduce me to the controversy over these two officers and others whose reputations are matters of contention, so that, like a commander weighing different courses of action, I have had to consider the arguments on either side. One of the most memorable (for me) passages in the book is in the "Author's Preface" when Barnett refers to generalship as "possibly the most complete human activity, since [it] involves all the intellectual, physical, and moral power in a man."[13] *The Desert Generals* can be used as a tool to aid in thinking about tactics and warfighting, leadership and character, and the problems of organization and training. Barnett's writing often enables us to follow the thoughts of the commander, to stand at his side and see the battle both through his eyes and through those of the historical narrator. The record of command of the British forces in North Africa mirrors somewhat that of the Union Army, the Army of the Potomac in particular, in that so many commanders were replaced. Of the five officers under discussion, one became a prisoner of war, three were relieved, and only one, Montgomery, did not have his command cut short by summary relief or capture. Even though they were experienced and highly regarded officers, the challenge of an independent command exercised under pressure from both an often-brilliant adversary and a demanding higher headquarters and political authority proved too much for Generals Alan Cunningham, Neil Ritchie, and Claude Auchinleck.

In this discussion of *The Desert Generals*, I will focus on Richard O'Connor. O'Connor in North Africa provides an excellent example of the combination of care and enterprise, of the planner combined with the gambler that seem to characterize the most successful combat leaders. O'Connor began with a campaign of limited objectives, but he developed over time a vision of a more ambitious objective. The poor leadership and dispersed positions of the Italians opposing him seemed to present the opportunity for a decisive victory, but O'Connor did not count on these advantages to ensure his success. He carefully trained his men and rehearsed for the planned attack. The men under his command were regular army veterans, and some of the best soldiers who fought in North Africa in World War II, but he recognized that even these excellent soldiers needed to be made familiar with the conditions of the desert and the tactics that would be employed. He carefully positioned an advance force where it could hold open the gap in the Italian lines that he intended to exploit, and he established forward magazines to keep his advancing troops supplied. The advance force served as the stationary element for a forward passage of lines by fresh troops. O'Connor maintained the pressure on the Italians, but he did so while also paying careful attention to the physical limitations of his own forces. He split marches in order to give tired troops a rest, and he continued to use the passage of lines maneuver, deferring the "culminating point" that can slow or halt an advance through fatigue, losses, and limited supply. O'Connor's attack on the Italian center around Sidi Barrani resembled a successful gambit in chess. He occupied the middle squares, allowing an attack from a strong base and impeding an attack by the enemy.

O'Connor's leadership style was somewhat reminiscent of Wellington. Unsmiling and seemingly omnipresent, he communicated to his soldiers the sense that he was fully committed to victory and to safeguarding their lives. He was in constant motion, conducting personal reconnaissance, talking and listening to subordinate commanders and the fighting troops. His decision to continue the attack after losing the veteran 7th Division to another command was a sign of character and also of his confidence in the plan that he had evolved. His reputation at this point was secure due to his earlier victories, and he would not have been blamed if he had curtailed the advance at this point, but hard work, careful thinking, and imagination had given him belief in a greater victory as yet unachieved.

O'Connor's tireless efforts to read the battlefield eventually cost him two years as a prisoner of war when he was captured with another general on a reconnaissance patrol. He tried to escape repeatedly, and he was eventually successful, gaining his freedom in time to be given command of a corps in the Normandy campaign. He was less successful in this role than he had been in the desert. Perhaps the rigors and dullness of captivity had taken their toll on him, physically and mentally. It appears that he may not have been able to make the mental adjustment to the conditions of the Normandy campaign, which were so different from those of North Africa. As opposed to the independence and emphasis on maneuver in the African desert, conditions in Normandy offered little room for maneuver or surprise and were characterized by tight Command and Control. Perhaps, as suggested by British Army officer Sam Cates in his monograph on O'Connor, O'Connor's superiors could have employed him more wisely, for example, allowing his corps wider boundaries to allow him to exercise his penchant for maneuver.[14] However, O'Connor might have been reasonably expected to adjust himself to the new conditions.

If there is one undying lesson of officer thought, it is the need to continue learning, to gain flexibility rather than set patterns of thought from our experience. This lesson is underscored for me by my long acquaintance with *The Desert Generals*, one that has been enriched by my more recent reading of other materials that cover the same period, events, and personalities. The Greek philosopher Heraclitus observed that we never step into the same river twice. The waters are different, and so are we. So it is, or should be, with the way that we read the ever-changing world around us, and our ever-developing selves.

THE MILITARY MEMOIR

The military officer memoir deserves a special place in the field of military history as a means to develop officer thought, because the memoir provides the most uninterceded insight into the officer's mind. A great memoir can put the reader into the historical context and inside the head of the memoirist in an almost uncanny way. As with all writing and all language, one must allow for a degree of disingenuousness in the memoir. Few people are immune to the temptation to make themselves appear wiser or better. Mark

Twain once said that what made memoirs so revealing was that the more the writer tried to conceal his own nature, the more it came through clearly! Most military memoirs are frankly undistinguished, and many are blatantly self-justifying. Sir John French's memoirs of his command of the British Expeditionary Force in World War I, *1914*, written after his relief, was called by military historian Sir John Fortescue "one of the most unfortunate books ever written."[15] A few memoirs are worthy of being read by every officer, although many more may be rewarding, especially if one has a special interest in the period or person.

The personal experiences of war and the thoughts that accompany them have been related in many military officer memoirs throughout history. The genre at least has roots in the work of such distinguished soldier-writers as Xenophon and Caesar. The military memoir was a popular form by the time of Shakespeare, and it has been a mainstay of popular literature, including a few notable classics, ever since.[16] Memoirs describe the soldier's experiences in putatively personal and factual terms, but soldiers have also written poetry, plays, and novels that draw on their experiences of war, and they have gone on to become military historians, making use of their personal experiences to give authority, empathy, and verisimilitude to their writing.

In effect, all personal accounts of war aim at the titular intention of Karl Marlantes's memoir, *What It Is Like to Go to War*. Military memoirs and other accounts of war experience also tend to specialize in different aspects of war and military service. Much military writing by soldiers is concerned with solving the military problems of warfighting. Some, like Marlantes's book, are more concerned with the spiritual and moral dimensions of war and combat, aspects of war experience that are partly cognitive, if not entirely subject to the unaided reason. Still, as Marlantes points out, people can be prepared for these spiritual and moral dimensions by a thoughtful approach to training and by leadership in the field. Of his training as a Marine, Marlantes says that he learned the moves but not their meaning. Officers are usually concerned to protect their men from the physical dangers of war, but they are less aware and adept at giving them the tools to deal with the inevitable loss of innocence, the "shadow" cast over their lives by the experience of killing, loss, and fear. Marlantes identifies several methods to alleviate some of the costs of war experience. In effect, these are literal extensions of the officer's obligation to look after her subordinates. Marlantes's methods include ritual post-combat reconciliation with the enemy, particularly with their dead. He imagines a ceremony at which an officer or sergeant might recite the following words,

> Bless these dead, our former enemies, who have played their part, hurled against us by the forces that hurled us against them. Bless us who live, whose parts are not yet done, and who know not how they shall be played.

Forgive us if we killed in anger or in hatred. Forgive them if they did the same. Judgment is yours, not ours. We are only human.

Among American memoirs, the most famous and influential is that of Ulysses S. Grant.[17] His book has perhaps set the pattern of subsequent American officer memoirs, and it was consciously imitated by at least two other well-known personal accounts, those of Pershing and Eisenhower.[18] Grant had been a very dedicated reader of novels since his days as a cadet, and he later took to the reading of history as well, recording in a ledger all that he had learned from his reading in a day.[19] Grant's memoirs are modest and ingenuous in tone. He does not attempt to write a complete account of the Civil War or of the other historical events that he lived through, but he rather limits himself to things he actually saw. His judgments are insightful but restrained. His description of an episode in the defense of Washington is characteristic. Grant praises General Lew Washington for moving quickly with inexperienced and outnumbered forces to conduct a spoiling attack on a Confederate advance that threatened the capital, but he admits that it is uncertain whether it was Washington's attack that gained the time necessary to mount a more organized defense. Grant is sparing of criticisms, especially of his subordinates, and when he recalls relieving General McClernand he is careful to explain the reasons, but he does so unjudgmentally. On the other hand, he is scathing and funny in his description of Jefferson Davis's self-declared *superior military genius* (Grant's italics) which he says was an advantage to the Union army! Most significantly, at least for our estimation of him, Grant grasped the moral import of the Civil War and the wickedness and damaging effects of slavery, an institution that he saw as both unjust to the enslaved and harmful to slave owners and the economy and culture of the south.

Another distinguished military memoir that deserves attention as revealing and exemplary of officer thought is *Defeat into Victory: Battling Japan in Burma and India, 1942–1945* by Field Marshal William Slim. One reason why Slim's memoirs are so valuable is that he fought under such terrible disadvantages. For much of his time in command of a corps and later an army, the Japanese were more numerous and generally better trained and organized, especially for the jungle fighting that characterized most of the action. They also enjoyed air superiority. The forces under Slim's command were a combination of British, Commonwealth, and allied troops, among whom the Chinese were most numerous. The Chinese were good fighters and even usually well led, but the employment of Chinese forces faced a complex political situation as well as cultural differences concerning adhering to schedules and expressed commitments. Most important about Slim's memoir is the degree to which he lets the reader into the workings of his mind, often admitting his mistakes, uncertainties, and confusion. The following passage is worth quoting at length.

This was not the first, nor would it be the last, time that I had taken over a situation that was not going too well. I knew the feeling of unease that comes first at such times, a sinking of the heart as the gloomy facts crowd in; then the glow of exhilaration as the brain grapples with problem after problem; lastly the tingling of the nerves and the lightening of the spirit, as the urge to get out and tackle the job takes hold. Experience had taught me, however, that before rushing into action it is advisable to get quite clearly fixed in the mind what the object of it all is. So now I sat down to think out what our object should be. . . . Were we going to stage a last-ditch stand to hold part of Burma? Or were we, now that Rangoon was lost, going to concentrate on getting the army, by a series of planned withdrawals, back to India intact? Were we hoping that the Chinese, added to the resources we had left, would give us strength to counterattack successfully? On the answers to these questions would depend very much how we carried out any immediate operation; all would be conditioned by the overriding object of the campaign. What that was we did not know. Indeed it was never, until the last stages, clear, and I think we suffered increasingly in all our actions from this.

Slim's reflections are a model exposition of the inner experience of making military decisions in an atmosphere of setback and uncertainty frankly exacerbated by a lack of strategic direction from above. His frequent use of the semicolon, as opposed to the full-stop in this paragraph is telling. There was too much that he simply "did not know" to allow him many conclusive statements. An officer reading this passage may be heartened to know that she is not alone in experiencing a sinking heart at the accumulation of "gloomy facts." She might also be instructed by Slim's words about sitting down to think before rushing into action. Finally, his observations about the "overriding object of the campaign" should be borne in mind by anyone planning or conducting military operations. Throughout his memoir, Slim clearly lays out the courses of action he considered and the steps that he took. His description of his efforts to overcome the extremely difficult problems of supply, health, and morale he encountered when assuming army command are a model of clarity, common sense, and creativity. Slim leveraged resources from his higher command and created more efficient procedures to approve supply requests. He made use of some of the latest and ongoing medical research to find cures for the diseases of the jungle, at the same time making prevention a responsibility of command, the neglect of which could be cause for an officer's relief. He also decentralized medical services and moved them closer to the combat units. Of improvements in morale, Slim notes, "They began, as most things do, as words." He worked to overcome the challenges to communications in his polyglot army, and to understand the cultural differences of the various national contingents, appreciating each group for its strengths and unique charm. He made sure that the support services were not neglected in morale-building. Slim frequently reminds the reader (and himself) of the necessity for "hard thinking."

HISTORICAL FICTION

Before I leave the subject of military history, I'd like to say a few words in favor of historical fiction. Historical fiction is sometimes consigned to the lower orders of military professional reading, as a category most suitable to junior personnel. The experience of reading historical fiction may not be as demanding as that of reading historical or other nonfiction books, but that does not mean that it is necessarily less beneficial. Fiction has a unique capacity to stir the mind and imagination. We live in narrative, and a convincing narrative must often be called upon to serve a convincing argument. Certain works of fiction become part of us, permanently informing our thought processes. This may be especially true of our early reading; for many young adults, fiction forms a rite of passage into the adult world, and for the future officer, historical fiction is often her introduction to the military profession. Ernest Tucker's *The Story of Knights and Armor,* a collection of illustrated historical vignettes from Roman through medieval times, was an early influence on my desire to become a soldier. The stories were simple but written with a kind of nobility of feeling, almost always featuring a young soldier who makes a rocky start but does well in the end through pluck and brains. (I knew that would be me!) Another early favorite was *The Silver Branch* by Rosemary Sutcliff about soldiers in Roman Britain. The main characters are an army surgeon and his friend a young centurion. The political situation in the story is complicated, but their soldierly faithfulness to each other through a change in emperor and various plots and coups leads to their just reward. Robert Graves's *Sergeant Lamb's America* was my introduction to the British regimental system and to another side of the story of the American Revolution. Graves was an infantry officer in World War I, and in *Sergeant Lamb's America* and *I, Claudius,* a novel about the eponymous Roman Emperor, his depictions of soldiers are knowing and sympathetic. The good officers whom Sergeant Lamb encounters (and the good outnumber the bad) have the courage and common sense that would distinguish them as capable leaders in any time. For all young people, becoming an adult means coming to terms with the fateful and eventually fatal conditions of life. For the future officer, the relationship with mortality assumes even more immediate importance. Through reading, he sees that death is, in the words of the Scottish major in the novel and feature film *Tunes of Glory,* his "stock in trade." Another story that stayed with me was that of the Greek soldier and runner Pheidippides, who conducted epic runs before and after fighting in the Battle of Marathon (490 BCE), falling dead from exhaustion in front of the Athenians after gasping out, "Rejoice, we conquer." When I started to run distances myself (to prepare for officer training), the story of Pheidippides would come back to me as inspiration and a relief from boredom. It was also a reminder to my youthful self of the full measure that might be expected of soldiers. Another classic runner's tale that I learned later was that of the future emperor Galba running beside Nero's chariot for twenty Roman miles in full armor!

Our early reading can continue to have an influence in maturity. Marshall and Eisenhower both read western novels all their lives. These stories of the West, the kind of stories they had grown up with, must have provided mental relaxation from their cares and responsibilities, but one can also imagine that they were a kind of continuing metaphor for the work they did. Like the solitary cowboy or lawman, bearing arms but restrained and even reluctant in their use, bringing peace to the town, the two generals experienced the loneliness and remorse of roles thrust upon them by dire circumstance. Marshall and Eisenhower likely read the works of Zane Grey, among others. In the Marine Corps of the 1980s, the western novels of Louis L'Amour were favorite reading.

The influence of story and fiction on how we think and what we believe is inevitable. We should be conscious of this influence, but it is neither to be despised nor discarded. The old stories of knights and cowboys can reconcile us to difficult and painful tasks. For the officer, stories may help to make her more resistant to debilitating doubt or cynicism, upholding some of the early and enduring idealism of military service.

OFFICER EDUCATION AND THE HUMANITIES

Through its dependence on narrative, prescriptive, and lyrical language, in its historicity and close ties to questions of value, military thought is dependent on the humanities. Military experience has also provided the humanities with some of its most valuable themes and texts. The humanities are valuable to the officer in a variety of ways in her roles as a leader, as organizer and warfighter. In his introduction to David Hackworth's *About Face: The Odyssey of an American Warrior*, Ward Just, war correspondent and author of the excellent study of US Army culture *Military Men*, cites a section from Marcel Proust's *Guermantes Way* as "The best single explication of tactics that I have ever read."[20] Proust's narrator is visiting his friend Saint-Loup at the garrison town outside Paris where the latter is performing his military service.

Saint-Loup has been attending a course on military history taught by a Major Duroc. Duroc presents military history as a text that successive commanders imitate and adapt to the tactics of their own battles. In addition to the "whole geographical context" of military operations, a commander must consider enemy traditions, habits, and doctrines. The soldier feels, or ought to feel "the vigilance, the judgment, the profound study of the Higher Command, you are as much moved by them as by the simple lamps of a lighthouse . . . an emanation of the spirit, seeping through space to warn ships of danger." Ironically, some of the "advanced" twentieth-century military thought cited with approval by Saint-Loup involves an embracing of the offensive that will prove to disastrous in 1914. A further irony is that the intellectual Saint-Loup, although he is a committed soldier, is also a *Drefusard* who rejects the army's prevailing reactionary and anti-Dreyfus ideology. (Dreyfus was the eventually exonerated Jewish artillery captain who was convicted on trumped-up charges of espionage and sentenced to Devil's Island, and whose case became a major *cause celeb* that highlighted some deep divisions in turn of the century France.) It is a paradox that the critical intelligence that enables him to think deeply about tactics (and clearly about Dreyfus) may also make him an outsider in the military community, although even his intellect, education, and reading cannot save him from being wrong sometimes!

My own experience of using the humanities to instruct officers is derived mostly from teaching midshipmen at the US Merchant Marine Academy. The mixture of maritime and military at Kings Point made for a challenging, diverse environment in which to teach leadership, and the focus of the curriculum on technical subjects could create some ingrained prejudice against the humanities in general, but using the humanities as a text or lens with which to address leadership could also serve to legitimize both subjects, opening up the discussion of leadership beyond its military application, and demonstrating against skepticism that the humanities can be useful and even necessary.

In a class that I co-created and taught with English professor Melanie Ross at the Academy called "Pen, Cutlass, and Sword," we alternated readings from military works like *The Armed Forces Officer* (1950/1975) and canonical literature like *Pride and Prejudice*. The argument we made for juxtaposing these works was wrapped up in an emerging discovery that, in the words of Correlli Barnett, the "secret" of leadership "lies not in managing 'human resources' but in cherishing human relationships," and that both *Pride and Prejudice* and *The Armed Forces Officer* both had a great deal to say about human relationships.[21] (We also did not neglect the historical and textual military aspects of Jane Austen's most famous novel, with its background of the wars against Napoleon, and first publication under an imprint that specialized in military titles.)[22] *The Armed Forces Officer* exemplifies the need for wide reading and continued self-education on the part of an officer. As the book confidently asserts, "the study of human nature and of individual characteristics within the Armed Forces becomes a major part of his training. That is the prime reason why the life of any tactical leader is so very interesting, provided he possesses some imagination. Everything may become grist for his mill." Professor Ross and I also devised and taught a class on the sea narratives of Joseph Conrad. Aside from seeming to us highly appropriate for the Merchant Marine Academy, works like *Heart of Darkness* and *Typhoon* communicate powerful ideas on leadership under conditions of moral darkness and mortal danger.

These reflections may raise the question of how broad a field an officer's education should cover. After all, there are limits to time and energy, and enough to learn even in the purely military sphere. Is the officer also expected to be a cultivated person with some knowledge of art and history, or is this just window-dressing, even an anachronistic holdover from the conception of the officer as an aristocratic dilettante whose social obligations outweighed his military duties? For the foregoing reasons concerning language, values, tactics, and leadership, I would argue, not irrelevant at all, especially if one considers the importance now being discovered (or perhaps rediscovered) of the merging of disciplines and areas of endeavor as essential to "synthetic" thought. Related to the idea of "consilience," the meeting of art and science, there is a growing awareness of the importance of not limiting oneself to a narrow field of knowledge. The humanities may be said to provide the best bridge between the practice of any profession and its larger import and impact on the lives of men and women. An officer may benefit from a study of economics, or mathematics, or a branch of science, but absent the humanities something vital will be missing. The humanities round out one's view of existence. Properly considered, they are an antidote to insularity and exceptionalism. The humanities are a vehicle both to impart values and also for receptiveness to changes in values. Narrative literature and poetry focus on the individual, on foibles and familiarity. All stories are alike in that they are made of words and are concerned with diverse but recognizable human concerns, but it would seem that we need a lot of stories to fully understand the human subject that is the basis for all systems of belief and governance, all professions and organizations, all public and private acts and interventions, all armies and armed conflict. Perhaps the most important function of the humanities is to hold up a mirror to ourselves. Self-knowledge is vital to an officer, lest decisions and relationships be burdened by self-delusion, by posturing or lack of authenticity.

A succinct and convincing argument for the importance to officers of a broad humanities education is made by Robert Kaplan in his editorial piece, "The Humanist in the Foxhole."[23] Kaplan holds up as an example of the "soldier aesthete" the recently deceased Patrick Leigh Fermor, whose broad reading and sincere interest in many cultures, in obscure facts, places, and texts, lent depth to his ability to move among and to mobilize native peoples as a special operations officer during World War II. In Josiah Bunting's article "The Humanities in the Education of the Military Professional." Bunting cites another special operations officer, Orde Wingate, on the "tyranny of the dull mind" and how this can be cured or challenged by a grounding in the humanities.[24] Bunting also quotes another famous proselytizer for humanities education, Cardinal John Henry Newman from his *The Idea of the University.* "It teaches him to see things as they are, to go right to the point, to disentangle a skein of thought, to discard what is sophistical, and to discard what is irrelevant." Bunting concludes by siding with John Rosenberg, who told West Point cadets that a liberal arts education might make them more sensitive to the value of things they would have to destroy. Bunting adds that it may also make them aware of the value of the things that they defend, and that "military victory must not be purchased in ways that utterly defeat the purposes for which campaigns are undertaken." Perhaps the most distinguished proponent of a humanities education was ex-officer Winston Churchill. As Jonathan Rose, author of *The Literary Churchill* puts it, "For Churchill, literary and strategic creativity were inseparable."[25] As an antidote to what he saw as their general lack of imagination, he wanted all officers to read Plutarch's *Lives.* Rose calls Churchill the foremost poet of World War II, and so he was. His language, often allusive and metaphorical, helped to define for many the nature of the struggle and their hopes for the future. Often a master of hyperbole, Churchill found in the Nazis and their evil cause a fit subject for his rhetoric.

Under the heading of the humanities, the canonical literature of the United States should be a part of the reading of an American officer. Along with the foundational documents already mentioned, classic American literature has formed what philosopher Stanley Cavell calls "this new but unapproachable America."[26] Two of the giants in this field are Herman Melville and Ralph Waldo Emerson. *Moby Dick* likely remains the one great American novel, and the whaling ship *Pequod* is, as critics from D. H. Lawrence have noted, a metaphor for America, with its themes of capitalism, uprootedness, racial difference, and religious belief. For the officer-reader especially, *Moby Dick* is about hierarchy and command, their rituals, use and misuse. With his essays, Emerson declared the intellectual independence of the young republic. His work does not define a nation so much as track a course of national and personal development, from the ebullience of "Self-Reliance" to the sadness and knowledge of "Experience."

The humanities in its relationship to officer thought might usefully be divided into two tracks: the narrative and the poetic. Narrative is the basic form for history and literary fiction. The cognitive benefits of narrative have already been alluded to. Drawing on research by others, literary critic Terry Eagleton describes several distinct benefits, to include enabling readers to think beyond the here and now, to process information, to anticipate risks and opportunities, and to prepare for setbacks.[27] Narrative is akin to diagnosis, to pattern recognition and problem-solving. By the poetic I refer to works in the humanities that are not necessarily in the poetic genre, but that address various seemingly irreconcilable values and unanswerable questions. Many such works have to do with human mortality, with the gap between our limited earthly lifetimes and the limitlessness of our desires and aspirations. Both narrative and poetic forms relate to how officers must think, especially in wartime, when the demands on decision-making and resilience are the greatest, and when paradoxes of the kind addressed in a poetics become most acute and immediate. A poetics as well as a narrative is needed to address the fragile, even tentative, endurance of the values for which soldiers fight, the impermanence of the things and people we value and love. The analysis of narrative and poetics is akin to diagnosis and to tactics, to an understanding based on incomplete knowledge and partly dependent on abstract and ineffable values, such as the worth of human lives, present and future.

There is an abundance of poetical works to choose from, new and old, works about war and those that have nothing to do with war. William Meredith was a Navy pilot in World War II who had a distinguished career as a poet and teacher until his death in 2007. In 1970 he published "Reading My Poems from World War II" in *Poetry* magazine.[28] Meredith recalls the beautiful and gallant images he created out of war, not to reject them exactly, although certainly to complicate them. The young poet "dressed as a lieutenant . . . wears his insignia with pride, nevertheless/You feel something is wrong; he is rendered with all the compassion Velasquez reserved for his dwarfs." Meredith says that his wartime poems "seem impelled by a moral purpose," which is that we not "blame the men/Even transformed into beasts in a stylized chase." The figure of the dwarf reappears at the end of the poem. His "eyes glitter as though in that whole scene/he saw no one worse than himself, and he prays for us all." The poem expresses through a variety of images the complex mixture of pride and guilt over complicity with war. The purpose of the chase is left in question. The image of the dwarf reflects a diminishment of humanity, but it is the dwarf who sees the humanity of all involved in the struggle ("no one worse") and who "prays for all." Perhaps along with a loss of stature, the dwarf-lieutenant-poet has acquired a wry knowledge. Do his eyes glitter with amusement, or like those of the murderers in *The Duchess of Malfi* "dazzle" with tears?

The officer does not only make use of the humanities. Her profession is in effect a branch of the humanities, a union of fact and value, history and language, influence, allusion, and creativity. The language of soldiers is often derided as dry, evasive, even disingenuous, but it may also achieve a poetic compression and guarded meaning. The repetitiveness and metaphors of military-speak, of leadership in a military setting, can be unforgettable. In the hands of a veteran practitioner, such language "comprehends all human tragedy," as the officer and novelist Evelyn Waugh wrote in his *Sword of Honour* trilogy on World War II. The soldier's calling often calls for poetry, and it has not been lacking in this regard.

> "Land of Song!" cried the warrior bard,
> "Tho' all the world betrays thee,
> One sword, at least, thy rights shall guard,
> One faithful harp shall praise thee!"
>   The Minstrel Boy[29]

My own experience of going to war in Iraq as a middle-aged Marine reservist wrung two poems from what I had considered a defunct poetic vocation. Both poems are bad and forgettable. I have shown them to few (and I won't inflict them on the reader now), but when I say that the titles were "I Asked for It" and "Fight to a Finish" you may understand the personal relevance that they had for me at the time. Along with the Homeric epiphany that I have already mentioned, these poems constituted an example of literature offering sense and reconciliation for a difficult, demanding experience, for the unforgettable sacrifices and destruction that I was witnessing and was also a party to. They enabled me to play my role as an officer, and they were also part of that role, in that they were an effort to comprehend what I beheld in professional, and in human, terms.

MORE WAR LITERATURE

In a sense the literature of the West and of the rest of the world begins with war literature and has (in the words of one distinguished literary critic) "never forsworn it."[30] There is almost an embarrassment of high-caliber, great, and near-great literature of war. Four groups may be said to stand out: the classical Greeks, the Elizabethans, the British World War I poets (some of them also memoirists), and twentieth-century American novelists.

THE GREEKS

The Western literary, cultural, and military traditions begin with the *Iliad*. The ancient Greeks treated the *Iliad* as moral scripture and military doctrine.[31]

From it came much of their nuanced, dialectical, poetical understanding of such military matters as causes and command, heroism and fear, chance and error. Long before Clausewitz, the Greeks had a poetic language and imagery for friction and the fog of war. In Ulysses, the man of both words and action, the commander and staff officer, the loyal subordinate and independent thinker, they possessed a prototype for officership that endures to this day. The Greek drama that follows the *Iliad* often re-imagines the Trojan War and Iliadic themes. The play *Ajax* by Sophocles takes off after the *Iliad* ends. When the armor of dead Achilles is awarded to Ulysses and not to Ajax, Ajax becomes enraged, plotting murder but, distracted by the goddess Athena into killing livestock instead, he eventually commits suicide. Under the "Theater of War" series, performances and discussion of *Ajax* have been shown to be very effective in the treatment of soldiers and veterans suffering from what has been termed "moral injury," feelings of shame and betrayal over the deaths of comrades, inept leadership, and the unequal distribution of rewards. *Ajax* and other Greek drama have been shown to be tools for commanders seeking ways to allow their soldiers to overcome the internal hurts of war. These performances have shown the way for other literary works to assuage, ameliorate, or inoculate against the effects of moral injury.

THE ELIZABETHANS

Elizabethan writers depicted war at a turning point in the English language, the beginning of the language spoken today and (some have argued) of a modern, humanist conception of existence.[32] As with the classical Greeks, with the Elizabethans we are present at the birth of a new way of looking at humanity, in aggregate, in communities, and as individuals. Many writers of the time experienced military service; in fact it has been interestingly hypothesized that Shakespeare may have been a soldier in his "lost years" that coincided with a period of heightened English military activity.[33] Whether soldier or no, Shakespeare's depictions of soldiers and war was extensive and profound, certainly representing one of his greatest artistic achievements and contributions to our understanding of human nature, history, and values. Like the literature of the ancient Greeks, Shakespeare's works have been shown to be extremely relevant to the challenges facing modern soldiers. Much of what we see in Shakespeare is the madness and rage that can upset the mind of even the most controlled and careful tactician and leader. In *Coriolanus*, the title character's mother, the formidable Volumnia, reminds him that he was willing to employ deception in war, and begs him to hide his contempt for the plebeians when speaking to them. But this the belligerent Coriolanus cannot do, and his lack of self-control leads to his banishment, downfall, and death. Some of Shakespeare's foremost soldiers are villains, like Iago and Richard III. They are clever, but the unscrupulousness and indifference to others that they take to be a strength is their undoing. Others are clownish, like Falstaff and his companions, whose stupidity as much their cowardice and shallow cynicism make them unsatisfactory as men as well as poor military material.

However, Shakespeare's plays contain many examples of good soldiers who are well-trained and well-intentioned, even if ultimately tragic or unsuccessful. *Henry V* is Shakespeare's most sustained tribute to military thought and professionalism. Henry's intelligent leadership, his emphasis on both the morale and the discipline of his army keep his forces together over a long campaign of "marching in the painful field." At Harfleur, Henry does almost exactly what Volmnia refers to in her speech to Coriolanus, cowing a besieged fortress with words rather than hazarding the lives of his men. At Agincourt, the English are forced to fight at a severe numerical disadvantage. Henry turns this vulnerability into a source of strength, telling his men that their small numbers bestow on each man a greater share of honor, and famously referring to them all as "We few, we happy few, we band of brothers." Henry also rejects the French herald's offer of ransom, committing himself to the same hazards as his men. Henry's soldierly instincts tell him that a smaller army, well-led, whose soldiers' "hearts are in the trim" can defeat a larger force, and he is right. Henry and the English cause are likely saved by the well-trained and conscientious officers in his army. One of them, the Welsh captain Fluellen, has studied the classical literature on war, and he frequently refers to Roman texts as providing guidelines for proper conduct and tactics. Although he is fussy and pedantic, of Fluellen Henry says, "Though it appear a little out of fashion/There is much care and valor in this Welshman" (IV. I, 78–79).

Other Elizabethan writers have better-recorded military service than Shakespeare's, and the relevance and accessibility of their works have been amply demonstrated by Marine officer Adam McKeown in his study *English Mercuries: Soldier Poets in the Age of Shakespeare*. Elizabethan soldier-poets could speak eloquently, in a language that is the origins of our own modern tongue, of the moral and material unhealthiness of the fortified camp, of the perils and uncertainties of counterinsurgency, of war on a shoestring of uncertain popular support far from home.[34] The period of McKeown's book falls directly in the middle of the "military revolution" famously hypothesized in 1955 by Michael Roberts.[35] During 1550–1650, the size, range, and firepower of armies increased dramatically; organization and tactics were refined. These changes gave armies powers that for a time seemed almost uncontrollable. Under the influence of neostoical thinkers led by Justus Lipsius, the military revolution became in large part a moral one, which called on the soldier to change his stripes from those of scourge to those of moral exemplar and protector of civilization. The mercury, the messenger, is a precious national resource in any time. As McKeown and Lipsius point out, second perhaps only to that of securing victory, a prime moral obligation of the profession of arms is to act as a repository of knowledge about war, its cruel dynamics and calculus, its deceptive simplification of human values, its uncertain outcomes and unanticipated consequences.

Another distinguished work of criticism on early modern war literature is *History and Warfare in Renaissance Epic* by Michael Murrin.[36] Murrin's work traces the efforts of the writers of the period to describe war and combat, adapting the epic form that had evolved in the medieval period to technological and social changes, most especially the growing importance of gunpowder weapons and the supplanting of the knight by the officer as the dominant military figure. He links the effort for soldiers and writers (sometimes the same person) to adapt to these changes in both literary and military senses. To wage war, to exercise leadership and decision-making, is also to write, to find a descriptive, directive, hortatory language that is sufficient to the causes and forms of conflict. The writing in this period, the tropes and rhetorical devices, see a diminished emphasis on heroic individual actions and more on planning, command, and group action.

WORLD WAR I

In his classic work on World War I, *The Great War and Modern Memory*, Paul Fussell titles one of his chapters, "Oh What a Literary War" (taking off on the musical and feature film *Oh! What a Lovely War* (1963/1969). Due to a variety of factors, World War I saw an outpouring of high-quality writing, of poetry especially, that was unprecedented at least since the Elizabethan period, and that remains unequaled in the century since then. Still, World War I is often seen as an eschatological event, a unique departure from the past. In addition, trench warfare is generally regarded as a futile and irredeemable form of warfighting, a tactical dead-end leading to a strategic deadlock, and an expression of the exhaustion of military thinking at the time.

And yet the literature of World War I may be both more continuous within the history of war literature and more relevant to officer thought today than its particularist and eschatological placement would indicate. As in other times, the literature of World War I may be read as working out questions of leadership and command, of the ways in which leadership is performed through writing, and of the relationship between the poetic and the military vocation. The poet's language and sensibility may seem to undercut the usual objectives of military thinking, but the poet also raises issues that sometimes must be faced if effective leadership is to be possible, and that can curb wishful or shallow thinking about war and in war. The good soldier and the strong poet face facts, and they may help one another do so. Both soldier and poet use language to engage with but also to keep at a distance the brutal facts of war, lest they become what they behold. In World War I, death, once tragic or elegiac becomes squalid and industrial. World War I presented enormous challenges existential, metaphysical, and ethical. These challenges may have been partly responsible for the very high literary quality of much World War I writing, since only great literature was equal to the questions of that time (and of our own?).

To depict the relationship between military thought and World War I poetry, I will discuss the work and careers of three good officers: Siegfried Sassoon, Robert Graves, and Wilfred Owen. Graves and Sassoon both belonged to the 2nd Battalion, Royal Welch Fusiliers, and both men, perhaps Graves in particular, caught the intense regimental spirit of this prewar, regular infantry battalion, and in different ways both adapted the values of the regular soldiers with whom they served. The iconoclastic Graves developed a highly individualistic ethos based on classical and historical sources. His mythologizing of regimental esprit de corps steeled him to endure multiple tours of duty in the trenches. Siegfried Sassoon soldiered heroically while venting his mounting disgust at war in poetry. In addition to these sentiments, fox hunter Sassoon shows an appreciation for tactics and terrain, for the implements and equipage of war. His declaration and later recantation of conscientious objector status may be expressions of his strong solidarity with his fellow soldiers expressed in different voices. In his life and work, Wilfred Owen navigated the paradoxes of war and the soldier until his death leading his company a week before the Armistice. Owen was a sensitive man who suffered some of the worst that the western front had to offer, but who also expressed gratitude at finding the strength to return to active service after his own period of exhaustion and convalescence at Craiglockhart Hospital. He is certainly the best poet and perhaps the best officer of the three. His densely organized poems regard closely the sights of war and get inside the troubled minds of combatants. More than any other war poet, he is concerned with the wounded warrior, with the psychic and physical toll of war and the obligation that they impose on survivors and society.

Robert Graves was eighteen and a recent public school graduate when the war started. He enlisted partly to defer his dreaded start "at university." He saw his first major combat with the 2nd Battalion, Royal Welch, a unit that had been spared heavy losses until that time, and so still retained a high percentage of prewar regular officers. Like all newly arrived subalterns, Graves received a chilly welcome, but he came to respect the disciplined courage and efficiency of the old soldiers. Graves created almost a poetic private religion out of elements of regimental traditions and esprit de corps. He published two books of poetry during the war, attracting a following that included some of his fellow soldiers. Graves's poems may be said to have answered a need for a combination of continuity and individualism. In "An Old Twenty-Third Man," he has two veteran legionaries of the Twenty-Third Legion discussing the new recruits. Strabo is bibulously dismissive and disdainful of the younger generation, but Gracchus corrects and chastises him, saying "the Legion . . . is all right" and adding "you'll not better them by drinking." (Graves's regiment had been numbered 23rd before the reforms of 1881, decried by traditionalists, had replaced numbers with names.) There are lessons here for the veteran and recruit, and they are echoed in a later poem, "Sergeant Major Money" in which the eponymous Money, left on his own by inexperienced or ineffective officers to rebuild an infantry battalion of raw recruits, tries his prewar best but is eventually murdered for applying regular army standards in a "new (bloody) army he couldn't understand."

Siegfried Sassoon was born into privileged circumstances. He attended, but did not take a degree at Cambridge, was an avid fox hunter and all-around sportsman. He wrote poetry before the war, but it took the war and the army for him to find his real vocation as a poet. He was perhaps surprised to learn that he also had a vocation as an infantry officer. He acquired the nickname of "Mad Jack," became something of a specialist in the trench raid, and won the Military Cross, a high decoration much less common than the more routine Military Medal. Then, unexpectedly, he declared his public opposition to the war and refused to participate further. Not knowing what to do with a war hero turned conscientious objector, and due in part to the nerve-shattered and tearful testimony of his friend Robert Graves, Sassoon was sent to Craiglockhart Hospital in Scotland, where he played golf and underwent treatment with shell-shocked fellow officers. After a few idle months, he volunteered to return to full duty. He was sent to the Middle East and then back to the trenches of France, where he was wounded in no man's land shortly before the Armistice.

A poem that illustrates Sassoon's divided personality, his pacific and belligerent impulses, is "The Kiss," apparently composed after a session of bayonet training in France. This poem is almost equal parts irony and enthusiasm, or it might be more accurate to say that the reception depends on the audience. I once told a group of Boston University English professors that if I had pasted a copy of "The Kiss" on the old shack of the Parris Island close combat section that once long ago had been subjected to my inspired leadership, I'm sure one of the drill instructors would have said something like

"That's a pretty motivating poem sir! Did you write that poem?" The English professors were shocked. The poem reflects a reasonable ambivalence between a soldier's fear and perhaps distaste on the subject of bayonet fighting, and the inescapable possibility that he might have to use his bayonet in combat, and with the spirit and will to win. The short lines and sibilant alliteration suggest speed and a paring down, a lightening of the consciousness for action, for killing. As Sassoon says in another poem, as if in an incantation, "Soldier, you must kill. Morning is red."

"Counter-Attack" combines an eye for tactical detail with an unflinching look on the fatal consequences of exercising leadership in combat. This poem depicts an incident in which a British unit, having captured a section of German trench, is subject to counterattack. Sassoon develops a picture of the tactical situation with the eye of a fox-hunter-turned-infantry officer, and with a brevity and compression at once soldierly and the poetic: the clink of shovels as the defending unit improves its position, the placement of automatic weapons to anchor the defense. The poem illustrates a common dilemma of trench warfare, which was that, hard as it was to take an enemy trench, it could be even harder to hold, with men worn-out and diminished in numbers, in the face of preregistered fire ("traversing, sure as fate" are the words of the poem, mixing military language and metaphor), in positions facing the wrong way and accessible through the enemy's own approach trenches. (Sassoon refers to Germans coming up "the old sap.") The soldier at the center of the poem is killed defeating the counterattack, unheeded by the officer, the poet himself perhaps, who had ordered him to man the fire step.

Soldiering and officership did not come naturally to Wilfred Owen. No athlete, and of a lower social class than Graves and Sassoon, he nevertheless perhaps had in common with them that civil life in Edwardian England did not offer much that was very appealing or satisfying. By the time Owen arrived in the trenches, the fighting had truly descended into battles that were long slogs of attrition and unproductive assaults that went on for months. A particularly harrowing bout of outpost duty in winter is depicted in the poem "Exposure." Owen wrote knowingly in "S.I.W." about the approach of a soldier's breaking point and, suffering from "shell shock" and possibly a combat stress casualty, he wound up in Craiglockhart where he met fellow patient Sassoon. Owen showed him his work, deferring to him, Sassoon remarked, as to a senior officer. Sassoon told Owen to "Sweat your guts out writing poetry." Owen recovered, returned to France, was given command of an infantry company, and was also awarded the Military Cross. He continued writing poetry and corresponding with Sassoon, until he was killed in action a week before the Armistice at the head of his company. Before he was shot, he had just told one of his soldiers, "You're doing very well!"

Owen wrote a number of poems about combat, to include some on the officer's role as leader and tactician (see "Spring Offensive" and "Apologia Pro Poemate Meo") but he might be said to have specialized in poems about soldiers who had been severely wounded, and his perhaps greatest poem, "Strange Meeting," is about soldiers who have been killed. Owen's poems about the wounded were no doubt inspired by his own time in hospital, but many soldiers had this experience, Graves and Sassoon included. For Owen, the act of suffering and the experience of pity were very close to his vocation as a poet and his role as an officer. His hospital poems include "A Terre," "Mental Cases," and "Disabled." The speaker in "A Terre" seems to be suffering from both physical and psychological wounds. He is addressing a visitor who is also a poet ("That's for your poetry book"). In his yearning for one spring, or even for life as a "dug out rat," the speaker may be an allusion to Homer's Achilles in Hades, who says that he would rather live on earth as a slave than be lord of all the dead. The poet visiting the sick, doomed man is discharging a moral obligation, one still important despite that he cannot comfort this man in his despair. (Unlike Achilles, he has no son whose deeds on earth, as related by Ulysses, comfort the dead warrior in the underworld.) In war, it may be the best who suffer most, a point made in "Mental Cases," whose minds are "ravished" by the dead and the "multitudinous murders" that they have witnessed. This idea is enlarged upon in "Insensibility," in which the speaker condemns those who "by choice made themselves immune/To pity and whatever moans in man." The officer who ceases to feel the pity of war (in Owen's famous phrase) loses humanity, contact with his fellow mortals, and the right to lead.

Had he survived, it is easy to imagine Owen taking a compassionate postwar interest in the lives of the physically and mentally wounded. A professional caregiver for part of his prewar civilian life, and an ex-shell-shock patient himself, his poetic vocation would have made him someone especially able and sensitive in helping his fellow veterans.

Mortality is much of what warfare and military leadership are all about: how wars are decided, who wins; death is war's coin and consequence. As soldier-poet Philip Sidney suggests in *Defense of Poesy*, perhaps only poetry is capable of containing the paradoxes and moral mazes of the experience of warfare at firsthand. Poetry is uniquely instructive; lyrics stay in the mind after dry lessons are forgotten. I recall the junior officers whom I encountered during my participation in Operation Iraqi Freedom-1 who were reading the World War I poets. One told me he always carried a copy of Sassoon's poems. As I've said, my own threadbare poetic vocation was briefly reawakened by war. I am admiring as a failed poet and sometimes soldier of the success of the men I've spoken of in making strong poetry of their war experience. If it is an officer's job to educate people about war, these soldiers did their job and fulfilled their role. Poetry is a means for our heroes to stay humane, not viewing their role too narrowly, as not merely "managers of violence" (to paraphrase Samuel Huntington), but as soldier-poets of the sublime.[37] Even if not a poet, a leader may aspire to go beyond anecdote and narrative to develop his or her own poetics of leadership, the song behind the words and actions.

The junior officers of World War I were the senior commanders of World War II, the Montgomeries, Pattons and Marshalls, and the Rommels too. Many of these men came out of war determined to do better than their elders. They thought and innovated widely in the interwar years, developing improved tactics and means of Command and Control that were more effective and responsive than those of World War I. The war poets were part of the legacy of World War I that the survivors carried with them, a legacy that included a renewed appreciation for the costs of war and the results of doing your job in a limited way, without empathy or imagination. If, as biographer Jonathan Rose maintains, Winston Churchill was the principal poet of World War II, spinning off apt phrases and images to describe a myriad of events and circumstances, perhaps George C. Marshall was the master storyteller, the narrator as well as the architect of victory.[38] The skepticism and irreverence toward higher command expressed by the war poets in what are sometimes described as antiwar poems was in fact shared by some of the brightest junior career officers of the time. Some of the tactical lessons of World War I were unfortunately grasped very well by the Germans, although the larger import, the humanity most expressed in the work of Owen, was mostly lost on them.

WORLD WAR II AND VIETNAM

Another period of high-quality war literature occurred in the second half of the twentieth century. Among American novelists, some of the great authors and their works that reflect on officer thought in World War II are James Jones and his "Army Trilogy," beginning with *From Here to Eternity* (1950), Kurt Vonnegut and *Slaughterhouse-5*, Norman Mailer and *The Naked and the Dead*, Leon Uris and *Battle Cry*, Joseph Heller and *Catch-22*, Herman Wouk and *The Caine Mutiny*, and Thomas Heggen's *Mister Roberts*. All these books were made into feature films in the 1950s and 60s. Another work, *Twelve O'Clock High* was a mediocre novel but an excellent film still used to teach leadership to cadets and officers. A persistent theme in these works is the dilemma of the officer in the service of a democracy and citizen army.[39] Another frequent subject is the need for the officer to strike the proper relationship between his military superiors and the soldiers under his immediate command. Many of the officers are intelligent young men new to the service who are working out the terms and demands of their new roles. They must decide what aspects of the military hierarchy are valuable, which of its representatives are trustworthy, and which practices and individuals need to be questioned or even resisted, sometimes on behalf of the rights of their subordinates. The protagonist of *The Caine Mutiny*, Willie Keith, is an intellectual and aspiring English professor who for a time falls under the influence of Thomas Keefer, another officer with literary interests. The similarity in their last names suggest that Keefer is, if not quite a double, then an alternative self, a path that the younger Keith might choose. Keefer's hold on Keith is loosened through language when Keith discovers that the approved Navy technique of decoding messages is faster than the one Keefer had devised, arrogantly scorning the official procedure that he believes was created for "idiots."

The World War II novels and films also depict officers coming to terms with the sacrifices that must be made for victory, and with the dehumanization and trauma inflicted on friend and foe. Even in a notably just war, ethical issues emerge. The practice of bombing of cities is called into question in *Twelve O'Clock High* and in the books by Vonnegut and Heller. Infantrymen Jones, Uris, and Mailer all depict the murder and mistreatment of prisoners. All the books depict debased and demeaning sexual relationships. In all the works, officers make decisions in tactical situations and in matters of assignment, awards, and promotions. The extended narrative form of the novel provides the means to depict and discuss the rippling, complex consequences of their actions, although the fog of war and the impermanent nature of military communities may descend to impede complete knowledge. The most complete World War II narrative is undoubtedly Jones's. His trilogy (a tetralogy if one includes the short novel, *The Pistol*) concerns the lives of a group of evolving and renamed soldiers from the pre–Pearl Harbor regular army in Hawaii, to combat, to their return wounded to stateside hospitals and bases. The main characters are enlisted men, but their relationships with and treatment by officers is an important part of their lives, strongly influencing the character of their service and their feelings about the army. A corporal in *Whistle*, the last book of the trilogy, deserts out of disgust at the unfairness and ineptitude of his company commander. In the same book, a respected "old-army" colonel tries unsuccessfully to save Prell (the descendant of Prewitt in *From Here to Eternity*) from his self-destructive behavior.

The war in Vietnam produced a new generation of war novels. Two excellent examples by officers are Josiah Bunting's *The Lionheads* and James Webb's *Fields of Fire*. Webb's book focuses on the platoon and company level, with occasional interactions with higher headquarters. The problems faced by the officer-protagonist Lieutenant Hodges are mostly those of small-unit leadership and tactics. His training and instincts seem to have prepared him well for these kinds of challenges, but this does not prevent a war crime from being committed by members of his platoon. In fact, it is suggested that the strong esprit de corps that he has built in his platoon may have contributed to an atrocity committed in reprisal for the murder of fellow Marines.

Bunting's *The Lionheads* is unusual in that the novel's principal characters are concentrated in the middle ranks of captain through colonel. Bunting was an army officer who served in Vietnam. The officers he depicts are a mixture in terms of character and ability, but they are often, good and bad, depicted as thinking more of the institution than of the mission. This begins at the top, with the employment of the riverine craft assigned to the "Lionhead" division. The craft are slow and vulnerable compared to the helicopters used to transport the rest of the division's combat troops, but they are an "asset" that has the army's stamp of approval. To omit them from operations or point out their deficiencies would excite high-ranking disapproval, so used they must be, even at the cost of soldiers' lives. The highest-ranking character of *The Lionheads* is also its villain. General Lemming is in command of the "Lionheads." As opposed to the rather hapless General Curzon of C. S. Forester's *The General*, the novel of World War I on which Bunting's book was apparently modeled, Lemming is highly intelligent and competent as a tactician. In contrast to Curzon's anti-intellectualism, Lemming has a collection of classic books on military history that travel with him wherever he goes. We get a degree of insight into how his mind works. He has an instinct for the battlefield and the ability to squeeze information and results from his staff. He is contemptuous of their tendency to turn out snap solutions, pushing them for a correct answer, but while pretending to be asking for others' ideas, he is often seeking a reflection of his own thoughts. Lemming is ruthless, not just toward the enemy, but with his own soldiers. No dissent or interference will be allowed to put him in a bad light with those who will decide on his promotion and next assignment. The theme of *The Lionheads* is the separation of "remorse from power," as Bunting writes at the book's beginning, in a quotation from *Julius Caesar*. The reading habits of some of the main characters are revealing. The intellectual General Lemming (one of a literary line of brainy but dislikable, amoral generals that includes Tolstoy's Napoleon and Norman Mailer's General Cummings) is a nightly reader of his collection of classic military history. In the narrative, he is working his way through Douglas Southall Freeman's *Lee's Lieutenants*. One of his aggressive and effective but casualty-prone brigade commanders reads mostly field manuals. The militant Major Claiborne is a frequent reader who travels, like Lemming, with a collection of military books. The upper-class and able but slightly eccentric Colonel Robertson is a reader of Trollope and other nineteenth-century novelists. Almost defined by the books they read, it is perhaps a pity that the reading habits of these officers are not more diverse. Each man seems to read in a genre that reinforces his own tendencies of vainglory, groupthink, or iconoclasm. Robertson tells Lemming that he would like Trollope, but we have no indication that Lemming gives Trollope a chance. Reading works of this kind might make him see the exercise of authority in more complex ways that could undermine his single-minded ambition. Although Bunting is clearly sympathetic to Robertson, the literate colonel might benefit from a slightly less dilettantish approach to his profession, perhaps alternating Trollope with Freeman.

A late arrival to the literature of the Vietnam War and perhaps the best literary work of any genre to come out of the war is Karl Marlantes's *Matterhorn*. A feature of *Matterhorn* that makes this work especially interesting for purposes of this study is that the main character, Lieutenant Mellas, although far more self-aware and sympathetic than Lemming and the others of that ilk, is a notably intellectual officer. He lacks the hunting instincts of his fellow platoon commander Lieutenant Goodwin and the natural way of handling men of the company executive officer Lieutenant Hawke, but Mellas is thinking all the time. He enjoys the "intricate planning" involved in setting his platoon in the defense.[40] Mellas is cool, but he is not cold, and in fact he gains in empathy and identification with his fellow Marines the longer he serves, changing from a young man who identifies with power to one who is more interested in the human and ethical aspects of leadership. One of the aspects of *Matterhorn* that makes it so outstanding is its range of insight. Although written from the perspective of a junior officer, the novel creates characters up and down the hierarchy who are believable and to varying degrees sympathetic. Battalion Commander Lieutenant Colonel Simpson is inept and alcoholic, but he is also hampered and harried by demands passed on to him by his higher headquarters. His Regimental Commander Colonel Mulvaney is far more able, and he is also motivated by fierce esprit de corps, but his ability to control events or protect the lives of his Marines is limited by the intractable terrain and weather, a determined enemy, and a failing strategy that he recognizes is devolving into killing for its own sake. All these tactical leaders, from lieutenant to colonel, must make decisions in an environment in which "all choices are bad in some way."[41] As with the best of all war writing, the narrative and poetic qualities of *Matterhorn* lay out the often tragic terms of the choices and consequences of military leadership.

WRITING TO THINK

As many of the foregoing samples of military writing illustrate, serving and former officers have contributed some of the greatest works in the genre of war literature. For the officer considering doing some writing of her own, this legacy may even seem daunting. Who am I to presume to enter such distinguished company? There are other difficulties involved in writing by officers, among them limits on time and energy, and hesitation to upset conventional ideas. Thankfully, there are now both greater encouragement to write and many more venues than existed in the past. For my own part, writing has been indispensable in the development of my ideas and capacity for thought. Writing requires concentration and clarity. The writing, drafting, editing process exposes gaps in logic and in knowledge.

• 3 •

Obstacles to Thought

$\mathcal{I}$n war, it's hard to think, and it may be that it is hard even to think about war. I remember with some embarrassment the red rage that overtook me after 9/11. I was ready to lash out at anyone even remotely connected with the attack, and I went through a period of emotional xenophobia. I was a Marine reservist, and I was spoiling for a fight. The implications of this widespread mood, which was shared by many in positions of authority, have since been made painfully clear. Any number of inherently mystifying and cacophonous forces make clear military thinking difficult. Some of these factors are related to the elements of Clausewitz's friction: fear and fatigue, movement and uncertainty, wounds and losses. Some of the most crippling impediments to good military thinking may lie within, with personal and psychological factors that precede the battlefield, although they may be exacerbated by war and combat, and even by certain enduring aspects of military service, the separate culture of armies, and perhaps what Orwell called "the essential horror of army life." In this chapter, I will discuss both internal and external impediments to thought and the officer's efforts to overcome them.

THE HISTORY OF INCOMPETENCE

Failures of command and leadership in war have been the subject of a considerable sub-genre of military history, with many works on the subject appearing after the American defeat in Vietnam and a new generation of books coming out in the aftermath of the withdrawal of US forces from Iraq. Some of these works follow what has been called the "'bloody fool theory' of military history," but others have taken a more nuanced and psychological approach.[1]

65

The classic of this genre is *On the Psychology of Military Incompetence* by Norman Dixon, a distinguished British psychologist. Dixon's book was written in 1976 and reissued with a Foreword by military historian Geoffrey Wawro in 2016. Dixon's thesis is that the officer ranks tend to attract and to cultivate authoritarian personalities. These individuals tend to be overly respectful of authority and of orthodoxy, and in positions of power they do not welcome suggestions from subordinates, especially if the suggestions are notably creative or challenging to established practices. They may be inflexible, since to change their minds is to admit error. Such people may not be "bloody fools," exactly. At least some incompetent commanders have been quite intelligent by other standards and in other spheres, but they have been rendered incompetent by inner fears and conflicts. Another more recent book on the psychology of military incompetence is *Command Failure in War: Psychology and Leadership* by Robert Pois and Philip Langer. The authors of this book, one a psychologist and one a historian, see the phenomenon of military incompetence as more complex, and not simply a problem of authoritarianism. Both books devote chapters to British high command in World War I, with close attention to Field Marshall Sir Douglas Haig. Haig had been a competent corps and army commander in the early years of the war. He was promoted to command British forces in France after Sir John French was relieved. Haig commanded the British Army through the battering, attrition battles of 1916 and 1917, and then on to victory in 1918. For Dixon, he is virtually the "poster-child" authoritarian commander: not very bright, insecure, guilty of implanting in his subordinates a "terrible, crippling obedience" to orders that were often "vague."[2] This is the conventional picture of Haig, although one that has come in for revisionism. Pois and Langer argue that Haig's imperturbability in the face of months and years of terrible losses for limited gains (in territory, and in terms of damage inflicted on the enemy) was a necessary trait, and one that he shared with many of his countrymen, officer and enlisted. Haig commanded the British Army to victory. They never in any numbers mutinied or refused orders to advance. Most British soldiers went home with their pride and allegiances intact.

Haig's stolidity may have fit the strategic circumstances and British national character all too well, especially in an era of extreme nationalism, fueled in Britain by the spectacle of empire and an education system that stressed discipline and muscular Christianity. At a military level, better solutions to the problems of the offensive were likely available than those employed at the Somme and Passchendaele, but Haig and his fellow senior commanders (in a manner satirized in the fictional General Curzon by C. S. Forester in his novel *The General*) made it a virtue of not discovering or being distracted by them, at least until 1918, when improved British tactics, as well as German exhaustion and the arrival of the Americans, enabled victory.

Pois and Langer discuss other examples of commanders in whom psychology might have had a complex effect of success or failure. Frederick II's arrogance may have led him to defeat at Kunersdorf, but it also might have impelled his bold, startling victory at Leuthen. McClellan's fear of failure led him to achieve much in a successful business career and as an army organizer, but it could cripple him as a warfighter.

Although the authors of *Command Failure in War* profess a slightly different interpretation of how psychology influences how officers make decisions, and although their view of officers (and perhaps of human nature) is not quite so dim as Dixon's, all three writers appear to agree that psychology can have an influence on how officers think and decide. Some of the examples cited by Pois and Langer suggest that certain types of psychological states may impose limitations to thought that are useful. However, if the commander lacks awareness of his own psychology, this may be a hit-or-miss proposition. The circumstances of the western front in World War I may have helped to promote a man of Haig's temperament to top command, but it is at least troubling that Haig appears (if all three authors are right) to have been driven in his decisions as much by his own psychology as by an objective consideration of the military situation.

MEN IN GROUPS

Aside from internal, psychological factors, what are some of the external pressures on officer thought? Of course, the two categories are related. Like all people, officers are shaped by their environment, and like all occupations that of an officer is to a degree self-selecting, although the motives to seek a commission in the armed forces may be very diverse. Two enduring characteristics of military organizations are that they are hierarchical and mostly male. The hierarchical nature of the military may impede dissension and the advancement of innovative ideas that go against conventional wisdom or implicit preferences of the commander. To the traditional element of hierarchy has been added in recent times that of careerism, although the desire for favor and advancement is far from new. Careerism not only tends to reinforce uniformity of ideas, it can encourage officers to value their careers and those of others over the furtherance of the mission and the maintenance of important professional and ethical standards. This appears to be a notable trait of the US armed forces since World War II. Reliefs of senior officers have been few, with most for conduct rather than performance, and many impelled by the political leadership, as opposed to the officer ranks policing its own.[3] High-ranking officers may benefit from what has been called "preferential attachment" or "cumulative advantage."[4] Senior officers have been successful in negotiating the military hierarchy. In effect they are sometimes seen as exemplars of the virtues most prized in the military, even beyond their desserts. Although they are supposed to be held to a "higher standard," if the status and reputations of senior officers are threatened, even by their own misconduct or ineptitude, the military hierarchy may seem to close ranks to protect them.

There are understandable reasons why officers tend to protect one another's careers. Unlike other professionals, the officer has few options in seeking outside employment. A doctor or lawyer who finds herself in uncongenial surroundings can move to another practice or firm. An officer might seek a transfer, but her evaluations will follow her from the old command, as will the prevailing service culture. An officer who finds herself really out of step can request a move to another branch, but this is not always possible, and again it may not be a solution. There is the option of working for a private military contractor, but this may involve a sacrifice of pension and benefits, a loss of esprit de corps, of prestige and the idealistic motives associated with the role of commissioned officer as compared to that of a "gun for hire," even one in the employment of the US government. Despite the foregoing, no officer's career should be weighed more heavily than oath and mission.

The male dominance over military organizations has been modified somewhat in the past two decades, but men continue to constitute the great majority of military members and of senior military leadership. More than this, since military service is an activity with close, complex ties to maleness and perceptions of masculinity, hypermasculine or macho attitudes are dominant throughout the armed forces, with even some female members imitating masculine behavior or downplaying or effacing their gender identity in favor of one that is gender-neutral or masculine. Military forces have arguably benefited from, and even exploited the equation of military service and masculinity. Testosterone-fueled aggression has its uses on the battlefield as it has on the playing field, and the instinct for comradeship on the part of young men can also contribute to the unit cohesiveness that wins wars and battles. Such instincts and tendencies unchecked by discipline and restraint can have dire consequences, however, even leading to lawlessness and atrocity. On a cognitive level, the military dominance of men and of male attitudes can further limit the diversity of views, discouraging dissent and accountability. Conformity may come to be the price of cohesiveness. The "male option" may sometimes default to the course of action that is most violent and direct, deriding and overriding what may be more sensible measures as not so much ineffectual as effeminate. This behavior may be seen in frontline units, but it can also be practiced at the higher headquarters or other scenes of military planning and decision-making far from the battle. These settings are presided over by men self-consciously directing fighting done by others, and a desire to compensate for a "wimp factor" can have an influence on decisions. An insecure man may be led to opt for the more bellicose option to allay private feelings of weakness. Perhaps even more dangerous is the genuinely insensitive man, who has adopted conventional male "toughness" to such a degree that it has become unconscious and habitual.

The cult of toughness can have more subtle effects, creating an internal, unofficial hierarchy that can be divisive. This tendency is at the center of retired officer James R. McDonough's *The Defense of Hill 781: An Allegory of Modern Mechanized Combat*.[5] In McDonough's ingenious allegory, a deceased lieutenant colonel is given the chance to redeem himself and exchange purgatory for heaven by correcting his past leadership failures. The colonel had been a highly qualified airborne infantryman who had neglected and even mocked those he considered less soldierly than himself. In a series of exercises, he learns to value the contributions of all in the unit, to include support personnel, the less fit and experienced, and to show his appreciation openly.

The male tendency to suppress emotions may be intensified in the military environment. There is some justification for this, given the strong, and perhaps debilitating and distracting emotions that war and combat can bring. As I've already noted, George C. Marshall reminded officers that they could not be people who felt deeply but who thought only on the surface. A theme of the John Ford western *Rio Grande* (1950) is the emotional austerity cultivated by the officers. Sentiment and song are left to the enlisted men and the very few women on a frontier army post. On the other hand, it might be noted that the maintenance of health and housekeeping and other "maternal" practices are part of an officer's duties. Bullying, negative managerial practices, for example, satirized in the David Mamet play *Glengarry Glen Ross* (1992), are out of place in a military setting. In the Mamet play, the members of a real estate sales department are visited by a mysterious, abusive emissary and faced with summary dismissal if they do not abide by the rule of ABC ("Always be Closing") and make sales on a single rain-swept night. Officers can relieve subordinates from positions or of specific responsibilities, but soldiers cannot be summarily "fired" from the armed forces. Their rights as citizens are given emphasis by the fact that they serve the nation, and by the Constitutional oaths sworn by officers and enlisted members. Members of the armed forces possess the dignity of those who bear arms; their training and weaponry give them a last resort to treatment that they might come to consider as intolerable. Many a military bully has changed his ways when faced with the prospect of going into combat with soldiers whom he has given cause to hate him.

Another potential obstacle to clear and creative thought, and to a sense of proportion, is the military concern for minutiae. Junior officers are taught to cultivate an "attention to detail." This necessary habit may become fetishized by the rituals of dress and drill: ribbons placed just so above the pocket, every soldier in a file pivoting on the exact same point on the ground. This is another example, like the "tactical mindset," of the habits formed in youth sometimes impeding mental development.

The path to becoming an officer is demanding on many levels. The aspiring officer is taught to ignore pain and fatigue; this can develop into a callous disregard for the suffering of others, if the officer does not make a conscious effort to be empathetic. If there is a philosophy at large among officers in general, it is stoicism.[6] This can be helpful in overcoming adversity, and in enabling the individual to surpass personal limits, but if it is projected excessively and habitually onto others, subordinates and the victims of war especially, it can lead to the officer becoming what he beholds, even losing a vital element of the humanity and compassion that fit him to be a leader. The challenges and sacrifices of military service may contribute to the self-righteousness that Anton's Myrer's General Caldwell in *Once an Eagle*, protagonist Sam Damon's father-in-law and mentor, calls "the occupational disease of the soldier . . . and the worst sin in all the world," one that "spawns arrogance, selfishness, indifference."[7]

THE MIND IN CONFLICT

The nature of armed conflict offers many obstacles to clear thinking. Anyone with even a limited experience of the war zone can recall the skewed perceptions, the misjudged distances, the incomplete and selective memories. This is what makes training so valuable, since it gives the soldier a few simple principles or actions to follow and perform as if automatically. These trained habits can be limiting as well as empowering, reducing tactics and other military subjects to formula, and causing soldiers to engage in trained, routine behaviors instead of taking more effective action requiring risk or initiative.[8] This tendency may present fewer problems at the lower levels of warfighting, since small-unit actions are somewhat amenable to formulas, and the speed at which they take place puts a premium on a good course of action executed immediately as opposed to a perfect solution deferred. At senior levels, the preference for well-worn solutions can be catastrophic. The senior officers who make operational-level decisions are mostly middle-aged men enduring the rigors of campaign, under the enormous pressures of command and other forms of responsibility, and in effect justifying the value of long years of preparation and selection for a chance that may come only once in a career. There is pressure to produce results but also to avoid error. Conventional solutions that fail may appear to be more defensible than unconventional solutions that fail or succeed only marginally. Officers may attempt to impose order on the chaos of the battlefield by an excessive adherence to schedules, to routine, to stereotypical solutions. They may also attempt to limit or close off their perceptions in circumstances that are frankly overwhelming. The effort to focus the mind is understandable and necessary, but it may also have negative consequences. An example of this is the tendency to dehumanize the enemy. This may be an understandable reaction against the idea that one is killing beings as fully human as oneself, but it may have the consequence of increasing violence and brutality, and the dehumanization of the enemy may expand to encompass the entire surrounding population, even leading the officer to place less value on human life in general. This can bring about what has been termed "moral injury": the loss of important values because of trauma, disillusionment, or the failure of oneself or others to live up to professed beliefs.[9] The understanding and treatment of this condition often go beyond the usual clinical methods, touching on ethical issues and bringing us back to the humanities.

The 1952 book and 1957 feature film *The Bridge on the River Kwai* can be read and seen as a case study in unhinged military incompetence. Subject to sweltering and prolonged solitary confinement and sensory deprivation by his Japanese jailer Colonel Saito, British colonel Nicholson, too tough and disciplined to give way to his captor, and having held himself together through very adverse conditions, emerges from his isolation with the fixed idea of keeping his battalion intact no matter what the cost. His privileging of the military organization over that which it is supposed to serve is typical of some military mis-thinking. In this case, the colonel aids the Japanese in setting his men to work efficiently on a bridge that is to have military purposes. Officers and men have their doubts about this cooperation with the enemy, but their exaggerated regard for authority along with their deep respect for the colonel keep them working diligently. The fact that the colonel earns the confinement that unhinges him by insisting that his officers not perform manual labor might suggest an exaggerated emphasis on officer exceptionalism. The excusing of officers from manual labor is likely based partly on class distinctions, although it has a practical basis too in the officer's role as planner and thinker. Ironically, the colonel and the other officers signally fail in this role, performing well at a tactical or technical level, but leading their men in a project that will benefit the Japanese army! Only when he is responsible for the death of a British (actually, Canadian) soldier trying to blow up the bridge does the colonel realize his mistake and redeem himself by tripping the explosive detonator with his bullet-riddled body.

Another, ancient depiction of blind error in war occurs in Virgil's classic *The Aeneid*. When the Trojans drag the fatal wooden horse into their city, some of them can actually hear the Greeks inside. As Aeneas recounts, "Four times the horse halted in the gateway, and each time weapons clanged within it. But we remained witless, and blind, and mad; we pressed ahead, and stationed the malignant horror within our consecrated citadel."[10] The Trojans, overjoyed at seeming peace and victory after ten years of war and siege, refuse to accept the fact that they are being tricked by the wily Greeks. Already intent on their celebration, their minds will not accept what their sense is telling them. The ability to face unpleasant facts is almost a job description for a military officer. When hope slides into unreality, she is doomed to bad decisions and a rude awakening.

Positive efforts to keep the mind ready to function under the stress of military service and war include self-care and self-knowledge. Getting enough sleep, exercising at least moderately as the situation permits, personal hygiene, care of equipment, eating and drinking moderately all seem to help soldiers to deal with stress and to think clearly. Cultivating a degree of self-knowledge can help to prevent the undue influence of personal and psychological factors in cognition. An officer has a professional obligation to rid herself of personal "immunities to change," of prejudice, resentments, and preconceptions, in order to become what has been described as a "clean machine," an agent intent on proper accomplishment of the mission rather than on the protection of personal and professional vulnerabilities.[11] Reading and religion can provide solace and relief from the pressures of war and military life. Few of these coping mechanisms are without possible side effects. Too much awareness or introspection can be distracting or enervating. In modern times, frequent communication with home and family can be a boost to morale or a depressing reminder of current loss and deprivation, of the uncertainty of the future. Perhaps the greatest asset is mature mental adaptability, which may be a challenge both for the very young and inexperienced and the older and habit-bound. Military life, in garrison and on campaign can bring satisfaction and fascination as well as fatigue, pain, and fear. Simple, undemanding humor can be comforting and even serve as a tool of leadership. Surviving and thriving under difficult circumstances often involves a degree of self-forgetting, an intention to help others, to see the circumstances from their perspective, and to lighten their load in some way, however small.

· 4 ·

Officers and the Intellectual Virtues

$\mathcal{T}$he classic approach to thinking is represented by Aristotle. Indeed, the rationalist tradition in Western thought may be said to begin with Aristotle. Aristotle distinguishes excellence in an occupation from true human excellence. However, he also acknowledges that certain occupations, such as those of physician and politician, may call for a broader knowledge that encompasses an understanding of human nature.[1] For this broad study of officer thought, Aristotle's explication of what he calls the intellectual virtues will be especially useful. For Aristotle, the five intellectual virtues are science, art, prudence, wisdom, and intuition. Science is based on an understanding of certain enduring principles. Art, also referred to as skill, or *techne*, is a reasoned productive activity, one that makes things. Aristotle also acknowledges the debt of art to chance, which might be another way of saying inspiration, accident, or serendipity. Prudence is the power of deliberating and of making correct decisions. It may be said to be aided by the virtue of intuition. Prudence is unique among the intellectual virtues in being firmly rooted in moral goodness and in wisdom. The good and wise may not always be prudent, but the prudent are always from among the ranks of the wise and the good. The officer has need of all five intellectual virtues. I will return to prudence as one particularly neglected and essential, but I will here briefly introduce the other four. Following this, I will engage in a more detailed discussion of each virtue in order.

THE INTELLECTUAL VIRTUES, BRIEFLY

Science and war have been allied at least since the time of Archimedes. Officers have often had to think like scientists to understand such factors as movement, weather, projectiles and propellants, and the health and care of the body. Officers are empiricists: testing weapons, formations, and tactics in training and in battle to find and improve the methods that work.[2] More problematic is the idea that officers are scientists in the sense of following immutable principles of war. Although principles of war have been taught and putatively applied since first enumerated by Sun Tzu, they cannot be verified or relied upon in the same way as scientific laws.

The military profession has also been described as an art, and the officer has some need of the tools of the artist. The officer's task is creative as well as destructive. If under art we include craft and skill, then fighting skills and the use of weapons fall under art. The mastering of fighting technique and the creation of new techniques also call for art. At a higher level, the military commander may have occasion to draw on the artist's chance discovery. Chance, as Von Clausewitz famously said in describing his "remarkable" trinity, is the domain of the army, while the state and people are respectively associated with reason and the passions.

Following Aristotle, Thomas Aquinas refers to military command as a form of intellectual and moral prudence. Aquinas's arguments on this subject emphasize the ethical demands of war, and not for commanders only, but for all those exercising a degree of choice. The exercise of command and the military profession in general are necessarily rooted in ethics, first in concern for the lives of others, friends and enemies, combatants and civilians, but also in the pursuit of a just cause. I will argue that it matters much more innately than it does for the artist or scientist that the military professional exercise prudence. (Perhaps political and military science courses and departments should be renamed departments of military and political prudence!) The morally imprudent scientist or artist may get into trouble eventually, and one might even argue that his imprudence can be reflected and detected in the work, but characteristically imprudent military commanders and officers are a danger to all and unworthy of their authority. They do not lead but drive. They endanger and disgrace the cause they serve. They recklessly and heedlessly expose their soldiers to danger and flout the protections against harming prisoners and other noncombatants.

It might be said that the officer, as one engaged in an active occupation, has need of prudence rather than wisdom. Does the officer require wisdom per se? I will argue that she does. Wisdom is the engine of prudence, but the officer who views wisdom in a purely instrumental way, who does not cherish wisdom to a degree merely for its own sake, is unlikely to acquire the full measure of wisdom that prudence requires, especially given the diverse demands of her profession. Also, soldiers do not only or always act. They also write and instruct. The accumulated knowledge of the military profession would be much poorer if officers had not privately and publicly reflected on their service, on their relations with civil society and political authority. Even the soldier in the field is a "mini-philosopher" (a lover of wisdom) weighing conflicting values along with competing courses of action.[3]

Aristotle appears to use the Greek word for intuition in a different sense from the meaning given to intuition by moderns. For moderns, intuition is seen more as an insight into people's motives and feelings. For Aristotle, intuition, *nous*, is an apprehension of first principles, an instinctive feel for the relevant moral issue in a question or circumstance. *Nous* might be translated as moral intuition. In my discussion of intuition, I will refer to both modern and Aristotelian definitions and to a third. The officer may, with time, acquire a kind of intuition about tactical situations and also about the culture and standards of the organization, about what is possible and permissible.

THE OFFICER AS SCIENTIST

The marriage of science and war is almost as old as organized warfare itself. It has been a rocky relationship, however, with scientists and officers often holding one another at arm's length, inhabiting very different professional cultures, and even appearing to hold differing values. Soldiers have often seen themselves as bearers of tradition, as representatives and upholders of the social and political hierarchy, while science has often been an abettor of change, a challenge to tradition and to religion, although not necessarily by intention. War and soldiers have need of science, for its union of empiricism and induction, of observable fact and reasonable theory. Officers may recruit science or even apply some scientific methods, but, as the philosopher Gaston Bouthoul observes, there is no real science of war, which he hypothetically would name "polemology," but only a collection of historical facts, perhaps capable of giving the illusion of a science.[4] Still, officers and scientists have often cooperated, and more than this, officers have often come to think like scientists with respect at least of some aspects of war's demands.

The infusion of scientific thought into the thinking of officers perhaps begins with the work of scientists as advisers to military commanders. The first famous scientist to put his abilities at the service of a military operation was Archimedes (287–212 BC). Archimedes is famous for the contrivances he created for the defense of Syracuse against a mighty Roman task force during the Second Punic War. The devices that he made and deployed for the defense of the city: the cranes, catapults, and fortress improvements, were not new. What was new, according to Brett Steele and Tamara Dorland, the editors of *The*

Heirs of Archimedes: Science and the Art of War through the Enlightenment, was that Archimedes is responsible for "infusing military thinking with rigorous mechanistic reasoning."[5] He anticipated the Roman moves, set up effective countermeasures, and coordinated the defenses of the fortress into a unified whole. Archimedes is identified with the origins of systematic approach to warfare on the part of military organizations. Dorland and Steele organize such systematic thinking into four domains: acquisitional, operational, tactical, and political. The definitions that they provide of tactics and operations are essentially the conventional ones in which tactics is concerned with individual engagements and operations with the campaign. Acquisition and politics are closely related and maybe even mixed, in that both are concerned with obtaining and utilizing resources. Whether Archimedes's mathematical genius and ingenuity in effect translated into extraordinary ability in the four military domains is open to debate, but there is no doubt that his efforts severely discomfited the Romans, who had expected a quick victory. Archimedes's application of a scientific approach to warfare was something new, and it has been imitated by many others since, making the Greek "discovery" of rational inquiry and of empiricism (with its origins in Aristotle) only slightly older than the use of these methods to warfare. The disparity between science and war is driven home in the death of Archimedes. In a scene that may express the arrogance of both the soldier and the scientist, and perhaps the respective limitations of scientific and military thought, Archimedes was killed at the end of the siege by a Roman soldier sent to take him captive, and whom the scientist ordered not to disturb the circles that he was drawing in the ground. The legionary, likely fed up after a siege that Archimedes had helped to prolong for eight months, and maybe drunk on looted Syracusan wine, gave the scientist his last lesson in tactics, that the sword counts as well as the circles.

THE FATE OF THE SOLDIER

Archimedes and the Greeks generally began a rational and empirical approach to warfare that would never quite be lost to the West.[6] The conservatism of the Roman Empire and the strict hierarchies and religiosity of late antiquity and the Middle Ages inhibited the exercise of scientific thought and the development of a profession of scientists. The emphasis in these periods was more on craft and skill than on science. In technology, some innovations took place, such as the trebuchet and the use of stirrups for horsemen. The revival of science in warfare could be identified with Leonardo, who as an artist *cum* engineer may be a pivotal figure in military science as well as the archetypal "Renaissance man." There is controversy among historians as to how much interaction took place between scientific and military thought during the seventeenth-century "scientific revolution."[7] Recent work on the subject tends to promote the importance of scientific thought, both as an enabler of technology and through what might be called its "second order" effects on cognition. In his book on military command in the seventeenth century, Erik Lund says that war became a "science of practical experimentation" and officers "speculative thinkers grounded in empiricism."[8]

Throughout the early modern period, and accelerating into the eighteenth century, science was on the minds of officers on many levels. The topics of military science included mathematics, ballistics, engineering, education, theory, and doctrine. One mathematical application was the design of formations that supported the complex infantry firing systems of the period. Mathematics was also used by gunners to enhance the accuracy of the evolving artillery. Both artillery officers and engineering officers became distinct groups in this period, often disregarded by officers of the more traditional infantry and cavalry, but gaining in prestige, due in part to their demonstrable credentials and competence. The military academies that came about during this period often specialized in producing officers for the new technical branches. Writing on military subjects increased steadily during the early modern period, and grew very fast after 1750, especially in France, where a characteristic national theoretical bent expressed itself in military writing as in other areas.[9] The Encyclopedists in France devoted lengthy articles to military subjects in their seminal effort to catalog human knowledge. Much military writing stressed the practical, vocational aspects of warfare, but some writers ventured into theory; among them were Raimondo Montecucolli, Jacques-Antoine-Hippolyte, Comte de Guibert, and Henry Lloyd. One issue discussed by all these writers was that of the proper balance between shock action and firepower. Guibert actually designed formations and drill movements that would strike a proper balance depending on the situation and allow for rapid change from column (which favored movement and shock) to line (which allowed for more firepower).[10]

A scientific mindset among some officers survived the Enlightenment, continuing into the nineteenth century in part through the writings of Antoine-Henri Jomini. Jomini was a great admirer of Napoleon, but in his idol he may have perceived more science than was really there. Napoleon observed some basic principles in war. He recognized different forms of fighting depending on whether he was numerically inferior or superior, assuming a central position in the former instance and splitting his army to hold with one force and strike with the other in the latter case. Jomini took theory to another level, however. He compiled principles of war, and he was a proponent of viewing the battlefield through a lens of interior and exterior lines, bases, and key points. His assertion that while strategy may be considered a science, war could not, since it is subject to too many chance factors, may presage the acknowledgment in modern science of such principles and chaos and uncertainty. The distinction between war and strategy has sometimes been overlooked, but it is a necessary corollary to scientific thought on war. Strategy is concerned with what is calculable and predictable in war. This may constitute only a small percentage of what happens in war, certainly less than half, since one half lies within the province of the adversary, although his efforts at control are subject to the same limitations as our own, to misfires and misdirection, accidents and bewilderment.

The man who was unquestionably the most famous theorist of war arose in this period. If it is theory plus observation that distinguishes the scientific approach, then Karl von Clausewitz was a scientist, although he was likely more than that. Clausewitz and his high-born and very intelligent wife Marie inhabited a remarkably erudite milieu of Prussian and European society, in an atmosphere friendly to philosophical thought.[11] Clausewitz may be credited with evolving, after many previous writers on war had perhaps tried and failed, a science of war that was nearly equal to its contradictions. He named as friction the element that causes operations in war to go awry. Friction is caused by violence and fear, by movement and fatigue. Soldiers and military writers had been acquainted with these things for millennia, but until Clausewitz they had had no theory with which to make sense of it and attempt to account for it. Clausewitz's was the "remarkable trinity" of government, people, and army represented respectively the elements of reason, the passions, and chance in war. This triangle expressed elegantly the paradox seen but less well comprehended by Jomini, the unbridgeable gap between military force and the ends it putatively serves. Finally, Clausewitz theorized about the role of force in war, leading some to see him as at least an apologist for heavy-handedness and even atrocity. Really he was neither. Like those who had come before and those who have followed, Clausewitz could not develop a fully satisfactory, verifiable theory that could lead to consistent results like those obtained in the lab. If Archimedes is the beginning of science in war, Clausewitz stakes out the limit. Like other highly intellectual scientists and mathematicians, he evolved into a philosopher of his discipline. His achievement as a scientist blends into philosophy in effect by subjecting his own historical and empirical methods to critique. Clausewitz does not wear out the connection of science and warfare, or even rule out the possibility, however remote, of a true science of war. His ideas have been improved upon and refined, but never supplanted.[12] In this sense he may be an even more eminent figure in the field of war studies than was Einstein in physics, the man whom many would give the title of preeminent scientist. Clausewitz pushed the boundaries of the knowable and verifiable in war.

Most American army officers of the antebellum period were trained at the US Military Academy at West Point. Writer and Canadian officer Ian Hope advances what might be called a minority view of military science in his study of the military education received by American army cadets at the antebellum West Point. In *A Scientific Way of War: Antebellum Military Science, West Point, and the Origins of American Military Thought*, he argues that West Point preserved the scientific Enlightenment approach to warfare to the benefit of a generation of officers who went on to command the armies of both sides in the Civil War.[13] In fact, the term for this approach, amounting a doctrine, is military science. Hope argues that the scientific approach to war, grounded in a curriculum that stressed engineering and mathematics, was responsible for American military excellence in the nineteenth and into the twentieth centuries. Although he finds that much of the scientific approach to war remains among American officers, he believes that it has been diluted by an excessive adherence to Clausewitz, amounting to a loss of clarity about military operations and war.

Another nineteenth-century soldier-scientist was French Army colonel Ardant du Picq. In *Battle Studies*, du Picq roots his observations in history and personal experience. Writing in mid-century, du Picq saw the need for changes in training, organization, and tactics because of the power of new weaponry. These would increase the duration and intensity of fire, necessitating greater emphasis on cohesion and initiative and a new kind of leadership. The constant was the heart of man, allowing historical examples to retain relevance, as with Clausewitz, not because they were repeatable, but because war remains a deadly struggle fought by mortal beings. Du Picq practiced empiricism, famously asserting, "To verify, observe better, to demonstrate, try out and describe better. To organize, distribute better, bearing in mind that cohesion means discipline."[14] Du Picq was killed at the head of his regiment early in the war with Prussia in 1870, perhaps leaving his work incomplete, since his published works were mostly compiled from notes he had left behind.

So far, our consideration of the officer-as-scientist after Archimedes has focused mostly on writing and teaching. Are there identifiable examples of officers acting, planning, and conducting operations in the manner of scientists? Given the scientific or science-inspired writings of soldiers on war, can we say how the theory was applied, and how the habit of theorizing from observation was carried into practice? Before I discuss a couple of examples of officers arguably thinking like scientists, I will list some hypotheses, based in part on the foregoing examples. A very general one is that while the products of science and the scientific method may be very useful to officers, science cannot fully comprehend war, and to understand war, and not merely to deliver military victory, is the officer's real task. Victory may at times be simply unattainable, or not worth the price, or be no victory at all, but a crime successfully committed. Ideally, the officer will be able to recognize this situation before the conflict is joined, and be in a position to avert an unwise or unjust conflict, but he may lack the foresight, support, influence, or authority to do so. In such cases, the officer may find herself fighting a war that should not have started. What then? Whatever the answer, science does not provide it. A scientific approach to warfare on the part of officers sometimes is noteworthy for what it omits as much as for what it includes. It may tend to pedantry, pseudo-science, or amorality. On the other hand, the divorcement of science from warfare, or of officers from scientists, may lead to mystification and unreality. This may be especially true in peacetime when wishful thinking can predominate, but during conflict, the "fog of war" may rise very high, at times clouding the minds of even those far above the fray. Those in the close fight see that reality, but they also feel the most, and sometimes too much. The officer who moves often between the command post and along the front lines may have the best chance of taking in the right data, but this can be a dangerous, exhausting, and time-consuming activity. Even to attempt an accurate science of war makes heavy demands that only some officers can sustain for long.

The German General Staff provides an object lesson in the pursuit of war as a science. Originating in Prussia in the early nineteenth century and given impetus by Prussian defeats at the hands of Napoleon, the Prussian version was the model for other general staffs, especially after the German defeat of France in 1871. After World War I, the victors paid the compliment to the German General Staff of insisting that it be disbanded. It was revived, at first in secret but later, after the rise of Hitler, openly, and again it confirmed its reputation in World War II by overseeing victory after victory, and later by staving off defeat by materially superior opponents. Candidates for the staff were junior officers who were subjected to rigorous selection and education that stressed historical study, theory, and wargaming. General Staff officers divided their time between service with troops and with the headquarters in Berlin. The staff developed war plans and new tactics based on an analysis of history, of their adversaries, and on the exploitation of technological developments. Their theory owed a large debt to Clausewitz, perhaps especially his concept of friction. Prussian planning and execution stressed maximum flexibility, simplicity, and the initiative of subordinate commanders. Their grasp of the trinity, and of Clausewitz's dictum that war is policy pursued through other means, was not so secure. Starting with the elder von Moltke, who reigned as chief of staff from 1858 to 1888, and ending with the rise of Hitler, the Prussians nearly reversed the subordination of the army to the state.[15] The primacy of the army in Prussia was not the invention of the General Staff. It went at least as far back as Frederick II in the mid-eighteenth century, but the theorizing of the General Staff and the success of their scientific methods gave this reversal further justification. The militaristic nature of the Prussian monarchy helped to develop the General Staff, and the General Staff in turn abetted German militaristic tendencies. A scientific approach based on Clausewitzian theory and European military history led the General Staff to undervalue deception and intelligence. The General Staff never developed a global strategy. If the General Staff approached war like scientists, in effect reducing war to a science, their focus on their own proven methods and expertise appears to have left little room for reflection or restraint. Erwin Rommel once said that General Staff officers were like marble: smooth on the outside but black at heart. The German propensity for innovation also sometimes became a willingness to embrace the frightful. Aerial bombing of civilians, poison gas, the flamethrower, and "unrestricted" submarine warfare were all German innovations of World War I. Not all of these can be laid squarely on the doorstep of the General Staff, but these men had an impact on German military thought and practice all out of proportion to their numbers, and they stand as a warning of what a certain kind of narrowly instrumentalist dedication to war can do.

It could also be said that officers in the years leading up to World War I suffered from a lack of science. In place of empirical observation and induction, much of the military thought of this time comes across as murky speculation and strident denial of lessons that should have been learned from the experiences of the Boer War and the Russo-Japanese War. The chief lesson was (or should have been) the great increase in defensive firepower brought on by magazine-fed rifles and the machine gun. But officers chose (borrowing from the ideas of Fredrich Nietzsche, Charles Darwin, and Henri Bergson) to insist that this development could be overcome by the stronger will, the dominant tribe, *elan,* and aggressiveness in attack.[16]

The marriage of scientists and officers likely came to a height in World War II, and it has left behind a strong legacy in the form of various organizations and institutionalized practices. Whether officers have come themselves to think more like scientists, following in the tradition that Archimedes may be said to have bequeathed to the civilian codebreakers at Bletchley Park or the bomb-makers of Los Alamos, is a more complex question, but one that can in general be answered in the affirmative. The direct descendants of such scientific-military cooperation can be found in think tanks like the RAND Corporation and the Defense Advanced Research Projects Agency (DARPA). Another World War II invention was the field of Operational Research (OR), which used probability to predict enemy actions, aiding the allies in the Battles of Britain and the North Atlantic.[17] These developments highlighted tension as well as cooperation between the officers and scientists. J. Robert Oppenheimer, the scientific head of the Los Alamos project under the military director General Leslie Groves, had his security clearance revoked after the war because of alleged communist ties and security violations. Bletchley Park codebreaker Alan Turing was convicted under antigay laws in Britain and died a probable suicide. The uniformed service chiefs were opposed to the creation of DARPA (originally ARPA) because it seemed to infringe on their own domains. (All, for example, claimed space as their rightful territory.) It was America's foremost former officer, President Eisenhower, who, acting on the principle of unity of command, overrode the service chiefs' bickering and established ARPA in 1957.[18]

In "Is Military Science 'Scientific'?" Glenn Voelez issues a warning against excessive scientism among officers.[19] Citing the work of Nobel-laureate economist Frederick Hayek, Voelez, an army lieutenant colonel when the article appeared in the *Joint Forces Quarterly* in 2014, decries pretensions to "competence" and "expertise" based on a misapplication of scientific methods. Voelez writes, "the fixtures of doctrinal orthodoxy have created an aura of pseudo-scientific in the military planning process." As antidotes, he suggests considering methods from other fields such as biology, epidemiology, and meteorology, and cultivating an atmosphere of skepticism, intellectual honesty, and scholarly accountability.

As I have already observed, the hubris of military science is far from new. It may have reached its height during the war in Vietnam and under the direction of the numbers-crunching Secretary of Defense Robert McNamara, whose commitment to quantitative measurements of success allowed the war to go on its un-winning ways. In this case, one far from unique, bad science was the servant of fears and feelings, of an unwillingness to fail or to be held responsible for failure, of an excessive investment in methods that had worked in the past, of personal loyalty taking preference over wider responsibilities.

In applying science to war, there may be a high persistence of what could be called, with again thanks to Aldous Huxley, the "ape and essence" factor, of the rational, even brilliant human mind at the service of the irrational and atavistic. Arguably, however, scientific schemata and methods may be helpful, even humanizing, perhaps especially if they are not trusted too implicitly. One of the activities that the military has tried to reduce to a science is that of planning. The planning process is described differently in the doctrine of the various services and in joint services doctrine, but there are considerable commonalities. The steps in the planning process usually involve framing the problem, mission analysis, developing and gaming the courses of action, and selecting a best course of action. If science provides predictable results, then the planning process is far from scientific, since it may yield widely different courses of action, but in fact this is part of its purpose, since the different courses of action proposed by a staff to a commander are supposed to be distinguishable. Two groups of officers may also evolve divergent "best" courses of action, due to differences in interpretations of the facts, and influenced by personality and service culture. Of course, as philosophers of science from Karl Popper to Paul Feyerabend have noted, even "hard' science is not immune from cultural and psychological influences. To the extent that science involves procedure backed by theory, the planning process may be said to be scientific, even to represent a form of scientific experimentation. The military has also borrowed quasi-scientific managerial tools from the business sector: flow charts, critical path analysis, measures of performance and of effectiveness.

Finally, the military is not alone in trying to impose scientific rigor on the inherently unpredictable. Economists and social scientists may be said to do likewise. As suggested by Glenn Voelez, these represent exactly the kind of inexact science that the military might profit from studying. The definition of science as "organized common sense" offered by T. H. Huxley is perhaps helpful. The military has made common cause with sociologists and anthropologists. Social scientists Morris Janowitz, Samuel Huntington, and Charles Moskos have studied the military community, often with a distinct focus on the officer corps. In recent years, military forces have hired anthropologists to gain a better understanding of local culture. Science and war continue their ancient, uneasy relationship.

THE OFFICER AND *TECHNE*

The Greek word *techne* used by Aristotle to describe one of the intellectual virtues had a meaning and connotation difficult to render in English. *Techne* meant craftsmanship as well as art, which for the Greeks were inseparable, if not synonymous. Today we are likely to make a sharp distinction between art and craftsmanship, and to a lesser degree between the artist and craftsman. In this view, few craftsmen are artists, and while some artists may be craftsmen, they need not be, or at least not be very distinguished as such. In this discussion, I will be speaking of the officer as both an artist and a craftsman. *Techne* also denoted manual skill, which upper-class Greeks like Aristotle tended to despise as fit only for social inferiors. In fact, neither the artist nor the craftsman enjoyed much prestige in Greek society. Even individual skill at arms was something about which the Greeks were somewhat ambivalent, as something more suited to a mercenary or military arts instructor than to a full-status citizen-soldier. It was *arête*, excellence of character, not *techne*, that was supposed to win the fight. The meaning and the ranking of *techne* (as art/craft/skill) has changed in our time, but not entirely out of recognition. Whatever else, *techne* is an intellectual virtue that requires some manual skills for expression. The balance of the mostly mental to the manual shifts as we move from art to craft to skill. Some of the preference of the ancient Greeks for mental over manual ability has survived into our own time. For convenience as well as clarity, I will discuss the officer as artist, as craftsman, and in relation to manual skills in succession, and then sum up their relationship, commonalities, and usefulness.

THE OFFICER AS ARTIST

It has been common for centuries to refer to war as an art. Three great military classics by Sun Tzu, Niccolò Machiavelli, and Antoine Jomini are given the common titular translation of "The Art of War." War has been the frequent subject of art: literary, "plastic" (pictures and sculpture), and musical. Sometimes, the artist and the soldier have been the same person. Starting in the twentieth century, many armies have possessed official art programs staffed by artists in uniform. Art about war has had an enormous effect on those who bear arms, helping to define how officers and other soldiers see themselves, perceive the causes for which they fight, go about their work, think, and act. This begins in the West with the *Iliad* and Greek drama and chorus, with the Roman *Aeneid*, with Greek and Roman statuary and architecture (to include the sculptures and structures made specifically to celebrate victory and extol military virtue and heroes), the Spartan fife, Roman martial and triumphal music.

Officers and other soldiers have been inspired by art. Have they also, consciously or not, imitated the artist? To what degree is (or ought to be) thinking by officers akin to that of artists? Is war at all an art? If the essence of the relationship between war and science is the union of fact and theory, that between war and art may lie in the creative act. This presents a difficulty, maybe especially for moderns, in that to describe war as something creative or beneficial seems much too complimentary of war, and even to venture on an aesthetic appreciation for the acts and scenes of war that they do not deserve. Sun Tzu saw war as natural as the seasons and in its own way as beautiful. Machiavelli advised Renaissance princes and patrons on an activity that was an inevitable part of the ruler's repertoire. Jomini celebrated the virtuosity of his hero Napoleon. Is it callous to call war an art? It might be argued that for an officer to perceive her role as artist is to humanize the practice of warfare, to lay stress on creative ends rather than destructive means: the liberation of a people, the defense against aggression, the return to peace. Like the artist, the officer may sometimes envision a better world or way of life, keeping in view a progression toward a background of peace beyond the conflict that is in the foreground. Armed conflict itself may call for creativity, and other artistic borrowings like imitation, *hommage*, the employment of motifs, symbols, and narrative. Officers may be in effect stage managers and artistic directors, given the inescapable performative aspects of war. In his memoir, *Good-Bye to All That*, Robert Graves quotes a fellow infantry officer on the aesthetic and combat-effectiveness qualities of drill.

> 'Arms-drill as it should be done,' someone said, 'is beautiful, especially when the company feels itself as a single being, and each movement is not a synchronized movement of every man together, but the single movement one large creature. I used to get big bunches of Canadians to drill: four or five hundred at a time. Spokesmen stepped forward once and asked what sense there was in sloping and ordering arms. I told them that in every division in which I had served—the First, Second, Seventh and Eighth—there had been three kinds of troops. Those that had guts but were no good at drill; those that were good at drill but had no guts; and those that had guts and were good at drill. These last, for some reason or other, fought by far the best.'

To cite the poet G. M. Hopkins, there can be a spare beauty to the soldier's gear, in its combination of functionality and symbolism.[20] The soldier's trained body is also a fit subject for aesthetic appreciation. As a counter-intelligence officer at Gallipoli in 1915, the writer Compton Mackenzie compared the lean, tanned Australian and New Zealand Dominion soldiers to the illustrations of classical Greek warriors by John Flaxman, calling them, "as near to absolute beauty as I hope to see in this world."[21] George Patton was an officer especially drawn to the aesthetics of military life, expressing himself in his poetry and a love for elaborate uniforms and for the sublimity of the battlefield itself. Patton was not alone in seeing in war a sublime aesthetic of its own. Other eminent officer-artists have included Alexander, Napoleon, and MacArthur. These were men to whom the aestheticizing of war was an important function of command, and who brought a creative flair to military operations that could be inspired, but that could also lead them astray, neglecting such prosaic matters as logistics and administration, sometimes the needs and limits of their soldiers. The artists of war may become self-creating and self-mythologizing, attempting to impose a vision that runs counter to reality and morality. Some officers have been aesthetes. Men like T. E. Lawrence (in *The Seven Pillars of Wisdom*) and Patrick Leigh Fermor have been motivated and empowered to lead guerrilla movements partly by an aesthetic appreciation (even, in Lawrence's case, an erotic interest) for the indigenous people and culture. War can be a struggle for the values of civilization, to include its artistic heritage. This was embodied by the officers and soldiers involved in recovering, preserving, and restoring works of art to their owners in World War II and in the modern Middle East. Officers have looted or despoiled art as well as rescued it, either for monetary gain, out of cultural envy, philistinism, or fear of the freedom and other values art seems to represent.[22]

The most important aspect of the artistic persona for officer thought is in the area of creativity, both as an antidote to mere destruction, and for the capacity to invent, to depart from formulas and doctrine. This has sometimes been reflected in how officers have been trained, and in the ways they have planned and executed. Given the general culture of obedience and conformity that prevails in most military organizations, it may be necessary to continually stress creativity as part of the officer's equipment. George C. Marshall, the man often credited with educating the pre–World War II officer corps, stressed creativity as a necessary ingredient to problem-solving and leadership at the various levels of warfare.[23] He rewrote the elaborate instruction manuals and formats for orders that stifled creativity, and he expressed impatience with subordinates who failed to come up with ideas of their own, who meekly agreed with Marshall's own ideas or who needed constant guidance and reassurance. His famous statement that no one ever had an original idea after mid-afternoon may be apocryphal, but it highlights the value he placed in creativity, even over the nose-to-grindstone diligence so valued in the military. The best military plans may be said to have an aesthetic simplicity and coherence, a unity in diversity that permits flexibility and initiative while pursuing victory like a leitmotif in a musical score. Amateur painter Winston Churchill said that strategy was like composing a canvas, where "few or numberless parts are commanded by a single unity of conception."[24] Even the planning process step sometimes described as "framing" evokes the activity of the artist. Military deception is a practice often calling for the talents of the artist and the craftsman. The tools of deception have changed considerably in the modern age of sensors and surveillance, but the essentials of a convincing, purposeful narrative, realistic imagery, and a plan to exploit future possible enemy mistakes remain.

In his monumental novel of the Soviet Union and the siege of Stalingrad in World War II, *Life and Fate*, Vasily Grossman reflects on the sudden transitions in warfare, the rapid shifts from triumph to disaster that take place in the mind, impelled by a shifting sense for the unity and effectiveness of our own forces and those of the enemy. "Often," Grossman writes, "it is the understanding of these transitions that gives warfare the right to be called an art. This alternating sense of singularity and plurality is a key not only to the success of night attacks by companies and battalions, but to the military success and failure of entire armies and peoples."[25] A short time later in the narrative, following a conversation between senior and subordinate commanders that is mostly concerned with details of tactics and reinforcements, the narrator reflects, "Another moment and it seemed that they might begin the one conversation that really mattered—about the meaning of Stalingrad."[26] Grossman does not say so, but this reflection on the meaning of the battle places warfare in the category of art in the sense that it is the subject both of creation and interpretation. Like Tolstoy's *War and Peace* for the Russian empire, Grossman's account will come to define the Russian and Soviet people and state, perhaps by cementing their characteristic mutual identification and inseparability. The historical significance of Stalingrad and World War II are, like works of art, subject to interpretation and reinterpretation. Along with the memorials, the literature and art that they inspire, wars and battles themselves are in this sense works of art, vortices through which are rushing different forms of meaning: aesthetic, moral, historical, infinite.

I had a personal encounter once that gave me an idea of the different forms the memory of Stalingrad could take. On a cool New York morning in the 1980s, I was home on leave, staying at my mother's apartment house in Manhattan. I left the building to go running, and the doorman, a large individual with a heavy accent, pointed to my sweatshirt, saying "USMC, United States Marine Corps!" I asked how he knew this, thinking that as a foreigner, perhaps a recent immigrant, knowledge of the initials of the smallest military branch in the Defense Department had probably not been part of his upbringing. He was a soldier too, he said. He had been a member of a 155mm artillery battery in the Soviet Army in World War II. I had recently read a book on Stalingrad, and I impetuously asked him if he had been in the Battle of Stalingrad. I still remember his response. With a kindly, patient expression, he waved a finger at me. "No, no," he said, "if was at Stalingrad then, would not be here now." His division, it turned out, had been pulled from the Stalingrad sector about a month before the battle began. He believed that if they had stayed and been there from the beginning of the epic fight, it is most unlikely that he would have survived. I've forgotten what book it was I read on Stalingrad, but I don't think I'll ever forget that brief conversation.

THE SOLDIER AS CRAFTSMAN

Craft is generally considered the inferior of art. The historian Edward Gibbon slightingly said that the Romans had raised war to an art but then debased it to a craft. Art is capable of creating something new, while craft recreates from set patterns, getting them right and perhaps juxtaposing them, but staying within limits, awaiting perhaps the artist, or the artistic, creative craftsman, to make possible a new form of craft. Even if it ranked below art (in a hierarchy that not all would acknowledge), most will allow the value of craft, both for its own sake and sometimes as necessary to execute artistic projects. This is true in the military world as well. Some military craftsmanship makes things, as with military engineering. Such activities as the care of uniforms and the routines of life in the field and on campaign are akin to craftsmanship, as are the use of weapons and other fighting skills. In the military hierarchy, the officer is more kin to the artist, the noncommissioned officer to the skilled or journeyman craftsman, with the junior enlisted man the noncomm's apprentice. Enlisted members may be more skilled as craftsmen than some officers, although the officer who neglects the basics of soldier-craft may find herself embarrassed and dependent when she needs them, and in any case may forfeit credibility if her inferiority in craftsmanship is too marked. My first infantry company commander told me that lieutenants should concern themselves with field skills and not trouble their minds with tactics or the higher levels of military thought. Looking back, he may have had a point. He had a notably brainy set of platoon commanders, it seems to me, and he was likely applying a corrective to our tendency to overintellectualize. There is also danger in "dumbing-down" the military profession. The junior officer coming from college will often find herself among people with less education than she. There will be a temptation to reduce the range of her vocabulary, to adopt the language, attitudes, and the sometimes simplified worldview of the soldiers she leads and commands. Some officers feel the need to talk down to their soldiers, to say what they believe is expected of them rather than what ought to be said. This is an understandable tendency in the junior officer, although one to be avoided, and it is inexcusable in a senior officer. The counterarticulate, disingenuous, or mock-ingenuous officer will be unmasked for the fake he is.[27] Worst of all, he limits the potential and problem-solving ability of the soldiers under him.

The officer exists in part to raise the level of military thinking and performance above the level of craftsmanship. The redoubtable Swiss pikemen have been described as a military force that lacked officers, but that relied on the equivalent of senior noncommissioned officers to run their organization. Perhaps as a result, and for all their courage and skill, the Swiss failed to adapt their dense, slow-moving formations to the threat of effective artillery, so that in their final battles they suffered enormous casualties and were defeated.

The need for craft sometimes must be stressed in the essentially amateur and citizen armies that arise in wartime. This may be especially the case for revolutionary armies, which must eventually come to terms with the fact that ideology and revolutionary fervor are not enough to win battles or freedom. The new American Revolutionary Army gradually embraced its own version of professionalism, which included an artisanal approach to the craft of soldiering, drill, and care of weapons and equipment, all under the flexible tutelage of enlightened foreign officers like von Stueben, and eventually under a native-born officer corps. Much later, Leon Trotsky would be at pains to remind Red Army soldiers that they had better learn how to grease their boots as well as grasping communist dogma.[28]

The crafty approach to soldiering and officership may yield benefits beyond those of getting the details right. A focus on the details may be a soldier's psychological and even ethical salvation. Any experienced officer knows that some simple task can be a refuge for someone in combat or on campaign who is feeling discouraged or helpless. In *Warcraft and the Fragility of Virtue: An Essay in Aristotelian Ethics*, G. Scott Davis equates soldierly craft with an individual virtue that is divorced from politics and ideology.[29]

MANUAL AND PHYSICAL SKILLS

Under "craft," but somewhat apart as well, are the purely manual and physical skills involved in soldiering. These are like craft in that they involve the hands and the rest of the body directly, but different in that they involve not so much skill as semi-skilled, trained, and ingrained habits. Physical exertion, the wearing of equipment, negotiating terrain and machine spaces, the deprivations of rest, sleep, food, and water are all facts of life for the soldier to which the body and mind must be accustomed and inured. These skills may seem out of place among the intellectual virtues, but to display endurance, to continue to think with clarity on cold, rainy nights after days of marching and fighting, these are mental as well as physical habituations. The Spartans were among the first to recognize the importance of regular and realistic physical training. Spartan boys in training were kept on short rations to increase their foraging and scrounging skills and to accustom them to hunger. Spartan training methods were so effective that they were imitated by the other city states. No one believed in physical training more than did the Romans. A Roman republican or imperial legionary trained constantly. If he could not meet the standard for timed marching under a prescribed load, he risked discharge less than the *honesta missio* (honorable discharge) and the benefits he might receive (under the empire) for twenty years' service. For all the changes and the replacement of human labor by machines, many of the physical demands of military service remain. The wearing of protective gear, the carrying of equipment, and long hours of work in the cockpit and crew space impose physical and mental stresses the soldier must learn to overcome.

Physical training is not just conducive to mental discipline; research has shown that it may aid cognition. As noted by philosopher Damon Young, neuroscientists have discovered that exercise increases "innovation and problem-solving." The act of running and walking can open the mind to new possibilities, connections and intersections of ideas, paths for the mind as well as the body to travel. This may not be automatic, but it can be cultivated, maybe especially given periods of rest and "reverie" alternating with exertion.[30]

INTUITION

In his chapter of the *Ethics* on the intellectual virtues, Aristotle treats with intuition only briefly. This is perhaps natural, since intuition is the least intentional or procedural of the virtues. By definition, it happens quickly. This is not to discount intuition. Intuition sees what can't be demonstrated or even fully explained. It involves a grasp of first principles. It may not be too much to say that without intuition, the other intellectual virtues, even the moral virtues, would be severely hampered and even impossible. Without the feel for rightness and purpose, guiding the agent like an unseen hand, how much of science, art, prudence or wisdom would be possible or productive?

Military people have tended to prize intuition more than have the members of other professional groups. Clausewitz's belief in the great complexity of military problems led him to commend a feeling for these matters that went deeper than words. The later Germans, with their propensity for stringing words together, invented the term *Fingerspitzengefühl* to describe the feeling at the fingertips that a tactical commander was said to experience in the form of a warning of danger or, more likely, as the "instinct for the jugular," the sense of an adversary's vulnerability. Distinguished combat leader Hal Moore makes faith in one's instincts and intuition axiomatic.[31] The nature of military operations would seem to demand the exercise of intuition. Military operations simply contain too much of the imponderable and unpredictable to be reduced to the more deliberate and drawn-out processes of the other intellectual virtues, and they are too bound up with first principles, like the value of human life itself, to be free of intuition's special claim on those matters. Perhaps most important, military decisions, especially on the battlefield and tactical level, must often be made very quickly.[32]

The implicit military faith in intuition, in the ability to make accurate snap decisions without conscious deliberation, may even be excessive. In fact, people and professions in general may have too much confidence in intuition. This point is forcefully made by Nobel economist Daniel Kahneman in his book *Thinking Fast and Slow*. Kahneman's experience and research included military units (he was an officer in the Israeli Defense Forces [IDF]) and other organizations that work in hazardous, high-stress situations. His data indicate that it requires numerous similar experiences to develop a dependable instinct for correct actions. Real intuition comes slowly. For example, it may take ten thousand hours of chess-playing (or five hours of daily play for six years) to be able to assess a game "at a glance" in what I have already referred to as "pattern recognition."[33] This has special implications for military officers for three reasons. The first is the almost infinite variety of physical environments, political and cultural contexts, and tactical situations that an officer may encounter. The second is the fact that military officers usually only experience actual operations (as opposed to training) for short periods. Even in wartime combat experience is not continuous, but is dependent on assignments and deployments. Finally, the military organization often treats soldiers and officers as interchangeable parts, as generalists rather than specialists, which may hinder the accumulation of the ability to practice pattern recognition.

Officers need to take the limits of intuition into account. Some of the limitations of military intuition may be unavoidable. No one would wish for a world always and everywhere at war to provide military officers with experience! Kahneman's conclusions are certainly a call for constant and realistic training in peacetime. This will not be new to officers, but it may, again citing Kahneman's research, indicate a need for training aimed at enabling officers and others to make good decisions. Perhaps more reflection, or debrief, is necessary too, with questions like "why did you do that?" or "what could you have done differently?" Officers must be able to diagnose situations and to fit them into their store of experience. Kahneman's work also supports the case for reading, since this is a way to further broaden the officer's experience. There may also be occasions to modify the military insistence on versatility. An example of this is provided by David Hackworth. As the commander of a battalion of mostly draftee soldiers serving one-year tours in Vietnam, he decided to have each of his companies specialize in a type of operation. Although Hackworth says that this policy made sense because of his young soldiers' limited experience, it might also be adapted for a battalion of regulars and veterans, whose practical experience might be as limited as those of soldiers with less time in service.[34] An argument for the importance of relevant experience and its significance in key officer assignments is made by Faris Kirkland, a retired Army artillery officer with service in Korea and Vietnam who went on to be a university professor.[35] He ascribes the superior performance of Marine units in Korea over those of the Army to the greater care shown by the

Marines in the selection of senior officers to combat command. The Marine Corps sought out officers for these positions who had commanded in combat during World War II. The Army followed a policy of "career equity," treating all officers of the same rank and branch equally, with the result that officers with little experience of command or of combat were commanding at the regiment, division, and even corps level. They not only lacked the capacity to make good decisions, they lacked the experience and confidence to question bad ones. So Army commanders responded to MacArthur's imperious and ignorant prodding by rushing headlong into an advancing Chinese army, while Marine commanders exercised greater discretion and were positioned and prepared to conduct an organized fighting withdrawal when the Chinese crossed the Yalu in force.

Although officers may only spend a small percentage of their time in service on active deployments, they spend their entire careers wedded to the military organization. Their most developed and dependable instincts likely have to do not with warfighting but with the tactics of navigating the military hierarchy. Such knowledge may be acquired and employed in a self-serving way, but it may also be put into the service of worthwhile projects and objectives. An example of this is provided in retired major general Aubrey Newman's *What Are Generals Made Of?* Newman recounts as a junior officer acquiescing in the *pro forma* discharge of a soldier with an undisclosed criminal record. The young Newman believed strongly that the soldier should be retained, but he lacked the confidence and administrative skills to register his opinion in an effective way. Later, as a more senior officer, he intervened effectively to improve a program intended to expedite soldiers' families joining them while on assignment in Europe. In this case, he was able to get beyond the regulations, in effect doing more than what was required in order to ensure that as many soldiers as possible could benefit from the program. The experienced officer's intuition about the organization is a political sense of "the art of the possible," but it may also be a moral one, like the *nous* of the ancient Greeks, a sense for the fitness of things, for what decency and honor require.

This is another way of saying that an officer should possess the instincts of a gentleman. Article 133 of the Uniform Code of Military Justice (UCMJ) makes it a punishable offense for an officer to conduct herself in a manner unbecoming a gentleman. What is a gentleman? In *The Idea of the University*, Cardinal Newman described a gentleman as someone who never inflicts pain. In fact, officers and gentlemen may at times need to cause pain, but by instinct they should do so unwillingly and only by necessity. This is not a luxury or nicety. It relates to the idea of moral prudence, which will be discussed in detail next. An officer can wield enormous power to do harm. She may tyrannize subordinates or use the awesome power of military weapons to visit unnecessary destruction. There are legal checks on this type of conduct, but they are not always effective, and they are likely better at punishing than at preventing bad behavior.[36] Only a person with the gentlemanly instincts to refrain from harm can really be trusted to wield the officer's authority in circumstances where the bars may be down, or the presence of a higher, supervisory authority distracted or remote. The attitude described by Newman also involves the desire to facilitate communication and action among others, to allow for the exchange of ideas, for disagreements without rancor, for initiative. The officer-as-gentleman exercises sets an example of restraint and creates discipline but also a sense of belonging and ownership. Among his many attainments, the gentlemanly George C. Marshall was a tireless facilitator of communications, whether patching up disagreements with the volatile Admiral Ernest King, putting a private at his ease, or asking a subordinate, "Why do you say that?" Marshall practiced his belief in open communications as an element of victory.

The existence of intuition raises the question of why some people seem to be simply better at certain kinds of rapid, accurate thinking than others, or better, even much better, than the average person. This question is addressed by the theory of multiple intelligences, an idea by developmental psychologist Howard Gardner.[37] Gardner posits seven areas in which individuals may have exceptional ability. These are linguistic, logical-mathematical, musical, spatial, bodily kinesthetic, interpersonal, and intrapersonal. These categories are fairly self-explanatory, with the possible exception of intrapersonal, which relates to self-knowledge. Ability in a certain area may be based on innate abilities, on education and self-development, and on occupation. An accountant will constantly be practicing his mathematical intelligence throughout his professional lifetime, and he will likely also have chosen that profession with the idea that he was good at figures! The officer would seem to have need of a wide spectrum of these abilities. Certainly, spatial intelligence is needed in the role as a tactician, but heading the list are likely intrapersonal and interpersonal, given the demands of warfighting and of leadership. However, no amount of intelligences, no matter how prodigious or carefully cultivated, is quite enough without a merging combination of the intellectual and the ethical.

MILITARY PRUDENCE

The idea of military prudence has roots in Aristotle, but it is directly attributable to Thomas Aquinas.[38] Aquinas devotes a small section of the massive *Summa Theologica* to the question "Whether military prudence should be reckoned a part of prudence?" He notes three objections. First, that warfare is an art, which (citing Aristotle) is distinct from prudence. Second, that although military affairs come under politics, so do other matters, such as trade, which are not of prudence. Third, that soldiers have need of fortitude rather than prudence. To the first objection, he acknowledges that war has aspects of art, such as in the use of "external things, such as arms and horses," but that as it pertains to the public good, it belongs to prudence. His argument against the second objection also invokes the "common good" as an aim in warfare that relates it to prudence. Third, Aquinas says that the direction of war requires prudence as well as fortitude. As noted by Gregory Reichberg, the arguments of Aquinas concerning war and prudence have been neglected, eclipsed by other descriptions and metaphors for how soldiers think. To revive this idea for modern readers, a few words of translation are necessary. Prudence, *prudentia*, meant more to the ancients and later writers in Latin than it does to modern English speakers. Latin was closer to its origins and more understood to be imbued with moral values than are modern languages. The lives of the ancients were a series of moral tasks like the labors of Hercules. Today, in common use prudence is almost synonymous with caution. When we pair it with "moral," it is to emphasize its status as more than mere caution, and as a moral as well as an intellectual virtue. When we speak of military prudence, we are positing a prudence that is not mere caution, but that has already accepted the unavoidable hazards and mischances of war. It is these very elements of armed conflict that make moral prudence perhaps the *sine qua non* of officer thought and the exercise of military leadership and command. To think of leadership in war as science, art, or craft (or as a business, as proposed by Clausewitz, or as a form of play or sport) may be helpful and even truthful, but these metaphors fall short without the addition of moral prudence. Art is concerned with things to be made, prudence with things to be done. Art (and also science, craft, business, or sport) do not require complete virtue in a person, but prudence does. Prudence is a "thick" conception of virtue that calls for character plus skill. Further, the truly prudential commander would not seek victory alone, nor a narrow national interest, but a common good. Aquinas's identification of military prudence accords with his precepts on just war. Just as skill is not enough for true excellence in a commander, justice and law are not enough to limit conflict and secure a moral order among nations. There must be amity as well. The officer who thinks as an artist or scientist, even if subject to law, but who lacks the virtue of military prudence is more likely than the prudent commander to confuse ends and means, to act in a short-sighted way, or to surrender to expediency.

As a moral and an intellectual virtue, moral prudence is a matter of navigating between extremes. Few have greater need for this principle than the military commander, who is constantly performing a balancing act between undesirable courses and outcomes. In military operations, the apparently better course is often the lesser, since it will be too obvious and anticipated by the enemy. The need for progress and victory must be weighed against the cost and the tendency for force to escalate, and the need to exert superior force against the potential for excessive, engulfing destruction.

Every now and then, a midshipman at the US Merchant Marine Academy, thinking that he'd hit on a brilliant idea, would tell me, "You know, sir, Hitler was really a great leader!" I would generally start off by saying that, just going by the record, Hitler had not performed very well. Twelve years into his reign, German armies were defeated, German cities were in ruins, and Germany itself was covered in a special kind of shame from which it may never fully recover. Beyond this, I might say, a proper definition of leadership, certainly one which we can embrace at a service academy, *entirely excluded* Hitler and his actions, which should be classed under tyranny, or demagoguery, as not just vexed leadership but really the opposite of leadership. Leadership brings people forward, toward the better angels of their nature (to paraphrase Lincoln's First Inaugural Address). It cannot appeal to the worst in us, to our resentments, prejudice, or lust for power over others, tendencies that lie dormant in all, and that only need the right spark to consume us and our public lives.

A leader who is incapable of moral reason, or who is indifferent to moral issues, or who lacks moral courage, isn't a leader at all, but a tyrant and despot. He is the enemy of real progress, of the common good, and such a person in a position of authority may be far more dangerous than someone who is merely incompetent. We may sometimes fall into the trap of thinking that if someone is technically competent, or if we agree with him on policy, if she has tried to reach out to us, if we see some of ourselves in this person (if perhaps not our better self), then this should make up for even serious shortcomings in what I've called moral prudence. This is a dangerous path.

Employers and teachers are coming to realize that this kind of thinking puts the cart before the horse. Officers need not be saints, but they must be people who are willing to confront the unavoidable ethical questions that are running through the decisions they make and the example that they set. An officer's education and practical experience give her an instinct for prudence, but like other virtues that may be partly innate or existing it should be cultivated. Military officers should also teach prudence to those they instruct, lead, and advise. This is even more critical in the times when brinkmanship and imprudence amounting to impudence become the orders of the day.

PRUDENCE IN HISTORY

Some of the famous prudential officers of history were Caesar, Charlemagne, Washington, Wellington, and George C. Marshall. Being human, they were all imperfect. In some cases, their prudence may have deserted them, but their careers are marked by a sustained moral-military prudence with respect to their roles as officers, commanders, and national leaders. Caesar and Charlemagne were military commanders who also built and maintained diverse empires. Caesar's ambition may have outrun his prudence in the end, although he was a victim of the endemic political violence of late-republican Rome as much as of his own hubris. Before his death, in his conquest of Gaul, he had husbanded a relatively small force, remote from its base in Rome, winning battles while limiting bloodshed, weighing force and clemency, sustaining support from Rome and winning over the Gauls so their country became a bulwark of the Roman Empire for over four centuries. He may be said to have demonstrated moral prudence both as a commander and an administrator. He avoided the search for personal glory that overtook some Roman commanders, and he would not commit untrained troops or outrun his supplies. He once delivered an Aristotelian-style lecture on military ethics to the centurions of a legion.[39] He gave positions of responsibility to local chieftains, treating them as allies rather than subjects. In both military and civic roles, he may be said to have adopted existing Roman practices and raised them to the highest level so far, laying the groundwork for the Western empire.

Charlemagne did not ensure the survival of his empire after his lifetime, although in this he too was perhaps defeated by his times. While he lived, the Frankish Empire was a rare example and source of stability in a period of rickety, warring fiefdoms. Charlemagne may have best exhibited prudence in providing balanced economic, logistical, and recruitment systems that were both sufficient and sustainable, and in his overall military goal of European unification, not just the raiding or conquest that were typical of the period in which he lived. Charlemagne's organized approach to economics and to warfare depended on an educational system that he helped to develop that bred literate and learned servants of empire.[40] In this area, and in others, Charlemagne set the example, demonstrating his own love of books and learning, having books read to him at meals and encouraging the translation of books by clerics.[41] Even when an old campaigner, Charlemagne did not lose feelings of sadness over losses in war, which he nevertheless kept in balance through self-discipline. In *The Song of Roland*, Charlemagne is depicted as swooning when he learns of the deaths of Roland and the rest of the rear guard at Roncesvalles, but on the following morning he rises early to marshal his pan-European force against the Moorish enemy.

Washington and Wellington both displayed a distaste for the excesses of war in their own ways, and both retired to civil careers, Washington as president and Wellington as prime minister, that reflected the Platonic and prudential benefits of the harsh schools in which they were trained, not expecting too much, but holding fast on principle. Washington as a military commander demonstrated prudence in the offensive. After a series of disastrous defensive battles in New York, he realized that his army could not yet stand up to British firepower and bayonets, so he sought offensive engagements, as at Princeton and Trenton, in which he could create advantages of surprise and numbers. Despite an innately authoritarian and aggressive personality, he showed balance, learning to listen to advice and resisting the temptation to overreach after victories, training, and husbanding his army until it was the equal of the British.[42]

Wellington was proverbial for the concern he showed his men, both in matters of supply and on the battlefield, developing tactics, like the use of skirmishers and the two-rank firing line, that limited British exposure to fire and casualties. He showed enormous forbearance in dealing with often untrustworthy allies, as on the Peninsula. Willing to overlook failures in others, his own personal and professional honor was scrupulous. He once said of an act of dubious diplomacy that he would prefer to sacrifice every frontier in India rather than his country's reputation for good faith.[43]

George C. Marshall followed a similar course, and I would like to single him out briefly as exemplary of military prudence. As a young staff officer, Marshall saw the devastation of Europe in World War I, and he never afterward forgot or allowed others to forget the human cost and far-reaching consequences of military operations. By the time of his tenure as US Army Chief of Staff (1939–1945) as, for example, at Cairo, he demonstrated, as one observer noted, that he had "more mature judgment (and), could see further into the future" than the others in attendance.[44] As early as 1943, Marshall was considering the problems of postwar European recovery, his ideas later taking shape in what became known as the Marshall Plan. Marshall was as imbued as any military officer with the desire for victory, but he learned to balance this with a respect for the processes of government and a sense of what the world would look like once victory was attained.[45] There were times, as in the extension of the enlistments of prewar draftees, when clever shortcuts were available to attain the desired result. Marshall rarely if ever stooped to these, because he saw the long-term consequences that such methods often entailed: the surrender of trust, the unfairness toward those already carrying the heaviest burdens.

Military prudence is not limited to senior commanders or officers of high rank. The junior officer's need for prudence may be even more pronounced since her closeness to the action and to those doing the fighting can make shortcuts and expediency seem very reasonable. The leader of a patrol who takes fire from a village may be tempted to employ a disproportionate amount of fire in response. The adviser or counterpart to an indigenous forces commander may be drawn to tolerate illegal and immoral methods that appear to be the local norm, and that may even be effective, at least tactically and in the short term. Challenges of this kind may have a clear right answer, but others will have a more open-ended, equivocal quality that may call for frequent reconsideration and refinement. An officer engaged in operations that appear to him to have a doubtful chance of success may wonder how much risk or effort they require. In the case of a losing war or discredited strategy, what are prudent risks? An illustration might be found in the episode titled "The Last Patrol" in the fact-based *Band of Brothers* book and series. In "The Last Patrol," an officer is ordered to repeat a previous night's patrol that ended with a soldier killed for the dubious reward of two German enlisted prisoners. This is late in the war, and to run the same patrol again strikes him as hazardous beyond reason. He indirectly but unmistakably tells his soldiers to stay behind the wire but report the patrol as completed. His deception goes undetected, and it may be that only his enormous prestige, a standing based on his superb combat leadership, prevents the subterfuge from emerging or being used against him. Faced with the threat of exposure or blackmail, he might have been confronted with a whole series of moral dilemmas that had no good answers. Moral prudence is a necessity, but it cannot be proof against bad outcomes or unintended consequences.

Unfortunately, history also offers a rich source of examples of imprudent command. Sometimes officers who were skilled tacticians and adept at leading lacked the prudence to weigh gains and losses. All unjust wars have been imprudent, and even some just wars have been fought by commanders who failed in moral prudence. Robert E. Lee was clearly imprudent at Gettysburg, at least on the third day when he ordered Pickett's Charge, and he might also be accused of moral imprudence for leading his men in the unjust cause of the Confederacy. Erwin Rommel skillfully but recklessly pursued aggressive war in the mismatched service of what should have been a defensive strategy, and the charge of imprudence for leading others in an unjust war could even more forcefully be made against him, since bad as the cause of the Confederacy was, that of Nazi Germany was even worse. The charge of imprudence may be made against Mark Clark in his command of US forces in Italy. Although very intelligent and a brilliant organizer and planner, Clark's repetitious and unimaginative tactics in the face of heavy casualties, his unwillingness to listen to subordinates, and his tendency to shift blame when things went badly are all signs of imprudence, of a cognitive failure linked to ethical shortcomings.[46]

Literature also contains vivid examples of officers who possess intellectual virtues but lack the melding of the intellectual and the moral that may add up to military prudence. Tolstoy's Napoleon, General Cummings in Norman Mailer's *The Naked and the Dead*, and General Lemming in Josiah Bunting's *The Lionheads* are often capable and even brilliant, but undone by their lack of military prudence, which ought to temper and add heart to the officer and warfighter. Cummings's ambition and arrogance combine to ensure that he is missing for the battle he hoped would make his reputation. Lemming is a capable tactician who refuses to oppose the army hierarchy over what he knows to be the dubious use of riverine craft in the jungle, a misuse of equipment which costs lives. Lemming also believes that his mock-ingenuous pretense of concern for his soldiers is a convincing leadership performance, but he is dismissed at the end of the novel by a representative soldier as a "fucking prick."

The officer who surrenders prudence to prepare for battle will not fight well. As the veteran Enobarbus says of Mark Antony in Shakespeare's *Antony and Cleopatra*, "When valor preys on reason, it eats the sword it fights with" (III, 13, 240–41). In the film *Twelve O'Clock High*, doubts about the efficacy of strategic bombing contribute to low morale among the air crews of a heavy bombing group. The commander tries to address these, but he is never fully successful, limiting himself to measurements of success that are somewhat arbitrary and artificial. In the end, his greatest challenge may be to convince himself that the destruction and sacrifice are justified. He fails at this, and after the death of a loyal subordinate acting on his orders, he lapses into debility and speechlessness. He has steeled himself to dubious battle, suppressing his own doubts along with those of others, but his brittle valor finally comes apart.

Harry K. Brown wrote in his classic novel *A Walk in the Sun* that "war, without virtue in itself, breeds virtue."[47] War can be a place where prudence is learned, but the instilling of prudence cannot be left to chance or deferred to the actual clash of arms. It must be part of military culture and education, of reading and discussion. The foregoing examples are meant to merely suggest how to go about this. Moral prudence is more than mere caution; it sees clearly the unavoidable hazards of war. Along with warfighting skills and the will to win, the self-regulation of moral prudence should be part of the equipment of everyone who aspires to command, or to advise the commander.

MILITARY WISDOM

Earlier, I introduced the argument that officers should not only display prudence, but that, in the manner of philosophers, they should love and court wisdom. In the following paragraphs, my concluding remarks on the intellectual virtues, I will enlarge upon this argument, acknowledging some reasonable caveats and objections along the way. Wisdom I contend is something that is properly embraced and acquired over the course of a military career and lifetime. While science and *techne* in their different forms may be acquired by the young in a relatively short period of intensive study and practice, wisdom is usually the product of years of experience followed by reflection. The tragedy of Hamlet may be read as a cautionary tale of a young soldier more clever than wise. He weaves a web of words and tricks but "loses the name of action," creating a complex plot that results in his own death and that of other innocents, finally in the sudden fall of his kingdom and the invasion of a foreign army.

Wars are often, perhaps always, the product of human folly, but the army and war do offer opportunities for wisdom as for other virtues. They offer contact with settings and situations that ordinary life does not. In the army, people are thrown together in situations of dependency that can make even the bonds of family seem tenuous by comparison. Thousands of soldiers have written to convey their secret knowledge of war, and some of the greatest works in literature have been the result. It is terribly ironic that war's fascination is often only increased by these accounts. Some military leaders have been admired for their wisdom as much as for their ability at warfighting. There are also the literal soldier-philosophers, beginning with Socrates, and even ordinary veterans often display considerable wisdom in their stories and reflections on war in later tranquility.

Socrates was surely one of the wisest men who ever served as a soldier. There is no evidence that he ever occupied a leadership position, but he was a teacher and counselor of officers. In the early dialogue *Laches*, Socrates engages in a conversation with his eponymous interlocutor, an Athenian general, correcting and refining the latter's thoughts on education, on military training, and finally on courage. In this dialogue, Laches may be said to represent prudence and Socrates wisdom. Laches tends to go for the pragmatic answer. His definition of courage is that it is when a soldier keeps his place in ranks, but Socrates wants to go deeper, getting at the true nature and meaning of the topics under discussion. For him, courage is a kind of knowledge of what is and is not terrible. Laches, the practical soldier, might brush these considerations aside as irrelevant to his job as a military commander, but he does not. He recognizes the potential value of Socrates's approach.

Socrates as soldier-philosopher was the product of a society in which all full-status citizens served in the army, and of a time of seminal philosophical ferment. To find his equal, we may need to go forward to another period of citizen armies and intellectual change. Ludwig Wittgenstein is accorded the status of one of the great philosophers of the twentieth century. The Cambridge-educated Austrian philosopher returned to his native country to enlist in the army at the start of World War I, rising to officer rank. At the start of the war, his philosophical interests were mostly in the field of logic, but his military service and experience of leading others influenced a turn toward ethics, even toward mysticism. (I will return to Wittgenstein in the last section of this book on the officer-as-visionary.)

The American philosopher J. Glenn Gray received his doctorate from Columbia University and his army induction notice on the same day in 1941. He served four years in the army, was commissioned, and later wrote a highly regarded book, *The Warriors: Reflections on Men in Battle*. His work ranges over the experience of war from command, to combat and comradeship. Gray records much about war that was bad and regrettable. He deplores the coarsening of feeling often brought on by war, but he finally concludes that "war did not change us enough," that the power of the military experience to better individuals and their society had not been fully realized in his own case and in his fellow soldiers.

II

THOUGHT AND ACTION

$\mathcal{O}$fficers must think, but they must also combine thought and action in unique ways. This can be a challenge, since thought and action may sometimes seem to be at odds. This a difficulty famously expressed by Hamlet, one of a long line of intellectual soldiers, who worried that his propensity for thinking made him less capable of acting effectively.

> And thus the native hue of resolution
> Is sicklied o'er with the pale cast of thought,
> And enterprises of great pitch and moment
> With this regard their currents turn awry,
> And lose the name of action. (III, i, Ln. 84–88)

For the officer, thinking ought to develop the capacity for choice, providing as solid a foundation for her decisions as is available under the circumstances. The types of conditions under which an officer is called upon to think and to act vary widely. One of the central ideas of Morris's Janowitz classic work, *The Professional Soldier: A Social and Political Portrait* is what he sees as the contrast or competition between "managers" and "heroic leaders." In *The Rules of the Game: Jutland and British Naval Command*, Andrew Gordon makes a similar distinction between "regulators" and "ratcatchers."[1] It will be an assumption of this book that an officer may find herself serving in either role, and that the two roles should not be viewed as so much a matter of inherent personal characteristics as of circumstance. The experienced staff officer may find herself thrust into tactical command, or she may even seek out this role. The combat leader may return stateside to a tour at the Pentagon, as happened to David Hackworth following a tour in Vietnam, a situation he describes in his fine memoir *About Face*. Both roles call for hard thinking of somewhat disparate kinds, and neither is without calls to action. In the section of this work that follows, I will address these roles under the headings of organizer and warfighter, laying out the cognitive challenges of each, sometimes referring back to the advance preparation, intellectual virtues, and impediments to thought already discussed. Last, I will discuss the officer's role as a visionary, one who, due to the nature of her service, may be capable of making an expansive contribution to the cognitive, cultural, political, and moral life of her society.

· 5 ·

The Organizer

Good generals had to have the type of mind that saw all men as
masses, as numerical groups of Infantry, Artillery, and mortars
that could be added and subtracted on paper.

—James Jones, *From Here to Eternity*

James Jones probably understood the army better than any other major American writer. In this instance, the narrator of his famous novel of the pre–World
War II regular army describes the clever but amoral Captain Holmes, and a
mental trait shared by better officers than Holmes. Officers must be able to
think in terms of organizations, of groups of people, their equipment and capabilities. In his biography of General Lucian Truscott, physician and retired
officer Wilson Hefner titles his introduction, "To Think Like an Army."
Quoting historian Eric Larrabee, he says that the military unit must be an
extension of the commander's own brain.[1] Some insight into an organization
can be gained by studying its stated mission, organizational chart, and table
of equipment. Much more can be learned by spending time with the people
where they operate. The tools for assessing the capabilities and success of a
unit have grown very sophisticated, but few would discount the value of the
usually hard-won ability to size up a unit by listening and watching. Maurice
Baring was a forty-year-old journalist when he put on the uniform of the
Royal Flying Corps. With no training or previous knowledge of aviation,
he made himself an invaluable staff officer through his understanding of the
organization and (most significantly) its people. Air Marshall Hugh Trenchard
described Baring's contribution in words quoted by Group Captain F. D.
Tredey in a foreword to Baring's *Flying Corps Headquarters, 1914–1918*. "He
was a genius at knowing the young pilots and airmen. He knew more about

what mattered in war and about how to deal with human nature . . . than any other man I know."[2]

The performance of a unit depends on its command climate, a mixture of leadership, cohesion, and morale that is somewhat quantifiable but also subjective and elusive, partly because it may change faster than the weather, the result of victory or setback, losses or other changes in personnel, news and rumors, good and bad. Performance rests on many paradoxical elements. Some of them are the subject of long reflection in *Young Men and Fire* by Norman Maclean. Writing of a disaster that befell a group of the newly formed Park Service smoke jumpers at Mann Gulch, Montana, in 1949, Maclean describes the interplay of obedience and initiative that allows a group to respond to rapidly changes conditions. Based on this incident, in which twelve Smoke jumpers of a fifteen-man team lost their lives, the Forest Service revised the training of smoke jumpers, "to remove the contradiction between training men to act swiftly, surely, and on their own in the face of danger and, on the other hand, training men to take orders unhesitatingly when working under command."[3]

Still, smoke jumpers continue to die from fire. The challenge of creating groups able to function in extremis is never solved finally or completely. This enduring paradox plays out in several ways when we attempt to define the nature and functioning of military organization. In this chapter, I will discuss various cognitive challenges facing the officer in her role as organizer. These include command, selection, training and education, force structure, doctrine, and cohesion.

THE NATURE OF COMMAND

Command is the formal authority exercised by a single person over a military organization. Military organizations are sometimes referred to as commands. In this sense, a "command" (as noun) is defined by the fact that it is subject to command, and by the nature of the command being exercised, by the commander's own abilities, priorities, knowledge, and habits of mind. Military command may be unique in the degree of authority and responsibility it invests in a mortal being, but it is not unlimited, and it can be extremely complex and even vexed. Military command in the past was often based on hereditary, even on divinely bestowed authority. Even in ancient times, however, it was the subordinates in a military organization who ratified and lent their cooperation to the act of command apart from the pedigrees of the commanders. Although military command might be conferred by the circumstances of birth, subordinates and writers on war would distinguish between able and incompetent commanders. The difference between the good and the bad commander often has to do with her willingness to take in information from a variety of sources in the planning process and in battle. Brilliant prince though he was, Alexander undermined his authority by embracing an autocratic style of command. One of the most eloquent statements on the necessity of an officer paying attention to the ideas of her subordinates characteristically comes from Eisenhower. In his World War II memoir *Crusade in Europe*, he writes,

> There is, among the mass of individuals who carry the rifles in war, a great amount of ingenuity and initiative. If men can naturally and without restraint talk to their officers, the products of their resourcefulness become available to all.[4]

Some commanders have effectively kept their own counsel, consulting with subordinates sparingly and keeping their plans to themselves until they were well formed and ready to be issued. A distinguished example of this type of commander is Ulysses S. Grant. Grant was quiet but approachable. He chose his confidants carefully, Sherman foremost among them, and from his memoirs one gets the impression of an interior dialogue taking place, as he weighs options, not getting too attached to first impressions or any fixed ideas.

To be effective and enduring, command must have a moral basis. This is behind the high praise of the faithful centurion by Christ in Matthew. The Roman officer says that they do not need to go to his home to heal a servant. He is a man under authority and wielding authority over others, and he knows how orders are carried out even when the superior is not present. Christ exclaims that the centurion shows greater faith than he has seen in all Israel. Soldiers may be held to a bad cause by habit, discipline, comradeship, and leadership. They may tolerate or even become complicit in a bad cause, and inured to wicked acts, but immorality in a commander can undermine the motives of soldiers and fray the bonds that should hold them together. In *Macbeth*, Shakespeare has the Scottish nobleman Angus say of the title character,

> Those he commands move only on command,
> Nothing in love: now does he feel his title
> Hang loose about him, like a giant's robe
> Upon a dwarfish thief. (V, ii, Ln. 19–22)

Macbeth's position as nominal monarch and commander are rendered meaningless by his crimes that are leading him to madness, by desire for power without a sufficient moral motive.

Leo Tolstoy is notably anti-command, or it might be said he is skeptical (or agnostic?) about the effectiveness of command. In *War and Peace*, his near-meglomaniacal Napoleon tries to subordinate the campaign to his will, and he fails. The Russian commander Kutozov is much more modest about his ability to control events. He gives the French army space and time to disintegrate and it does.

To resolve the paradoxes and complexities of organization and of command, officers have evolved several practices and principles. I will discuss these under the headings of chain of command, unity of command, and Command and Control.

CHAIN OF COMMAND

The idea of a formal chain of command may have originated with the Spartan officers who were referred to as a "commanders of commanders."[5] The chain of command provides for instructions downward and information upward. A functioning chain of command ensures that a commander must communicate only with several subordinates instead of many. Like other procedures that aim at efficiency (those of parliaments and bureaucracies, for example), the chain of command can be limiting as well as empowering. Subordinates may be blocked off from useful access to a higher commander by intervening levels of command, with their sometimes jealously guarded authority. This jealousy may extend up and down. The commanders of subordinate units often resent the interference of seniors with their internal affairs, but senior commanders may see such intervention as necessary and authorized, even necessitated by the nature of command. Here, as in other areas, the key may lie in *prudentia*, in deference on the part of the junior, forbearance on that of the senior, on due respect combined with self-respect in both. The junior bears the burden of obedience, but the senior bears the even greater burden and responsibility of command. From him is expected the greater degree of prudence and wisdom.

UNITY OF COMMAND

One of the most important aspects of command is unity of command: the vesting of command in one person. Unity of command may be said to have had its origins in the ancient systems of command in which authority was conferred by high position in the social hierarchy, one usually conferred by birth. Whether exercised despotically or benevolently, the royal or noble commander could exercise command secure in the sense that the values of a hierarchical, aristocratic society were at his back. A Renaissance soldier might well say, "There is great hidden force in sweet command." *Noblesse* could also breed overconfidence, leading to disaster and mutiny, although even a defeated king or one in flight may remain or return a king. Later, as military command came to be based more on professional credentials than on birth (for a time these two may have been in balance), the principle of a single commander was upheld by both the tradition of royal command and by a sense that it was necessary given the nature of battle. The commissioned officer was clothed in the authority of the ruler by his uniform and by his commission, a document that bore the stamp of the monarch and that vested the officer with quasi-royal authority. War might admit of councils and parliaments, but battle called for quick decisions being made by one person. As the royal bastard Don Juan said before the naval battle of Lepanto, "Gentlemen, the time for counsels is past and the time for fighting has come."[6] Unity of command may seem to be inherent in the nature of military organizations, in which every unit seems to have its single commander who reports to another commander, but providing unity down through the layers of command, and across organizations of different types is a continuing challenge. The challenge of unity becomes greater in multidimensional warfare and multinational armies. There is ever diversity in unity. Culture, training, communications, types and ranges of movement may strain or amend unity of command. Command may always be collaborative, but weak or uncertain command rarely produces effective results. Command may be weakened by the limitations of the commander, by a lack of means for the commander to exercise command across distance and in the face of war's "friction," or because the members of an organization lack confidence in the commander's abilities, whether such lack of confidence is justified or no.

The movement toward unity of command at the highest levels in the US armed forces in the twentieth century and into the current day is brilliantly narrated in David Jablonsky's *War by Land, Sea, and Air: Dwight Eisenhower and the Concept of Unified Command*. Some of the challenges to unified command had been identified in World War I, but interwar American military training and doctrine had largely left the matter unaddressed. Fortunately, General Eisenhower gained through experience, professional education (to include his mentoring by Fox Conner), and a program of personal self-education, a firm understanding that unified command would be necessary to the Normandy landings and the operations that would follow. He recognized that the employment of airpower, the problems of continuing resupply of allied forces over the sea and across the beaches, and national differences would all present severe obstacles to effectiveness absent a single commander. Eisenhower's insistence on unified command was vindicated by the allied victories. In fact, his few lapses were often those of a failure to exercise the unified command with which he was empowered. A rare difference of opinion with Army Chief of Staff George C. Marshall arose when Eisenhower seemed about to give way to British insistence that a ground commander be interposed between him and the army group and army commanders in the field. As president and commander in chief, Eisenhower recalled the lessons of unified command and pushed for a unified command structure across the armed forces. Eisenhower knew that the changes he helped to implement in the national command structure were incomplete, and it was not until the mid-1980s that legislation further strengthened the prestige and authority of unified commanders. In his book, published in 2010, Jablonsky calls for a renewed discussion of unified command. One issue that is revived periodically is the placement of the Chairman of the Joint Chiefs of Staff (CJCS) in the chain of command. This is a role that the CJCS has never held. The chairman is principal military advisor to the president in his role as commander in chief, and the line of command goes from the president through the Defense secretary to the regional combatant commanders and the heads of the major functional commands like Space Command. As Army Chief of Staff in World War II, George C. Marshall exercised command over a huge army that included army air forces. Since then, fears of a uniformed career officer with the status of a "generalissimo" exercising command that would intervene in direct civilian control has helped to keep the CJCS out of the chain of command. The same argument can be made both for and against such an arrangement. The fact that the CJCS is a military professional with military knowledge acquired over decades, that he is likely to know and even to have a relationship with many of the other senior commanders, and to have a strong emotional attachment to the armed forces, to his fellow service members and to the symbols and rituals of military life may be thought of as either strengths or weaknesses. The chairman's professional knowledge could make him effective as a commander, but also enable him to conceal courses of action or noncompliance from his civilian masters. His loyalties might give command a human touch, but they could also make him excessively risk-averse, incline him to favor the interests of the armed forces over those of the nation as a whole, or to prefer what he considers as effective military strategy over the attainment of policy aims. Lurking in the background is the specter of a "Seven Days in May" military-coup scenario: unlikely but not impossible.

The issue of unity of command generally becomes more complex as one moves up the levels of command, but it is not absent at the lower levels. Some of the problems have been discussed in the section on chain of command. How much intrusion (or "assistance") from a higher commander to a subordinate is appropriate? The unity of command issue may also be raised when staff officers visit subordinate commanders. How much of the authority of the senior commander has been vested in the staff officer? I remember a senior lieutenant from the regimental staff issuing orders to my platoon during a field exercise while I meekly acquiesced. My company commander later rightly rebuked for this failing, one which I can say I did not repeat. (There were others, however!) The error was compounded by the fact that the staff officer's instructions, to repeat an attack that had already failed, were clearly mistaken, resulting in another decision on the part of umpires that we were repulsed with losses.

Another challenge to unity of command can be presented by units attached or in support of another unit. Not only are these units normally under a different chain of command, lacking familiarity and perhaps confidence in the adopted command, they also often possess specialist expertise that the supported unit may lack, resulting in dubious orders for their employment that may be met with resistance and lack of complete cooperation. The supporting unit may even appeal to their own parent command, possibly inciting a conflict among senior officers. In practice, command must be flexible as well as unified. The command structure, more of a web than a simple chain, must reflect a changing tactical, operational, and strategic picture, calling for transfers of units from one higher command to another and for changing relationships between supporting and supported units.

COMMAND AND CONTROL

Officers use the terms Command and Control together so often that they may sometimes forget that the two words mean very different things. Command and Control are even sometimes spoken of as if synonymous with communications. Properly speaking, command is exercised solely by the commander. In the great majority of military organizations, even those of coalitions, command will be vested in one person. Control is a multifaceted function of the staff of the commander. Command and Control are influenced by a relationship between a commander and the staff that can be complex in senses both organizational and highly personal. The commander will issue guidance as well as commands, and the effect such guidance has on the staff will depend on a variety of factors, to include the commander's overall credibility, signs of insight and confidence as expressed in language and nonverbal signals, and the inherent quality of the guidance. The staff conducts planning of future operations, and it supervises the conduct of current operations. In addition to providing control downward through planning and the monitoring and direction of current operations, the staff will provide information to the commander based on their specialist expertise and acquired knowledge of the situation, derived from personal observation and reports. The larger the organization, the larger the staff, and the further into the future it is equipped and expected to plan. Plans of large units can be enormously lengthy and detailed. In war they are subject to constant change, and even in peacetime they may be frequently revised. The ultimate product of planning is execution, and the first step in execution is the issuance of an order, which is usually written in larger formations. Over the past century and a half, armies have developed standard formats for planning procedures and for written orders. These have the virtue of preventing glaring omissions (Napoleon would sometimes forget to issue orders to entire corps!), although the format itself is no guarantee of creative or even clear thinking. Lengthy orders take much time and energy to write and also to read and disseminate. Excessively lengthy orders may go unread or unheeded. They may stifle initiative and the full exercise of command at lower levels. Still, the act of composing detailed planning documents and orders can be good preparation for the coming operation. As Eisenhower said, "Plans are worthless, but planning is everything."[7] In fact the substitution of PowerPoint and other media for detailed written orders has been noted by some as the enemy of thoroughness and clarity. Elaborate visuals can seem to substitute the medium for the message and form for substance. The life of an officer now includes periods of mind-numbing "death by PowerPoint," in a cycle much deplored but hard to break. PowerPoint or other varieties of electronic visual aids sometimes seem to seek dull acquiencence by rapidly presenting a sensory overload of data and images, preventing reflection or dissent.

As has already been suggested, a successful plan or order, and the exercise of all Command and Control, may be thought of as a form of narrative, one that must possess some of the same traits as a good story. Command tells a story of victory. The narrative of victory must exhibit verisimilitude and square with the facts of the situation as they are perceived by the soldiers who must execute the plan. The soldiers should not only believe the plan to be possible, it should possess a kind of narrative pull. It must in a sense be compelling, worth reading and worth carrying out, with at least the prospect of a happy ending.

SELECTION, TRAINING, AND EDUCATION

The formal preparation of officers can be categorized as selection, training, and education. Officer candidates and officers are subject to all three, and officers are also tasked with managing them. All three present cognitive challenges, and all are to varying degrees aimed at evaluating and instilling cognitive abilities. Officers who conduct selection, training, and education are likely to draw on their own experience when so doing (even imitatively), but they may also seek out additional knowledge from a variety of sources, civil and military. Officers have referred to psychologists and athletic trainers, educators, and outdoorsmen for advice on these matters. Selection, training, and education begin at entry level for officers. Enlisted members experience selection and training from the start, but enlisted education has been generally reserved for more senior individuals (although this is changing). All three continue throughout the duration of a soldier's service. Selection, training, and education are the means by which military personnel demonstrate and develop their ability to perform their duties. Selection, education, and training also ensure the perpetuation, transmission, and enhancement of abilities, skills, and knowledge. To the degree that it constitutes a profession, the military is entrusted with its own terms of membership, performance, and advancement. However, the conditions of officer procurement and promotion are also subject to outside influences. They are established by congressional legislation, and the appointment of officers is subject to congressional and presidential approval, even if only flag and general officer selections are generally subject to much scrutiny by Congress or the executive branch.

Selection

Selection standards for military service are both physical and mental. Military forces impose minimum standards for medical health, physical fitness, and mental ability. Recruits may self-select for different branches or be assigned based on testing or the needs of the service. Character counts, depending on the degree of selectivity that is being exercised. Armies prefer not to enroll habitual or violent criminals, although they have done so. Officer candidates more often than enlisted recruits are required to demonstrate character in a more positive way rather than by the mere absence of a criminal record. Selection for service continues in early training, when those passed by the recruiting officer may yet be found wanting. Selection goes on throughout a career, as military members are picked for promotion, for assignments, for advanced training and education. Group selection may be conducted to ensure that a unit is prepared for its duties on deployment or other assignment. Military selection is based on the premise that the soldier has not experienced his real test, combat, and even if he has, experience may not guarantee his good performance in the future, especially since his future responsibilities may be different and greater than those of the past. More than in most endeavors, merit in the military is fleeting and uncertain. The extraordinary demands of wartime may bring out the best, or the worst.[8] Given the relative infrequency of combat in most careers, military reputations may lie on the undependable basis of a small number of successes and failures, even on suppositions and prejudice. Military historian S. L. A. Marshall offers several warnings about being too confident in assessing potential in his classic *The Armed Forces Officer*.[9] He points out that even carefully selected persons may fail when put to the test, and that the most unlikely, those overlooked because they are shy, inarticulate, or don't look the part of a fighter, may step forward when others hesitate.

The experience of selecting and training officers for the Army Ground Forces in World War II illustrates some of the problems associated with preparing individuals for leadership roles.[10] The Army estimated that the officers from West Point and ROTC would suffice for the first 120 days after mobilization. When the OCS became the main source of officers, their task was at first fairly simple. Supply exceeded demand, and questionable candidates were simply dropped from the school with no chance at remediation. In 1942, however, the Army had discovered that the number of acceptable officer candidates was limited, and better efforts had to be made to make the most of the available pool. Preparatory schools were established, and a system of turnbacks was initiated to give failed candidates another try at all or part of the course. This resulted in some 9,000 officers for the Army who would have otherwise been lost. Questions remained concerning selection and the course of instruction for officer training. The use of standardized tests and educational requirements to weed out candidates with a low probability of completing the course caused some concerns that soldiers with leadership potential were being eliminated arbitrarily. The length of the course was a subject for debate. In addition to a pressing need to provide large quantities of officers, Army Ground Forces began with the belief that the course should be kept short in order to get the new officers out to their units as quickly as possible, where their most valuable experience would take place. Later, however, the decision was made to increase all branch OCSs to seventeen weeks from an average of twelve to thirteen. Another early assumption that was modified with time was that all Army officers should be qualified to serve in any capacity. Later, some individuals were commissioned strictly for noncombat, administrative, or technical roles. (This could not, however, completely rule out the possibility that any officer assigned to a theater of operations might find himself in combat, willy-nilly.)

Throughout the war, the main criteria for success appears to have been completion of OCS. This might be classified as a measure of performance rather than of effectiveness. The official Army history does not record a formal feedback loop so that OCS could respond to recommendations from the field based on the performance of new officers. A frequent comment of inspectors and other senior officers appears to have been that the greatest deficiency was not in technical competence but in leadership, which occupied only six hours of formal instruction at OCS, and opportunities to practice leadership in training were infrequent and unevenly distributed.

The collection of data on the performance of officers after their commissioning and early training has increased substantially since World War II. The US Military Academy may lead the way in its efforts to assess the performance of the products of their program, going out to commanding officers to collect reviews of West Point graduates, with the intention that such reviews might not only provide answers (for example, to Congress) to the question, "How are we doing?" but also provide feedback that might lead to specific changes in the curriculum. It is difficult to say how effective the data collection may be in this regard.[11] Changes may face opposition from strongly held assumptions and entrenched programs. An example of this from another army is provided by Daniel Kahneman from his service with IDF. As a young officer, Kahneman provided his superiors with strong evidence that an officer candidate assessment tool that they were using was ineffective. Many years later he returned to Israel and learned that the exact same test was still in use!

In World War II, the armed forces could draw from an enormous manpower pool to fill the ranks that were growing, at one point in the war, by 300,000 each month. On a smaller scale, the volunteer armed forces today face a similar dilemma of getting the most out of the available population, selecting and training effectively, and balancing training with the value of experience. Although the World War II buildup and the pressures to field a large force are unique, military forces still turn over at a rapid rate, with most enlisted members and officers serving for only a single enlistment or period of obligated service.

Training

As illustrated by the foregoing examples, if military selection is difficult, sometimes almost arbitrary, military training walks several fine lines that the officer who plans and conducts training must weigh and consider. Some of the paradoxes of military training are realism and confidence, obedience and initiative, mistakes and perfection, practice and assessment, large units and small units.

Military training must instill confidence, even imparting a desire to practice trained skills in combat, and also communicate a realistic attitude about the experience of warfare. The inexperienced soldier who is too confident, too eager for the fray, may find the sudden reality too great a shock to process. Objectives in training exercises are sometimes unrealistically ambitious compared to what would be attainable in war, where "Even the simplest thing becomes difficult." In World War II, it was found that too much realism, in the form of training areas ensanguined with animal blood, for example, could impair performance in combat. A frank acknowledgment of the additional stress, uncertainty, and "friction" of war should accompany training, and going into action a few simple ideas, repeated often, are more helpful than complex instructions. A Marine officer in Vietnam facing a fortified position for the first time, recounted that he could recall only the formula "Blind, Burn, Blast" from his class on the subject at The Basic School. Talking to newly arrived American soldiers in World War I, a British officer remarked that, "One rule is about all a chap can handle in a battle, and as good a one to remember as any is to keep touch with the chaps to your right and left."[12]

The tension between obedience and initiative has already been discussed in the example of *Young Men and Fire*. Training is generally considered to instill habits of action and obedience that are nearly automatic. Can initiative itself be a habit? Can soldiers be trained to exercise initiative? The best atmosphere for this may be one that combines a rigorous determination to be "brilliant at the basics" with an acknowledgment that it is simply not possible to train for every contingency. Training should reinforce the basics, the good habits and procedures, security, formations, immediate action on contact, and also present the unexpected. The basics of combat are sometimes summed up as "move, shoot, and communicate." These involve physical training, practicing the use of cover, weapons handling and fire support, and simple signals and orders. Once the basics are mastered, the unexpected can be inserted into simulations and training exercises. Some unit training is "force on force" involving an unpredictable adversary. Either two roughly equal forces are pitted against one another, or a small team of "aggressors" may be assigned to provide friction to an exercise. Some exercises are specifically designed to test and promote problem-solving, like the "Reaction Course" that often requires the creative use of improvised equipment to negotiate obstacles. War and combat present a combination of technical and adaptive challenges, and training should reflect this.[13] Technical challenges can be addressed by doing things that individuals and organizations know how to do. They are subject to competence in technical, administrative, or managerial tasks. Even some tactical situations are "technical" in this sense. Units perform "battle drills" to respond quickly to typical tactical situations, like the ambush or meeting engagement. Adaptive challenges require new ways of thinking. They go beyond acquired competence. Military forces that have trained to operate in a certain way, under certain conditions, or even with a certain aim in mind may find themselves faced with unexpected challenges. They may be loath to switch from what they know to what the situation demands. Adaptive challenges may also be presented in a fluid tactical situation in which a unit may move between the offense and the defense, or exploit an unexpected advantage, or react to an unexpected setback or enemy action (even to a new capability). Training cannot anticipate every challenge, but it can accustom soldiers to the inevitability of change and the continuing need for adaptation.

Training has undeniable ritualistic aspects. Some of the standards of military training may appear arbitrary and remote from the practical demands of the service. Up to a point, petty, arbitrary, or artificial difficulties in training may be justified in these terms, that they are meant to give the trainee a sense of transition to military life, of a step up in rank, or of membership in a specialized subgroup of the larger organization, but these "rite of passage" aspects of training must never be allowed to be a substitute for the instilling of useful knowledge or to undermine soldiers' rights, safety, or self-respect.

Education

The subject of officer education has been addressed in earlier parts of this book. In this section, I will be taking a meta-educational or institutional approach to inquiring into how officer education takes place. Officers are involved in education throughout their careers, as students, teachers, planners, and commanders. Most officers are college-educated. Their academic majors vary, although aspiring officers at the service academies and in ROTC take a curriculum of courses designed to introduce them to military organization, customs and courtesies, tactics and leadership. A service academy or ROTC graduate will normally be commissioned on the same day that she receives her degree. Attendance at an entry-level service school usually follows. This school will likely combine training and education, "hands-on" experience with classroom instruction and study. Some officers are sent out to the operating forces with little or no post-commission training, or perhaps with a stack of compact disks that they are expected to absorb in their off-duty hours! This is a foolish economy. Education is best done face to face, and the goal of pre-commissioning and entry-level officer education is to produce a competent ensign or second lieutenant, but it also should introduce a future or very junior officer to the military profession. Entry-level training is when the neophyte first learns to "think like an officer," although the process is incomplete without experience and reflection. If an officer remains in the service, she will attend service schools in effect on schedule and tied to advancement in rank. Other schools are not as *de riguer* but reserved for those requiring specialist knowledge. In addition to service schools, the armed forces outsource some officer education. Lawyers, chaplains, doctors, and dentists usually receive their professional education at civilian institutions. A few officers will attend graduate school on orders or in an extended leave status. Often, these individuals will join the faculty of one of the service academies, usually for a tour of duty but sometimes for the duration of a career.

As already noted, in general, the armed forces prefer to provide their own officer education, rather than have officers experience civilian education. There are practical and cultural reasons for this, but there may also be a price to be paid. When an officer candidate attends a service academy instead of a civilian college, or when an officer attends a service school instead of graduate school, the service branch has control over the environment and curriculum. This may be important, not just to ensure that all instruction deemed as necessary is included, but perhaps to omit influences on an officer that might be distracting or enervating. As military sociologists have pointed out, and sometimes approvingly, the military profession has tended to see itself as a thing apart. The impulse to "censor" what an officer learns may have roots in Plato, who wanted to protect the guardians from impious drama! The consequence of this approach to officer education may be education that is too narrowly focused and uncritical.[14] The authors of the article, "What sets the officer apart?" argue that the best approach to officer education is a "hybrid" that combines the discipline and acculturation of the soldier with the scholar's skepticism and instinct for doubt, navigating the Scylla and Charybdis of "social closure" and "liberalization."[15] By having officers teach officers in an atmosphere of military hierarchy, the services may even be in effect "recycling" rather than "evolving" in knowledge and attitudes. In such an atmosphere, the benefits of challenge and consilience may be lost.

FORCE STRUCTURE

Although the structuring of a military force is in a sense prior to the other subsets of organization that I have addressed in this chapter, I have placed it after discussions of command, selection, training, and education because force structure in effect assembles the pieces. Force structure begins at the top of the hierarchy and extends into the line of fire. Units go to war with the structure designed for them in peacetime, although they may be modified. One of the principles of force structure is that of command. The principles and practice of unity of command, a chain of command, and Command and Control have a decided influence of how military organizations and the supra-military organizations of government are structured. Command should be unified, but Command and Control involves a diversity of function, as specialist units and staff officers work at their own areas of expertise. Another dilemma of military organizations is whether they should be organized to fight or to train. For training, it may be preferable to keep units of the same type together, where they can have access to facilities and train under the supervision of experienced senior personnel. "Task organization" involves parceling out smaller units as attachments to larger ones for operations.

At the very top level, the problem for officers is determining how the Defense Department will interact with the other agencies of government most effectively. For officers, this may pose questions of civilian authority, civil–military relations, loyalty, teamwork, and the sharing of information. In this environment, officers are called upon to be politically savvy without becoming politicized.[16] Relations among the services may be even more fraught than those between military and civilian departments. Behind their outward similarities (officers of the different branches are indistinguishable to many civilians), the services have different cultures and sometimes competing interests. The interagency and intraagency problems are not matters to be resolved by well-drawn charts, but of human relations and varying degrees of willingness to understand another's point of view, of dissimilar people coming together to learn from and to reflect one another.

Although they perform other missions such as deterrence and peacekeeping, the defining activity of military organization is armed conflict and war. At the upper levels, organization must expedite effective command, creating a framework for good decisions and a mechanism to enact them. At lower levels, and closer to the fighting, organizations must be designed to bring resources to bear and to be resilient in the face of opposition and losses. This is illustrated in the successive reorganizations of the Army division in the twentieth century. The Army fought World War I with a very large division of four infantry regiments plus units of artillery, engineers, and other supporting organizations. The large division was thought to be necessary to sustain the casualties of the battles on the western front, but the "square" division was also found to be unwieldy and inflexible. After the war, the Army switched to a structure of three regiments. This triangular structure mirrored the internal organization of regiments and battalions, and it gave the commander more options for employment. (Tanks were omitted from the infantry division organization, on the mistaken assumption that their use would be the exception, not the norm.) The organization of the new airborne divisions presented particular problems. Well into the war, the authorized strength of the US airborne division was set absurdly low. In the field, this limit was routinely exceeded, even doubled, but it took the intervention of a division commander dispatched from the field to Washington in the midst of the European campaign before official organization caught up to practice.[17] After World War II, thinking that wide dispersion would be necessary on a battlefield in which atomic weapons might be used, the Army replaced the regiments with five Battle Groups as maneuver units. This really did not solve the problem of dispersion, and in fact it gave the division commander an excess of units to supervise, possibly exacerbating the challenges to Command and Control associated with dispersion. The "Pentomic" division was short-lived, replaced by an organization called ROAD (for Reorganization Army Division). The new division was a return to the "triangular" structure of World War II and

Korea, with the difference that in place or regiments, ROAD had three brigade headquarters to which a flexible number of maneuver and support battalions could be attached, depending on the mission. (And perhaps also on the commanding general's estimate of the brigade commander's capabilities.)

War and combat can have contradictory influences on a military organization. The ties of comradeship and commitment to the mission can be made stronger. But the pressures of war can be too much for some individuals and organizations, uncovering incompetence, lack of efficiency or energy. Until changes can be made, these deficiencies will impair performance. A key element of military effectiveness may be the agility with which an organization can restructure itself under the pressure of war and often in the face of established ways of thinking and entrenched interests.

DOCTRINE

The authors Dennis Drew and Don Snow usefully define doctrine as "what we believe is the best way to conduct military affairs."[18] I classify doctrine under organization along with command, selection, training, education, and structure because it is one of the given elements that prepare a military organization to perform a mission. Officers create and are subject to doctrine. They are expected to read and to understand doctrine, and most of all to adhere to doctrine when performing their duties. The form of doctrine varies along with its scope. In general, contemporary doctrine does not provide programmed answers, but is concerned with procedure, the steps of planning for different types of operations, and with major factors and elements to be considered. Each of the services has its own doctrine, and there is a growing body of joint doctrine. The aim of contemporary military doctrine seems to be that nothing is forgotten. Its weakness is that everything is included. Doctrinal answers to problems may look like "laundry lists" of actions that lack focus. The assumption may be that the creative commander will provide focus to a staff guided by doctrine, but this requires a significant mental adjustment on the part of an officer moving from a staff position (where most officers spend a substantial part of their careers) to command.

A fascinating account of the influence and evolution of doctrine is *The AEF Way of War: The American Army and Combat in World War I* by Mark Grotelueschen.[19] Despite three years of trench warfare in which European armies had learned that attacks could not succeed without abundant, planned firepower from artillery and other supporting weapons like mortars, machine guns, and light cannon, the American Army went to war in 1917 with a prescriptive doctrine that emphasized the rifle and bayonet as the decisive weapons of the battlefield. Even more surprising, many senior officers, to include AEF (American Expeditionary Force) commanding General Pershing, clung to this belief after the experience of American units proved the contrary. In an excess of faith in the unaided infantryman with his rifle and bayonet, AEF General Headquarters continued to promote and press for attacks with insufficient artillery fires and too few attached supporting weapons. Resistance to change was hardened by Pershing's authoritarian tendencies, and by a prickly patriotism that made it appear disloyal to learn from foreign officers! Fortunately, many officers at the division level and below heeded the advice of their French and British colleagues and learned from experience. After the war, there was still resistance to embracing the "firepower gospel" that the experience of World War I appeared to promote. This resulted in a post–World War I doctrine that walked a line between firepower and maneuver, one that may have served America better than did the firepower-intensive doctrines of some of their World War II allies.

As Grotelueschen's book recounts, doctrine is the official thought of the military, but it often evolves from informal sources such as journal articles, local publications, and (today) "concept" monographs. Official doctrine is not the only influence on military decision-making. Military organizations often have, in addition to doctrine, a cultural preference for certain "ways" of war. This phenomenon is discussed across the length of American military history by retired colonel Antulio Echevarria in his book, *Reconsidering the American Way of War*. He argues that the "American Way of War" as articulated by historian Russell Weigley belies a great diversity in the wars and conflicts of America. Weigley argued that the United States had developed a characteristic approach to warfare that emphasized overwhelming force and decisive action. Written in 1973, as America was coming to terms with the outcome of the Vietnam War, Weigley's book has had a large impact. It has been faulted, even by its admirers, Echevarria among them, for omitting a significant part of the American military experience of conflicts that were not decided by overwhelming force. America has fought the big, decisive wars that are the focus of Weigley's account and of much written history, but it has also engaged in small-scale, long-term operations.

America is not the only country that has arguably demonstrated a preference for a way of war based on a selective reading of its national history and culture. The ancient Greeks favored their own form of decisive combat using the phalanx of armored spearmen. Their "doctrine" was the *Iliad* and the body of Greek drama (tragedy especially) that dealt with armed conflict. The French of the eighteenth and nineteenth centuries had a somewhat sentimental preference for the bayonet over the bullet, an inheritance perhaps from writings on chivalry that had formed medieval military doctrine and that continued to exert an influence for centuries after. The British favored sea power, preferring allies do most of the fighting on land. This preference was in part a matter of geography, but it was also influenced by a sense of national destiny. "Rule, Britannia. Britannia rule the waves," in the words of the eighteenth-century apostrophe later set to music. Doctrine and the way of war may be influenced by what is called "strategic culture," the people and institutions that frame a nation's military policy. Historians like Weigley and the navalist Alfred Thayer Mahan may exert a considerable influence. Much American and Western doctrine is still influenced by interpretations of Clausewitz. These influences may be unseen, experienced uncritically as if part of the natural landscape, as enduring aspects of armed conflict rather than as the culturally coded choices that they are. Doctrine based in history may move too quickly from the descriptive to the prescriptive, violating what the philosopher David Hume calls the is/ought distinction. The fact that some wars have been fought in a certain way does not constitute a guarantee or even a strong likelihood that they will be fought in the same way in the future.

The best that doctrine, concept, way of war, or strategic culture can do is perhaps to frame and ask the right questions. What kind of conflict is this? What measures offer the best chance of success? Are these measures sustainable, and such that we are willing to employ? Perhaps the most important question is whether force is to be used at all, either as a threat or in actuality (and one can lead to the other). Officers' manage force, but they must also understand the unpredictable and uncontrollable aspects of armed force, which can assume a life of its own. Military doctrine may seem to rush to the assumption that the military option is inevitable or at least preferred, but it rarely is. A poetics of war, drawing on humankind's long and mostly bitter experience of armed conflict is as needed as a doctrine.

A POETICS OF WARFIGHTING

I have suggested in this work and elsewhere that previous societies possessed strong poetics of military professionalism. Greek and Roman histories give content and context to deeds of individuals and groups. The Greeks had a rich poetics in the *Iliad* and a large body of drama. The Roman poetics was partly derived from the Greeks but was also homegrown. Civic virtue and imperial destiny meet in the *Aeneid*. In the Middle Ages, from the *Chansons* of Roland to Camelot, the emphasis is often on fealty and ancestry.

What would a modern poetics of war and military officership look like? The military poetics of the past should not be forgotten, although they will be subject to a reinterpretation by each new generation, in the manner of what Harold Bloom has described as a "strong" poetics. The seeming uncritical celebration of the heroic of some literature of the past turns out to be more complex than it might appear. Modern works of the past century are more likely to be antiheroic, although again this appearance bears scrutiny. Modern war stories are more likely to have disillusion and flight as important themes. Less of sacrificial meaning is usually attached to death. A modern poetics of war, to be acceptable, and perhaps to preserve some cultural regard for military leadership, must it seems be ironic. This is illustrated in the poem by William Meredith cited earlier. Irony is a dominant mood in some of the best war writing of our own time, like the stories of Phil Klay's *Redeployment*. These works show classical conceptions of military leadership subject to stress and doubt, to skepticism concerning the value of sacrifice, to concerns for human rights and well-being that give a greater edge to the sometimes sentimental and passive reactions to human suffering of the literature of the past. The bar for permissible conflict has been raised, as has that for permissible conduct in war. What once seemed tragic inevitability now seems wickedness, or mere folly, an avertable, historically contingent catastrophe. The individual is more thrown back on himself than in ancient literature, in which the soldier is more likely seen as representative and exemplary in the context of a larger culture. Not that the cultural context is absent in modern works, but that it is more remote. Modern readers are also likely to read classical works on war differently than did the ancients, for example, seeing Achilles's actions as indicative of individual trauma and neurosis rather than as the will of the gods and of fate. Civilization still has need of soldiers to defend it and of officers to lead them. The writings by civilians and by soldiers on military subjects continue to reflect this knowledge in different ways, but the acknowledgment may be now somewhat more conditional, and even reluctant.

An important subject of a poetics of war and the military profession is bound to be leadership. At the center of a legitimate poetics of military leadership (as opposed to one that is mock-heroic, authoritarian, or fascistic) is a concern for human nature and personal relations. The responses, desires, aspirations, and limits of leaders and led (and these roles are often flexible) are of great importance, as is the significance of leadership as a political but also a moral act. A poetics of leadership may go beyond the familiar terms of transactional and transformational to the transcendent.

For example, the reader is at this point referred to the earlier discussion of reading for officers. A particular illustration may be made of Karl Marlantes's novel *Matterhorn*. The descriptions of the sufferings of the Marine company amid a tortuous landscape, internal racial divisions, and against a hostile, likely invincible enemy are poetic and unforgettable. Efforts to lead and direct in this setting face extremely complex obstacles that seem to defy solution. All the options are "bad in some way."

The greatest accomplishment of a modern poetics of war may be to recapture, in modern terms, some of the ancient sense of the tragedy of war, of its inherent sinfulness and independence from human control. War is not inevitable, but when war begins it will go on in an inexorable way, often making a mockery of the best intentions, skill, fortitude, and prudence.

COHESION AND BELONGING

> Discipline without *esprit de corps* is a damnable thing for which no humane person is likely to offer a defence; discipline based on *esprit de corps* is the dynamic of human progress towards any goal.
>
> —Charles Carrington, *Soldier from the Wars Returning*[20]

The nature of military organizations and of armed conflict promote a powerful sense of belonging among soldiers. In military language, such feelings are given the names cohesion or *esprit de corps*. Soldiers probably must of practical necessity identify strongly with their military organizations, since the threats to unity are also powerful. The battlefield, combat zone, even the barracks may be lawless and licentious places, and the forces of law and even of command may not be enough to hold a soldier in check or urge him on (as the situation demands) absent collective feelings of identification with her comrades and with the unit itself. The military unit is an abstraction that most military forces labor to make real, even to reify through symbols, ceremonies, and narrative. In *The Sand Pebbles*, ship's captain Lieutenant Collins gives a talk to his men on Flag Day comparing the nation to a length of cable, in which the individual strands and cords pull together tightly under the stress, as he says, of "hauling our history into a stormy future."

Cohesion and esprit de corps promote effective group action that, along with leadership, and (still) above technology, is a decisive element on every battlefield, land, air, and sea. To instill and sustain these feelings is therefore something that must never be far from the officer mind. This is a principle almost universally recognized but often neglected. Practice in this area has often run far short of the ideal. Units and commanders parade the colors and use the language of cohesion, but then often undermine the real sources of *esprit de corps*. The managerial personnel policies of the American military have sometimes seemed to stress competition over cohesion, the individual over the group, and to treat soldiers as replacement parts rather than as parts of a whole, who are defined by their membership as much as by the skills they bring as individuals. This was illustrated by the replacement policies of the Army in World War II, Korea, and Vietnam. Soldiers straight from basic training were often fed into units actively engaged with little effort to integrate or orient them. These men hardly had a chance to contribute to the units they joined before they became physical and mental casualties at a much higher rate than the original members. The more able and experienced division commanders held schools to introduce new men to the conditions on the line and to the units they would join, the regiments and battalions. In the World War II German Army, this practice was standardized.[21]

Unfortunately, some officers view enlisted members as simple and somewhat comic subjects, neglecting their individuality and even indulging in stereotypes. This results from a kind of inattentiveness, and it can make the members of a unit feel overlooked and neglected, their special talents, personal circumstances, needs and ambitions lumped together with others in their grade. Officers (some of them former enlisted members) who claim to understand the "mind of the enlisted person" are likely falling into this trap, which hurts both individuals and the unit. They must remember that the enlisted member is (to quote Kipling) "most remarkable, like you" if the full human potential of the military unit is to be realized. To again cite *The Armed Forces Officer*, the wise officer will never condescend to her enlisted subordinates but will treat them as "a group of his intellectual and political peers from any walk of life."[22]

For their part, enlisted persons sometimes think of officers as naïve and uninitiated, even divorced from reality. Such imputation is not without basis in fact! Officers must look to this as well: understanding that the perspective of enlisted persons is often different from that of officers. It is not that officers must surrender their own point of view, but that they must think of ways to understand and to empathize with the lives and feelings of the people who are doing most of the work and fighting.

Much mischief may also come of a soldier's loyalties. Soldiers may be pressed into countenancing or engaging in unethical or unlawful behavior out of an exaggerated desire to go along. Young soldiers whose values and identities are still being formed are vulnerable to this, but so are older veterans whose attachment to the organization and unit have grown strong over years of service, perhaps replacing other ties, as physical and psychological separation from home weaken the sense of any law higher than that of the pack, of the self-regarding profession. This tendency is virtually the central theme of some of the best works of modern war literature from *The Lionheads* to *Matterhorn* to *One Bullet Away: The Making of a Marine Officer*, the memoirs of his service in Afghanistan and Iraq by Nathaniel Fick. War is a social activity, but it must be more than this. It must also be ethical if the organization is to retain the ability to resist the demoralizing aspects of war and deployment: the sense of impermanence and abandonment, the disorienting effects of violence, the seeming randomness of death and wounding, the loss of innocence. Military command and culture must do more than promote unity, they must constantly stress moral purpose, even above the contingent demands of policy. What do we profit if we gain the world and lose our souls?

Soldiers going into war may be said to desire to believe in three things: that the odds of their personal survival are on their side; that victory is attainable; and that their cause is just. It may be that an army will fight on if at least two of these pillars remain, but if two or all three are significantly undermined, the army will become demoralized, either fighting in a savage, even self-destructive way, or losing the will to fight. Classic historical examples of this are the Japanese army in the World War II Pacific theater and the French army in 1917. The Japanese continued to believe in their cause, but lost faith in victory or survival, fighting on to inflict losses on the Americans until despair overtook them and they committed mass suicide, either literally or in hopeless "banzai" attacks. After the aborted Nivelle offensive, the French also lost confidence in victory and survival. Their faith in the cause for which they fought perhaps also undermined, their response was to mutiny, and only radical changes in tactics combined with repeated reassurances (and harsh disciplinary measures) convinced the soldiers to continue fighting.

Some of the drawbacks of military cohesiveness have already been discussed in the chapter on error and incompetence. Too much military belonging can tend to groupthink. It can also foster a kind of dependency of the individual on the military organization. Like prison recidivists or career corporate executives, officers can come to depend on the military organization for identity, for material, emotional, and spiritual support to an unhealthy degree. A dramatic example of this occurs in the novel and feature film *Fail Safe* (1962, 1964). When an Air Force colonel is ordered to hand over information to the Soviets to facilitate the shooting down of US aircraft mistakenly sent to their targets in Russia, he suffers a breakdown and assaults the general who has given the order. It is emphasized in the novel that the colonel is the son of a dysfunctional, impoverished family. He may be more than usually dependent on the uniform for feelings of self-worth. This is an extreme case, but in general military officers are people with a strong desire to belong. This can be beneficial and ennobling, but "the corporate sense" can be an enemy of clear thinking.

The relationship of the individual to the institution is partly a question of culture and partly a matter of individual choice. Former Foreign Legionnaire

Christian Jennings makes an interesting observation on the subject that may apply to other organizations that aim at cohesion and conformity.

> In encouraging people to think of themselves as legionnaires rather than individuals, the process of discrimination was fostered. As elsewhere, the difficult, biased people remained difficult and biased, while those with character and personality intermeshed with the system and thrived on it, still retaining their integrity.[23]

The attitude of the members of another, civil professional group to their profession is illustrated in some of the novels and short stories of Louis Auchincloss.[24] Auchincloss was a lawyer in New York for many years. In his writing, one can discern different attitudes toward the legal profession that are tied somewhat to the generations. The law, it appears, may be something in which either to lose oneself or to find oneself. Both approaches have their drawback and advantages. Most of the older lawyers in the stories (mostly written in the mid-twentieth century) tend to be single men whose entire lives are involved with their profession. The younger lawyers tend to be married and trying to balance work and family. The almost cloistered involvement in their profession of the older men may be limiting, but it can also result in deep feelings of accomplishment and comradeship. The lives of the young lawyers may be more balanced but also divided. The two groups might be compared to regular and secular clergy, respectively, those bound by the rules of their calling and those more of the wider world. Among officers, this kind of monastic dedication to the military profession has become quite rare, although its cognitive and affective benefits may be seen in the service of the man who is likely the foremost American officer of his time, James Mattis, whose tours of duty in senior command positions and as Defense Secretary have been marked by his deep knowledge of armed conflict, one cultivated in the absence of the distractions of family life.

Mattis made his reputation as an organizer but especially as a warfighter, and it is to that role of the officer that we next turn our discussion.

· 6 ·

The Warfighter

$\mathcal{T}$he officer's role as a warfighter is the most demanding, the most dynamic, and the least understood of the parts she will play. Most military training is given over to an officer's administrative or garrison duties and to the exercise of peacetime planning. Although some training is intended to be a realistic preparation for war, war, and combat especially, is notoriously hard to simulate. In an earlier section of this book, I addressed some of the ways that officers can prepare to think as warfighters. In the pages that follow, I will try to describe the mental experience of the officer-as-war fighter. What is it like to think like a warfighter? What kinds of mental schemata or attitudes are effective (and which may be limiting)? The mental demands of the officer's role in war are diverse, and they require a great deal of mental agility; as a warfighter the officer may be required to switch among the roles of personal combatant, tactical leader, and staff officer. Military forces and the social and political environments in which they operate are complex adaptive systems, the actions and reactions of which are very hard to predict.[1] The experience of war is an intensely personal matter for everyone, be she private or general, one that requires mental preparation and disciplined habits. To the personal business of thinking themselves through the day at war, officers add responsibilities that generally increase (at least in scope) as they move up in rank.

In this chapter, I will attempt to synthesize the writing on warfighting with my own education and reflection on the subject. I will address, in order, the areas of tactics, operations, and strategy. The terms tactics, operations, and strategy pertain to the different levels of warfighting. Tactics is concerned with the engagement, operations with the campaign and theater of operations, and strategy with the war. The three levels overlap. A running engagement over a series of days may combine tactics and operations. A war that consists of a single campaign in one well-defined theater combines strategy and operations. A tactician may have to consider the operational and strategic impact of her tactics, and higher-level commanders may involve themselves in tactics, providing training, guidance, and resources. Military officers functioning at the operational or strategic level have nearly always been trained as tacticians earlier in their careers, an experience not had by most civilians functioning as military strategists. The tactical mindset may be useful or a distraction for someone operating on a higher level of war. An appreciation for the tactical challenges of terrain, weather, and enemy resistance can help to rein in unrealistic expectations, but an excessive concern for detail, one perhaps formed in the habits of youth, can impede higher-level planning and execution. A general should be able to think as a platoon commander, but she can't spend too much time doing so! Strategy may drive operations and operations tactics, but in practice there is often an interplay between what is desirable at a higher level of war and what is possible at a lower level. The nineteenth-century Prussian chief of staff Von Moltke remarked that "in the case of a tactical victory, strategy submits."[2] Strategy must not (although it often does) set goals that are simply unattainable at the operational and tactical levels. Strategic goals may be too ambitious because they call for physical progress that does not sufficiently consider the factors of enemy resistance, terrain, or the physical and material limitations of one's own forces (as was arguably the case of the famous Von Schlieffen plan for German units invading France in 1914). They may call upon lower formations to perform tasks for which they are unprepared by training, equipment, or experience. The available resources may simply be inadequate to the task, as were the German forces committed to the Battle of the Bulge, or US and allied forces in the "Phase 4" follow-on to the invasion of Iraq. It is a paradox that an officer functioning on one of the three levels must cultivate an understanding of the other two levels while maintaining a focus on her own. The tactical, operational, and strategic levels of war must be in sync, and the maintenance of this synchronicity is a task of officers at all three levels.

For all that they overlap, I want to argue that the three levels of war are experienced differently at the cognitive level, as they are at the sensory and affective levels. The tactician must be frankly predatory and even homicidal in her approach to war, while guarding diligently against the potential to brutalize her that is latent in the very ways of thinking that make her tactically effective. The operational level is war at its most chess-like and professional, but still deadly and demanding, sometimes in unexpected ways. The operational is as much of time and space as of force, and it is the link between tactics and strategy. The strategist relates the military instrument to policy, a daunting enough task. He is the main go-between in the chain of command between civil and military. Fewer officers are required to think as strategists than at the two lower levels. Still, competent strategists in or out of uniform seem to be usually in short supply, or at least there are fewer, and perhaps fewer in the right places, than circumstances require. It may be beyond the reach of this book to rectify this deficiency, although it will at least be an ambition to imagine a solution.

Over time, a post-Clausewitzian approach to war has gained currency within the United States and many other armed forces. The concept of a center of gravity has been debated and refined.[3] A modern version of this idea calls on the enemy center of gravity to be a specific enemy unit or grouping of forces, the defeat of which is the key to the defeat of the enemy overall. This unit has a critical capability that makes it dangerous, a critical requirement necessary to the exercise of this capability, and a critical vulnerability in the means available to resource this requirement. This approach has the advantage of avoiding the interpretation (likely a misinterpretation), which is sometimes made of the idea of a center of gravity. Some commentators, either aghast or with approval, have taken this idea of a center of gravity to at least strongly imply that military operations must be directed at an enemy's strength, the "thickest part of the fence." It might be admitted that not every enemy force will conveniently arrange itself to fit the refined Clauswitzian pattern, but the search for the center of gravity and its elements, carried on with imagination combined with a proportionate respect for the available facts, can be a useful planning schema. It is applicable, as we shall see, at all levels of war.

The officer as warfighter constructs a narrative to supplant the competing narrative of the enemy. The officer tells a tale of victory, one that her own soldiers must believe and invest their lives in, and that even the enemy must accept as in effect inevitable, even finally desirable as a lesser of evils.

COGNITIVE CHARACTERISTICS
OF THE THREE LEVELS

Tactical thought is personal, especially at the lower levels of command. Operational thinking is communal, or even tribal. Strategic thought is bureaucratic, with all the advantages and drawbacks of bureaucracies. For the officer, all are hierarchical. The differences have to do with the size and compositions of staffs and the range of the commander's responsibilities, such that he becomes less able to exert personal command the farther up he goes in the levels of warfighting. The tactical level of command involves much one-on-one interaction among unit leaders. Tactical thought is also personal in the sense that the tactician is a part of the situation that he is trying to control, as are those with whom he is communicating, whether conferring, questioning, directing, or exhorting. At the higher tactical levels, thinking may take on some of the communal and less personal attributes of operational thinking. I have described operational thinking as tribal because it is at this level that we find the greatest concentration of military professionals. Although most operational commands are joint, and many are multinational (combined or coalition), they are staffed largely by military officers with years in the service who may share a common outlook. In fact, it may be an unstated aspiration among them to have the shared military profession overcome differences in service and nationality. The presence of the officer is somewhat diluted at the strategic level. The bureaucracies that engage in strategic thinking also consist of government officials and even academics, consultants, and members of "think tanks." In the realm of military strategy, the officer may be deferred to as the putative expert, but the degree of influence that she exerts is subject to many factors, to include the officer's ability to persuade. Military discipline may have an inhibiting effect on this influence as well, since officers tend to be more guarded than others in expressing their views, and they are less likely than others to openly disagree with someone in a superior position, since this goes against the habits of a lifetime and the authoritarian tendencies of many officers.

A question that has been regularly revived in military theory and history concerns the question of whether the focus of effort is on enemy forces or features on the ground. The usual consensus is that the enemy is the main objective, but some argue for terrain. It is undeniable that terrain is highly significant. As already noted, Ian Hope argues that the antebellum education of army officers at West Point served them well by focusing on terrain and lines of operation rather than on the enemy. This debate can be better understood by reference to the levels of war. At the tactical level, which is concerned with engagements, the emphasis is on the enemy and the effects of terrain on fires. At the operational level, the emphasis shifts to the effect of terrain and human-made features on movement. The strategist is the most concerned with the economic, political, and symbolic significance of terrain. At no level is the commander unconcerned with either the enemy or the ground, but the emphasis changes, and to function effectively commanders at all levels must understand that their counterparts at the other two levels look at the same map with different perspectives.

The three sections that follow address the officer-as-warfighter's role on the tactical, operational, and strategic levels. It should perhaps be acknowledged that the roles of tactician, operator, and strategist likely do not exhaust the challenges of the officer's role as warfighter. The protean nature of war means that the officer-as-warfighter may have to perform other roles. Some of these are holdovers from her duties as organizer, since these do not cease with the advent of war. The officer may be involved in the development and adaptation of new technologies even as the fighting is under way. The warfighter may have to serve as counselor and negotiator, as an interpreter and explainer of policy, and as the means of feedback in the case of policy that she sees as mistaken or misapplied.

THINKING LIKE A TACTICIAN

Perhaps no other cognitive activity so defines the military officer as that of the tactician. Tactics is not a specialty, but a way of thinking that transcends the differences of service branch and physical milieu. The tactical battle is subject to an almost infinite variety of influences, from the psychological to the sensory, cultural, and physical. As S. L. A. Marshall observes in *The Armed Forces Officer*, for the imaginative tactician, "everything becomes grist for his mill."[4] Even officers in the combat support or noncombatant branches are expected to have some understanding of tactics, so that they may serve and survive in a tactical setting. Officers who operate at sea, in the air, and on land are tacticians. Tactics is the basis of warfighting. Officers may gain experience at the operational and strategic levels, but they are trained as tacticians and serve in tactical-level assignments from the beginning. All officers in the armed forces must at least have a knowledge of tactics, and those in the combat and combat support arms should consider it their specialty.

Some tactical fundamentals apply equally to the sea and air as well as to the ground, and to the small-unit tactics practiced by the noncommissioned and junior officer as well as the grand tactics practiced by generals in command of very large, combined arms organizations up to division and corps. No ground, air, or sea officer can afford to limit his understanding to a single medium or dimension. The tactician must be familiar with the battlespace above, below, and upon the surface of earth and sea. The officer must resist the tendency for the technical demands of modern warfare to crowd out her role as a tactician. The officer must have a tactical mindset, in all its aspects, most especially not excluding the human: the motives, limits and capacities of those doing the fighting. As argued by B. A. Friedman in his book *On Tactics*, tactics has been undertheorized, with the result that the link between tactics and the higher levels of war has been neglected.[5] The best tactics can neither redeem a flawed strategy, nor succeed if they are out of sync with strategic ends. Tactics can become an obsession, crowding out the higher levels of war in the mind of the officer, but it can also be neglected, left behind as senior officers move on to the "big arrows" of operations and strategy.[6]

It is at the tactical level of war that the paradoxes of officership most accumulate. The tactical level is war at its most immediate and murderous. The tactician has need of some of the same instincts as the hunter or armed robber. At the level of the engagement, warfare would seem to devolve into aggravated assault on a large scale. This is where force is expressed in many individual acts of barely restrained violence. However, precisely because of the "point of the spear" personal violence of tactical combat, the officer-as-tactician must be at her most prudential. Very close to the action herself, she has the ability and obligation to control the destruction and death visited on her own soldiers, on the natural and constructed landscape, even on the enemy, since the utter annihilation of an opposing force is rarely attainable, necessary, or even desirable. In fact, as a military professional the officer's task is as much the containment as the unleashing of violence. The requirement to limit harm is in its way as besetting and vital a professional obligation as the physician's "First, do not harm."[7] The tactical level is both the most subject to real-time, immediate Command and Control and the most difficult to control, the level at which the elements of friction, the influence of fear, fatigue, and miscommunication are most in play. Tactical situations change and develop very quickly, and tactical leaders must be granted the degree of authority and initiative necessary to stay ahead of a changing situation. However, tactical leaders are often accorded less room for independent judgment than are commanders at the higher levels of war, due to their relatively junior ranks and to the innate disorderliness of the tactical milieu. In his article, "John Boyd on Clausewitz: Don't Fall in Love with Your Mental Model," Ian T. Brown[8] cites Boyd as taking Clausewitz to task for placing too much emphasis on the reduction of friendly friction, and not enough on the imposition of friction on the enemy. As in the questions of command with which tactical matters may be said to overlap, the views of junior and senior commanders on these issues may be quite different, with junior leaders claiming more independence and their seniors insisting on more authoritarian Command and Control.

The tactician is a puzzle-solver, assembling the parts of a tactical situation, even though inevitably some of the parts will be missing. The tactician is also a reader of a variety of texts: of terrain, of various signs of enemy activity, of written orders from above. He is a writer of instructions and notes, but speech is probably more important to the tactician than written language. He must communicate clearly, engage in dialogue and intuit the hidden meaning behind words, all through a barrier of friction, perhaps of deliberate obfuscation, sometimes across deep differences in culture and in a foreign language. To engage in combat is always to speak. One of the great points of S. L. A. Marshall in his writings on tactical combat is the importance of communication across the unit, not just from the top down, to develop situational awareness, unity of will and action.[9] Speech becomes increasingly urgent and difficult approaching the point of contact.

Although she is inescapably a killer, the tactician must cultivate sincere empathy. The feelings of her soldiers are a vital part of her professional knowledge, since these will largely determine how they function in combat. Also, the tactician must possess an "other side of the hill" ability to get into the mind of the opposing commander. This ability can be fueled by the study of enemy history and doctrine, but it should not be dogmatic or tied to stereotypes; the tactical situation is foremost. The tactician must believe that the enemy is as smart and adaptable as she.

Part of the tactician's picture of the battlefield must include the laws and rules governing the use of force. These include the orders she receives, relevant legal articles, and standing rules of engagement (often abbreviated ROE). The rules may be unwelcome, and applying and enforcing them can be seen as an additional burden on those already with the most to bear, even as an impediment to the mission and a danger to life. Restraints on the use of force come from on high, or more tellingly from well behind the lines. Like any instructions, they are not immune to questioning, even to disobedience, although the flouting of rules by an officer on any occasion both exposes him to disciplinary action and may serve to undermine his own authority. Rules limiting the use of force have been compared to armor, in that they may be uncomfortable and confining, but in that they also offer protection against the misuse of force that may hinder mission accomplishment and cause psychological damage. Even the most complete situational awareness, the most prudential and effective exercise of command, and the most scrupulous attention to the rules governing the use of force will not rule out the possibility that, while seeking to destroy the enemy, the tactician will hurt and kill noncombatants, destroy their homes, and disturb their lives in ways that may take years to undo, indeed that may leave scars that will never fully heal, but are passed on from one generation to another. Anyone with any experience of war on the ground has some knowledge of this, and it is very often a source of regret and doubt, even of moral injury if some deeply held value was betrayed by one's own or someone else's actions. The officer does not decide when wars will be fought, but, especially in his tactical role, he has very direct knowledge of war's consequences. It is left to him to ameliorate the unwanted consequences, and to remind others that the neat or surgical war is as much a fantasy as it ever was.

As S. L. A. Marshall also notes that, one of the lessons that the tactician must learn is not to expect too much, too quickly. This is in effect a rewording of Clausewitz's comments on the effects of friction. Actions on the tactical level are subject to the maximum of friction. In contact with the enemy, fear, fatigue, casualties, equipment damage, and the confusion, dislocation, and inertia that can result from these are at their greatest. The greatest source of friction is the independent will of the enemy. As noted earlier, study, planning, and an adaptive, open state of mind can reduce the impact of the opposing will, but it is a constant of war and combat in every age. The tactician will often have to be content with small gains that fall short of planned objectives. Different routes and methods may have to be tried and discarded if their lack of effectiveness has reasonably been established. Setbacks must be borne with a combination of patience and tenacity. In ground combat especially, the fight may at times be borne by only a small number of those nominally engaged in an action. Soldiers may be rendered *hors de combat* by many factors, to include their location, physical condition, situational awareness, and psychological state. Overall numbers still matter, as the combat effectives must be wrung out of the larger group.

The key to the tactical mindset may be a state of constant alertness, a restless desire to improve your unit's opportunities, a sense that there is always one more thing to be done. This mindset is behind General Mattis's often quoted remark, "Be polite, be professional, but have a plan to kill everybody you meet!"[10] Sometimes the tactical mindset can be surprisingly elusive. One of the first nights into Iraq during OIF1, I came into the medical tent surprised to find the corpsmen settled down for a night of video games. I told them to break out their weapons for a check and we talked about some possible courses of action to take if our position were attacked, a likely prospect under the circumstances, but one that had not occurred to them until I mentioned it. Sometimes, it may not be enough to have a plan to kill everyone you meet, but to fight people who have not yet made their appearance.

TACTICAL PSYCHOLOGY

The subject of tactical psychology is not at all new. From the earliest writings on war, there has been acknowledgment that the hearts and minds of combatants were the keys to victory and defeat. "All be ready if our minds be so," as Shakespeare has Henry V say on the eve of battle. There have even been some systematic efforts to understand the psychology of soldiers in combat, perhaps most persistently and successfully by S. L. A. Marshall. Still, it likely remains true that too little attention has been paid to the details of what psychological states determine how and with what success soldiers fight. This is not only a question of leadership, but of tactics, since most engagements are not won by killing all or even a sizable minority of the enemy, but by convincing the survivors that the game is lost. In *War Games: The Psychology of Combat*, British soldier-turned analyst Leo Murray does a deep dive into the area of combat psychology. Based on historical data, unit records, and interviews with numerous soldiers, Murray analyzes the four main battlefield behaviors of fighting, freezing, fussing (his word for engaging in activities that are merely routine or otherwise not suited to the situation), and fleeing. Understanding and anticipating the difficulties of "seeing straight" and "thinking straight" in combat should be part of soldiers' training, and overcoming them must be a goal of leadership. Taking in new information and instructions once an engagement begins seems to be especially difficult. "Tunnel vision" and other forms of sensory and cognitive impairments kick in. Cohesion counts, but leaders (formal and informal) must be close to ensure that soldiers are mirroring the correct behavior (fighting, rather than fussing, freezing, or fleeing). The confusion of the battlefield can also be exploited in a way to enable victory. Flanking attacks, speed, and incoming fire from multiple directions, mixing direct and indirect fires if possible, decrease the number of enemy soldiers willing to fight. Demonstrating the possession of a prestige weapon, giving pause, and having combatants in close proximity to the enemy gives them the opportunity and incentive to surrender, which (ethics aside) is more desirable than merely killing because of the potential value of prisoners and the contagion of the surrender-habit.

Murray is correct that flanking attacks tend to be neglected in training. They are too time-consuming, physically taxing, and hard to control. Flanking attacks with blanks lack the psychological payoff of one conducted with real bullets, but there is evidence to show that they are worth the trouble. I remember a flanking attack conducted at night during a training exercise in Spain that caught us by complete surprise. The company executive officer had an idea of what was coming, but neither he, the company commander, nor any of the rest of us were able to act in time to avert disaster. If it had been the real thing, we probably would have all been dead, prisoners, or in disorganized flight by morning. A successful flanking attack avoids the enemy's main fires, creates the conditions for enfilade fire, and most significantly makes the defenders feel disoriented, possibly abandoned, and already defeated. (It was a very educational night.)

Another area explored by Murray is the "is it worth it?" calculus. Fear is not the only reason soldiers hang back. They are constantly reevaluating the chances they take versus the possible benefits. Karl Marlantes frankly admits to taking an action in combat because he thought he would receive the Navy Cross. (He did.) The usual consideration, however, appears to be a weighing of the risk to the soldier against how his actions will further the mission and protect himself or his fellow soldiers. When an officer goes out to inspect his positions, or gets in a vehicle to visit another unit, or engages in personal reconnaissance, he is often thinking, "Is this trip really necessary?" Of course, necessity may be variously defined. Mission accomplishment and safeguarding the lives of his soldiers are the main considerations, but appearances matter too, and not just in the matter of combat decorations. The presence of an officer may be reassurance or "insurance" (against a lapse in discipline, for example). The officer should also be aware that her soldiers are often going through the same calculations when they are deciding whether to move from cover, to fire their weapons (perhaps revealing their location), or even just to raise their heads to survey terrain in the presence or the enemy or under fire.

Another point raised in Murray's book is that the enormous weight of the body armor and other accoutrements carried by modern soldiers sometimes renders the flesh incapable even if the spirit is willing. In the past, soldiers could considerably lighten their load by dropping packs, but the new weight is mostly part of their combat load, and not so readily jettisoned. Of course, greater protection can also boost a soldier's confidence, making him more willing to move forward or otherwise take action, but there is a limit to how much effect this increased confidence can have if he is exhausted by the weight of his equipment.

SUCCESS AND FAILURE

The tactical leader would do well to remember that, even as she heads down dead alleys or tries methods that prove fruitless, she is (or should be) developing an understanding of the tactical situation. A failed advance may seem to have sacrificed the element of surprise, but even failed attacks have had serendipitous effects favorable to the attacker. Properly and not callously considered, failure can breed success. Defeat has often been a spur to greater innovation, determination, and resourcefulness. This is one reason why action is generally favorable to inaction, although, like all military precepts, this statement contains its antithesis, which is the need for due consideration prior to acting, even if there is little time for thought. As Field Marshall Slim's memoir suggests, it is not just experience, but hard experience that is a valuable teacher, and it is a defensible generalization from military history that losers learn best.

One of the unknowns in tactical combat is the degree of effort or commitment that is necessary to achieve the objective. A target may need to be attacked multiple times, or a full-out assault be necessary to take the place of reliance on supporting arms. Not all combat is decisive. Shaping and supporting actions are needed along with a main effort, and even a main effort may have to accept limited gains.

Some of the decisions and dilemmas facing the tactician are illustrated by the challenging, even infamous World War II Italian campaign.[11] The allied solution to the mountainous terrain of the Italian peninsula and the skillful, dogged resistance of the German forces was to adopt frontal infantry attacks on a large scale and supported by pre-planned and on-call indirect fires referred to as "stonks." These methods may have seemed inevitable if costly to the generally unimaginative Allied commanders Mark Clark and Bernard Montgomery. It took the somewhat disregarded French to devise better methods that involved infiltration by light infantry forces kept supplied by mules that could operate in the roughest, but least-defended terrain.

The greatest challenge to thinking like a tactician may be the combat environment itself. The friction and uncertainty of this environment may make any decision or action seem difficult. An officer, faced with life and death decisions in such an atmosphere may succumb to sensory overload and inertia, especially in a crisis. This arguably happened to two other senior World War II commanders Lloyd Fredendall and Courtney Hodges at the Kasserine Pass and the Bulge, respectively, although Hodges bounced back in time to help retrieve the tactical situation and avoid being relieved from command.[12] The tactician may sometimes need to step back, even if this simply means walking a few yards off the firing line in order to regain perspective and see ways out of what may seem an overwhelmingly difficult situation.

"PRINCIPLES" OF TACTICS

> There is only one principle of war and that's this. Hit the other fellow, as quick as you can, and as hard as you can, where it hurts him the most, when he ain't looking.
>
> —Field Marshall Sir William Slim

In his memoirs, Field Marshall Slim recalls as a young officer cadet being seen reading a tactical manual by a sergeant major. The sergeant major treated the young Slim to the piece of advice quoted above. I plan to take this quotation (cited in Marine Corps Doctrinal Publication 1-3 *Tactics*) as my text for a further discussion of tactics.[13] Slim was a highly successful World War II commander who also had a great command of language, as illustrated in his rightly well-regarded memoir. As I have already noted, Slim is particularly good at laying out the thought processes that led up to the decisions he made as a commander (to include the times when he was admittedly mistaken!). His direct, often witty writings in war merit study. Like many other deceptively simple aphorisms, the injunction quoted above may seem simplistic or even reductive, but it is really quite complex and even profound. I will discuss this statement in two parts, the first to do with hitting, and the second with "not looking."

"Hit the other fellow, as quick as you can, and as hard as you can, where it hurts him the most."

Hitting hard requires the concentration of forces to support a single blow, rather than distributing force evenly and equally across the battlespace and objective, thereby spreading one's strength and administering a series of slaps instead of a hard punch. Speed is a subject I will address separately, but obviously speed contributes to the impact of the main effort, giving the enemy no warning and imparting momentum. Hitting where it hurts means locating the critical vulnerability, the weakness that undermines the enemy's strength, whether it is a gap in his lines, an exposed flank, or a deficiency in his tactics, Command and Control, or organization that can be exploited. Commanders also use different means to enlarge a gap or further weaken a vulnerability to set the conditions for the main effort.

To do this requires several things: good intelligence, an appreciation of one's own capabilities, of time and space, of the terrain and its effect on movement, on fires, on cover and concealment. At Blenheim in 1704, the Duke of Marlborough noticed that the French center was relatively weakly held by cavalry. Rather than launch an immediate main effort at the center, however, he launched supporting attacks at both flanks, pinning down the French forces there and goading the French commander to further weaken his center by reinforcing the flanks, one anchored in the town of Blenheim. Marlborough patiently waited for the flanking attacks to develop until the maximum French forces were drawn from the critical center, keeping his own infantry in the center under cover while they endured French bombardment. Finally, in late afternoon, he launched his main attack, breaking the army of the French and their Bavarian allies in two, driving off their cavalry and pinning thousands of French infantry in the town of Blenheim for capture.

"When he ain't looking."

Convincing the enemy not to look is an even greater challenge than hitting hard and fast where it hurts. Applying this idea, the tactician is a magician, misdirecting his audience to look somewhere else rather than where the real trick is taking place. Commanders employ several methods to make the enemy look somewhere else, some of them illustrated in the preceding narrative of Blenheim. Methods include deception, supporting arms, a supporting attack, covering fire, and again speed. Like much else in war, deception may be said to take the form of a dialectic. The thesis of enemy expectations may be said to meet the antithesis of the deception operation, resulting in a synthesis of the enemy's revised (and incorrect) perceptions. Discussions of deception often focus on the large-scale, famous examples of deception, like Patton's Ghost Army that helped to hold German forces at Calais even after D-Day, or the efforts to convince the German high command that Sardinia, not Sicily, would be the next allied objective after North Africa. But deception is also a matter for the tactician. As one of the most successful battalion commanders in Vietnam, David Hackworth routinely used deception.[14] It was standard operating procedure for units to appear to settle in before night but then to move to their actual nightly defensive and ambush positions under cover of darkness. Empty Huey helicopters deceived the Viet Cong as to the actual location of landing zones and objectives. Hackworth might also use nearly empty trucks to deceive the enemy as to his numbers, perhaps to convince an enemy that he was withdrawing an entire company when in fact most of the unit was still in the field occupying ambush or attack positions. A unit might appear to occupy a circle of defensive positions but then withdraw to an inner circle so that the enemy would needlessly expend ammunition and an assault on empty positions, exposing itself to the unexpected fires of the inner ring in the process.

Supporting arms weaken an enemy by causing casualties and destroying equipment, forcing him to take cover, deceiving or distracting him from the main effort. A supporting attack may do the same; if the enemy reinforces the objective of a supporting attack, he may draw troops away from the objective of the main effort, enlarging a gap or weakening himself where we mean to strike. Covering or suppressive fire has the purpose of forcing an enemy to take cover, throwing off his aim and limiting his movement. Indirect fire has its limitations. The overreliance of US forces in the World War II Italian campaign has already been noted. Few things can raise the spirits of hard-pressed soldiers like the sight of their own supporting arms firing in effect, but even in an era of precision munitions, supporting arms are very often insufficient by themselves. The maneuver unit is still normally the main effort.

In addition to strengthening the attack and reducing the time of exposure to enemy fire, speed can deceive the enemy as to the real location of friendly forces. Fast moving units have often arrived at an enemy's doorstep unannounced, unexpected, and finding him unready. "Where did they come from?!!"

The other, unstated half of Slim's sergeant major's advice is not to fall victim to the enemy's effort to hit us hard, fast, where it hurts and where we "ain't looking." This involves many considerations, and even more than the foregoing, these are the reasons why a tactical leader's job is never done. The things that will keep a unit from being hit, hurt, and taken by surprise include physical security, operational security, mutual support, and a reserve.

Physical security in the defense takes the form of observation and listening posts, patrols outside the wire, sensors and drones to detect enemy movement. On the move it calls for point, flank, and rear guards. Operational security requires good communications procedures and care about revealing plans and current operations only to trusted persons and on a need to know basis. A tactician will anticipate the enemy's efforts to find, expand, and exploit gaps in her position. It is impossible to be strong everywhere, but units can be both mutually supporting and to a degree self-sufficient. Units must be connected physically, or by fires and communications. A favorite target for attack is the boundary between two units, so the defense must be coordinated. As has already been suggested, it may be possible and desirable to present a gap where none exists, to appear weak, unprepared, or vulnerable while in fact lying in wait.

A reserve force is insurance against surprises. It is vital but not enough to have a reserve. The tactician must also plan for how it might be needed and used. A reserve is a reaction force, closing gaps, reinforcing units that are hard pressed, exploiting success. It may take an enemy attack in flank or rear. The Battle of the Bulge, in which the American army found itself in the unaccustomed position of trying to stave off and contain an initially successful large-scale German attack, indicates the importance of the commitment of the reserve at the proper time and place. American commanders like Troy Middleton had to resist the temptation to commit the reserve even when German attacks were successful, waiting to be as sure as possible that this was the main German attack and not a diversion. The decision of where to place the reserve had to balance competing goals of blocking, containing, or channeling a German advance, and even more wrenchingly, of which American units would be supported and which frankly had to be left on their own, perhaps sacrificed to heavy casualties, defeat, and capture. Historian Harold Winton says that in making these decisions, based on a "geometrical calculus" of the battlespace, commanders were "trading lives for time."[15]

In the defense and on the offense, whether trying to discomfit the enemy or avoid his own discomfiture, a tactical leader must continually exercise the "other-side-of-the-hill" imagination with respect to the enemy. This is a job for the commander as well as the intelligence officer. It is a military adage that time spent on intelligence is rarely wasted. In Vietnam, David Hackworth spent days in conversation with a captured Viet Cong officer to understand his enemy's motives and gauge his morale.[16] The effort to understand the enemy is related to the vital understanding of the nature of the conflict, on what it hinges on, and how it can be won. Through a greater understanding of the enemy, the thoughtful commander may also grow in self-understanding.

There are many ways to view a battlefield, but the clearest perspectives are the best informed. The word *reconnaissance*, French in origin, in its root sense denotes understanding, even empathy or gratitude, seeing through the eyes of another. To fulfill the role of tactician, the officer must undertake reconnaissance in this meaning, one not limited to the observation of appearances, but encompassing the meaning underneath and within. What are we fighting for? Do the means match the ends?

FLEXIBILITY

In her role as tactician, the thinking of an officer is perhaps less tied to rule and more dependent on flexibility and mental agility than that of any other professional activity. Neither procedures, principles, nor doctrine provide the solution to any tactical problem. Unlike the lawyer, to whom the words of which laws are made are all-important, the engineer, who must abide by known rules of stress and structure, or the physician, whose training inculcates strong guidelines for diagnosis and procedure, the military officer-as-tactician must consider a multitude of uncertainties tied to only a few givens. He must never get too committed to any plan, and the plans themselves must allow for change on the move. Good tactics allow room for maneuver, whether in offense or defense. Plans must be made with the inevitability of change in mind. Military doctrine makes use of the terms "branches" and "sequels" to, respectively, denote the unexpected threats and opportunities that may arise, and the new tasks and missions that we may be called on to perform in response to them.

A flexible mind and a creative approach to problem-solving are the tactician's best weapons. Grant said he'd never bothered to study tactics, but he looked at each problem and figured it out, not asking himself what Napoleon or Frederick the Great would have done, but what he and the Army of the Potomac needed to do. The study of tactics and military history may (of course) be valuable, but they are best thought of as presenting problems rather than solutions. This is also true of theory and doctrine. Without them, even the most adroit problem-solver may not know which problems to solve. As Friedman argues persuasively in *On Tactics*, the tactician must also be trained as a strategist, or else tactical victories may not serve operational and strategic ends. The tactician's own experience is probably his most valuable text. Through experience, the tactician may acquire mastery over a widening range of problems. He acquires an accurate intuition and the ability to "think fast" to engage in accurate intuition and pattern analysis.[17] Even experience can be misleading, however. Experience that is remote in time may be in effect rewritten or rendered irrelevant. The temptation to convert experience into formulas is dangerous. The Duke of Marlborough had won a great victory at Blenheim in 1704, but his subsequent battles sometimes appeared to be attempts to recreate the Blenheim victory, even when circumstances had changed. The frontal assault that had carried the day at Blenheim proved murderous against well-entrenched troops at Malplaquet in 1709. Marlborough won a victory at Malplaquet, but the tactical victory was so costly that it damaged the strategic prospects of the British and their allies against France.

SPACE AND TERRAIN

On a tactical level, space, distance, and the physical features of the land can have a decisive influence. Space and terrain offer impediments and advantages in the areas of fire and movement, the two enduring elements of the tactical battle. Some modern weapons and means of transportation can nearly eliminate the influence of space and terrain, but the stubborn importance of the physicalities of space and terrain remains. Combat forces are still armed with some weapons that are limited in range and to line of sight. No amount of standoff by a drone or missile can eliminate the possibility of a closer-up confrontation. In fact, the close-quarters confrontation still seems to be necessary to a decisive conclusion. War is about the people for whom and by whom it is fought, and eventually there will be "skin in the game" on both sides. The side that insists on holding the other at arm's length will find itself outflanked by some asymmetrical approach that does not respect self-serving assumptions and conventions.

The area in which a tactical engagement is fought offers several problems. It may be useful to consider the battlespace as a potential two-sided force multiplier, impeding or enabling either side impartially, depending on their physical location. When enemy losses and other measures of success are sometimes hard to gauge, terrain features and human-made structures offer tangible objectives. Most terrain features are impediments to movement. A featureless landscape would allow unimpeded movement in all directions. High ground, depressions, bodies of water, jungle, and forest all offer impediments to movement. Roads may enable movement, but they also channelize and create opportunities for ambush by the enemy. The possession of terrain features, of high ground especially can obviously also be of value tactically, since they offer cover, improved observation and fields of fire from on high or within, and obstacles to an approaching enemy, whether in the defense or offense, moving or stationary.

THE FUTURE OF TACTICS

Tactics has always been modified by technological changes. Technology drives changes in tactics, although it is up to officers and other soldiers to decide how new technology will be employed, how it will affect, not only tactics, but organization and training, even military ethics. The trend over the centuries has been an increase in the distance between shooter and target. In the past, traditional thinkers have often thought of these developments as spelling the end of courage and prowess in warfare. "What was the world coming to" when a kid with a sling can lay low a mighty warrior, or a common archer or musketeer defeat a wealthy, pedigreed knight with years of training? But the profession has adapted to these developments. Slingers, archers, musketeers, and aviators have been drawn into the fray, taking their chances like everyone else. The full impact of new technology remains to be seen or felt. With drones and long-range precision warfare, it may seem that some military professionals are so remote from the battlefield that they are barely soldiers at all, but video gamers, like the protagonist in the science fiction novel *Ender's Game*, deprived of the means to gain hands-on knowledge by the intercession and reliance on technology. On the other hand, the operators of drones may see much, loitering over their targets for days before striking, even forming an uncomfortable, remote relationship with the people they are planning to kill. It will be a cognitive and an ethical challenge for officers of the future to retain a human sense of war in the face of new tools that may tend to dehumanize. The cyber domain may seem to exist mostly at the operational and strategic levels. For the tactician, "cyber" may be little more than a new word for electronic warfare, but the more use tactical forces make of digital, online devices, the more dependent they become on them, the more vulnerable they will be to cyberattacks.

THE OPERATIONAL MIND

The operational level of war, the most recently named level of warfighting, is a middle ground between strategy and tactics. Operations is the business of the campaign, stringing together a series of tactical engagements to achieve victory over a longer time and a greater expanse of space. The prime consideration in tactics, the art of the engagement, is fire, "steel on target." At the operational level, space and movement move up in significance.[18] The mind of the operator is concerned with a large, complex, four-dimensional space. This may also be said of the tactician and the strategist, but it is at the operational level that calculations of time-space assume the greatest importance. The operational narrative of victory is an extensive geographical chronology, a narrative of victory over an extended but finite stretch of space and time, bounded by the duration of a campaign and the physical limits of the theater.

I have described operational thought as tribal. It is here that the officer, usually of middle or senior grade, most interacts, almost at times exclusively, with her peers in the military profession. There will be differences in service culture, of course, and even of nationality, but the participants in operational thinking will be likely to share some common vocabulary, doctrine, and to a degree an outlook as career military officers that cross service and national lines although, in fact, surface similarities may conceal more vital differences. The tribal nature of operational thinking tends to breed groupthink, to allow conventional wisdom and errors that might, to an outsider, seem obvious, to go unchallenged. This tribal tendency has arguably been responsible for some of the egregious operational errors in history. The failure of army staffs and commanders to anticipate the German attacks in the Ardennes that led to the Battle of the Bulge is in this category. Not only did planners and intelligence officers fall into line with the prevailing view that the Germans would not attack in force, but also in effect the Americans projected their own unanimity of thinking onto the adversary, imputing to the Germans their own reasoned calculation that such an attack had little chance of success. The American officers perhaps forgot that decisions were being made, not by military professionals like themselves, but by a cocksure ex-corporal, one who had never learned to think like an officer! In addition, even German military planners were in a much different state of mind from that of the Americans. The Germans officers faced an almost inevitable total defeat, one that perhaps could only be, if not averted, then ameliorated by a negotiated settlement following a risky, high-stakes, high-payoff gamble that the Americans, increasingly confident of success, saw as imprudent and uncalled for.[19]

At the operational level, the importance of the primary question posed by Von Clausewitz about the nature of the struggle assumes greater immediacy than at the tactical. A way of expressing the question might be to ask what must change in the current situation. Is defeat of enemy forces going to be enough, or will that leave other threats unanswered? Even if defeat of conventional forces is sufficient, what must be involved in that defeat? What is the shortest route to depriving an enemy force of its "center of gravity"? Is ground to be ceded or left to the enemy to gain time and limit losses, or is the ground itself of inherent value, for example providing roads and ports, or natural, industrial or population resources needed for the prosecution of the campaign, and not just as the fruits of eventual victory?

The plan of campaign is the product of an intense process of study, coordination, and simulation. At the operational level, most staffs are divided into "future" and "current." Planning will be conducted by the future operations section. When a plan is complete and has been approved by the commander, there will be a transition to the current operations section, which will exercise control over the conduct of the operation as it develops. This process of transition from future to current will begin at the outset of the campaign and continue throughout. Current operations may also in a sense transition to future ops, as the current situation, which is rarely static, provides the basis for missions to come.

Before the first engagement in a campaign, and throughout its duration, officers will try to "shape the battle," creating the conditions for the success of tactical engagements and their contribution to the success of the overall campaign. The relationship between tactical success and the higher levels of war has been the subject of disagreement. It may be said to constitute yet another warfighting dialectic. Prussian general Von Moltke's remark that strategy submits in the case of a tactical victory notwithstanding, the pursuit of a tactical victory could arguably be a distraction from the main objective of a campaign, as in the case of the defeat of an enemy unit that might have been bypassed and left to follow-on forces.[20] In modern times, shaping operations are often performed by aircraft, which degrade or destroy enemy combat and support units and attack the means of Command and Control. Although an operational commander ought to attempt to create conditions for tactical success, the tactician and the operator may find themselves at odds. The operator's concern for time and tempo may lead her to impose a timetable that is unrealistic on the tactical level. The operator is concerned with facilitating movement, but the tactician is confronted by the stubborn facts of difficult terrain, degraded transportation infrastructure, and (most important) enemy resistance.

Once the campaign is begun, a continuing effort on the part of the operators will be to defer the "culminating point." The culminating point (a term coined by Clausewitz) is the point at which an operation loses momentum.[21] There may be variety of factors contributing to this: casualties, physical and mental fatigue, logistical shortfalls, and damage to infrastructure. In an offensive campaign, the attack may outrun its supplies, while the enemy is able to fall back on hers. The culminating point may be conceptual, the result of a failure to plan effectively, of deficits in intelligence or understanding, of "reconnaissance" in the broad sense.

The importance of the time factor at the operational level gives the "main effort" a special significance. The main effort is normally assigned to a subordinate unit within the larger command. It has priority for fire support, combat support, and Command and Control resources, to include the attentions of the commander. The focus on a main effort is very important at the operational level, but too great an emphasis on the main effort can deprive the commander of flexibility. A famous debate on this subject occurred in the World War II European Theater, with the overall commander Eisenhower and Army Group commander Montgomery as the principal antagonists. Eisenhower persisted in maintaining a broad front, while Montgomery wanted a narrow front with most resources dedicated to him. The argument was summed up by Eisenhower in a letter to Marshall.

> Examination of this scheme exposes it as a fantastic idea. . . . The attack
> would be on such a narrow front that flanking threats would be particularly
> effective and no other troops in the whole region would be capable of go-
> ing to its support.[22]

Montgomery may have had a point, but the broad front gave Eisenhower
the ability to switch the main effort according to threats, opportunities, and
available resources. The preference for a single decisive blow or coup de main
can be hazardous. Lee's obsessive courting of a decisive battle may have been
his undoing, especially at Gettysburg. The American and allied invasion of Iraq
in 2003 was a reminder that even a decisive campaign may not end a conflict.
Significant victories are rarely those cheaply or easily gained.

SPACE AND TIME

At the operational level, the effect of space and terrain on movement assumes a relatively greater importance than their effect on fires, since the
operator mostly leaves the engagements to the tactician, and the operator
is also more concerned with the employment of fires that are not tied to
terrain, those of artillery and aviation especially. As in tactics, operations
usually focus on the destruction of enemy forces. This was the commander's
intent of theater commander Eisenhower in western Europe, for example,
as reflected in his orders to the American forces, which read in part, "You
will enter the continent of Europe and, in conjunction with the other Allied Nations, undertake operations aimed at the heart of Germany and the
destruction of her Armed Forces."[23] Eisenhower's directive mentions the
territories of Europe and Germany, making them a kind of aiming point, but
places most emphasis on the enemy forces. Cities may be the objective of a
campaign. Eisenhower recognized the significance of Paris, but he refused to
be rushed into taking Berlin. In doing so, he had to resist strategic guidance
that was understandable but probably unrealistic. The strategist, with her
greater spatial and temporal reach, may place greater emphasis on the long-
term economic or symbolic value of terrain than the operator or tactician.
Although the enemy must be defeated in war, war at the level of strategy
is ultimately about terrain, the land where people live, the buildings, roads,
and other infrastructure that provide them with shelter, employment, and
services, the farms that feed them.

An unwillingness to move in tough terrain can severely limit one's options. This may be especially insidious in a force that is overly road-bound,
airlift-dependent, or wedded to the employment of indirect fire, as was often

a fault of US forces, in Italy, Korea, and Vietnam. Seizing key terrain features before the enemy gets there is often a good "offensive-defensive" course of action. By placing tactical forces on high ground or other tactically significant terrain, the operational commander can shape the battle by conferring an advantage on his subordinate tactical commanders. Physical obstacles presented by terrain are almost always much easier to overcome than enemy resistance. Even the Alps have been crossed on a timetable, while the opposing will of the enemy is unpredictable, and more likely to be lethal.

There are other reasons for the importance of terrain at the operational level. The theater commander must often consider the residents of the countryside over which a campaign is conducted. What of the people who live on that ground? Can they bear enemy occupation if we leave the enemy in possessions of their homes? Terrain also contains or yields resources that may be militarily important. The usual focus on the enemy force may be modified in insurgency or unconventional warfare, in which a focus on the enemy may distract from security and nation building, raising the level of violence when it should be lowered. The conventional warfare focus on the enemy in an unconventional struggle may have been a flaw in U.S. operations in Vietnam and in Iraq. In Vietnam, Military Assistance Command Vietnam (MACV) in effect belied its own designation by emphasizing the independent employment of large American units to locate an elusive enemy that wisely avoided engagements except on the most favorable terms. (An approach that may have benefited from the writings of Sun Tzu and an Asian way of war.) The MACV investment in indigenous friendly forces and true counterinsurgency efforts was relatively slender. The results should have been predictable. In Iraq, punitive operations by US forces, again operating independently, too often took precedence over rebuilding local forces or establishing security.

Worldwide, urban terrain is increasing in mass and military importance. Urban terrain is tactically challenging but often essential on an operational and strategic level. Cities and towns are often transportation hubs, and they therefore loom large in the operational commander's calculations. A debate in military circles in the 1990s as to whether urban terrain should be bypassed or no turned out to be irrelevant. As US forces learned in Iraq, it is sometimes nearly impossible to bypass urban terrain, and in a city, the (human-made) terrain assumes a great importance, defining the tactician's challenge to a greater degree than combat in other physical *milieu*. With its multidimensional complexity, urban terrain directs and determines movement and channelizes fire to a greater extent than even the densest or most daunting natural terrain. Fortifications may be considered a specialized subset of urban terrain. Both must be addressed with a great degree of painstaking deliberateness.

Adding to the complexity of urban terrain is that fact that it is the habitation of dense concentrations of people, some of whom may be caught up in the fighting, become combatants, be exploited by combatants, or simply be cast in the role of victim, adding to the difficulties and burdening on the conscience of soldiers fighting in their home. Shaping operations and the use of fire support in urban settings are often problematic. The rubble left by supporting arms can be as good or better cover for defenders as the undamaged buildings, in addition to impeding movement. Cities are worth preserving. Soldiers' lives may be risked for the sake of structures that will be useful for future operations or the return to peace.

All warfighters employ maps. The operational commander's preoccupation with space–time and the large area that she must master give maps a special importance at this level. The tactician can depend more on direct visual observation, and the concerns of the strategist are less tied to space–time. The study of maps is a way to develop a detailed knowledge of the terrain. While stationed at the War Department early in World War II, Eisenhower and a fellow officer would spend their Saturdays pouring over the worldwide maps that were kept on file. For the operational commander, the entire theater of operations must be studied, since units may have to operate in unplanned locations. During planning, in a process sometimes referred to as intelligence preparation of the battlefield (IPB) the maps will be populated with enemy units, information on the population and places of cultural and economic significance. A problem with maps is that they are external, and if they remain so they are of limited usefulness. This may be even more the case with digital representations of the tactical situation, given their lesser tactility. The problem is again one of reading and learning to think. How to get the map information inside one's head, where it can be part of the tactical schemata? Field Marshall Slim records in his memoirs that he would copy out a simplified version of an important map, showing relative locations of key features and writing out distances between them. Significantly, his practice was to throw away these hand-drawn maps once he had familiarized himself with them.

In war, considerations of space are always related to those of time. The operator looks at space mostly with the question of how fast it can be crossed. The faster, the better. Speed is nearly always desirable in operations. Greater speed means less time of exposure to the fire of the enemy. It impedes the enemy's ability to react effectively to our operations, increasing our ability to impose our own will and narrative on the enemy. Time is so important that commanders' have been willing, and even justified, in employing the "geometric calculus" trading lives for time, sacrificing lives today so that (perhaps) no one has to die tomorrow.

PROFESSIONALISM AND THE OPERATIONAL MIND

The tribal or communal nature of operational thought perhaps highlights the strengths and weaknesses of the military profession. Since operations are dominated by career military officers, at this level we can sometimes see in focus the good and bad features of this tribe on display. Solidarity and purposefulness are weighed against conformity and excessive deference as illustrated by some of the historical examples already cited. To these we might add examples from our own time and experience, whether military or not, in which ritual has won out over reason and creativity. The greatest success of the American officer corps was World War II. The nation was fortunate that the small prewar officer corps had experience of selective and progressive professional education that was flexible and relevant enough to produce a cadre of operational thinkers to staff and command the corps, army, fleet, and theater-level organizations that won the war.[24] This was partly due to the fact that the war they fought was the one for which they had trained, in that it was a war of large and largely symmetrical forces against enemy nations that had begun to identify themselves (although not everyone saw this) decades before. In the future, we may not have this luxury. Even more than in the past, flexibility and creativity, the possibility of new technologies, methods, partnerships, and of operations aimed at evolving strategic objectives must be the emphasis of professional officer education.

STRATEGIC THOUGHT

For military officers, strategic thought is a subset, along with tactical and operational thinking, of their role as warfighter. However, strategic thought is distinct from the other forms of thinking in which officers must engage by virtue of its much greater complexity. It is also the way of thinking that most requires the officer to be self-conscious, or metacognitive, and in effect to distance herself from the kinds of thinking required for the tactical and operational levels of war at which she normally functions. In its complexity of ways, means, and ends, strategy is more than just another level of war. Perhaps this is why the record of strategy is so marked by error and failure. Failure in war is most often a failure of strategy. For the officer, this means all the effort, sacrifice, and success at the tactical and operational levels may well come to naught because of a flawed strategy. I will consider the nature of strategic thought and the officer's role in it to determine why this is so, and perhaps what is to be done.

Of all levels of armed conflict, strategy is most concerned with complex ends and long-term effects difficult to plan and foresee. The strategist works at the meeting of the irrational and the rational: force, or the threat of force, in the service of policy. As the theorists Deleuze and Guattari note, the so-called war machine is not an efficient instrument, but an unlikely fusion of competing opposites.[25] No single state owns the war machine, which is not complete until two (or more) opposing sides come into conflict. If war is a machine, it operates like a car in which one person steers while another (his deadly enemy), works the brakes and gas pedal! History, to include recent US history, is full of examples of military victories, deterrence, or dominance that had ambiguous results. Even the Allied victory in World War II, although it is considered one of the most important and decisive in history, destroyed three militant and acquisitive empires to set the stage for the expansion of a fourth. On the other hand, the Soviet Union created enormous conscripted armed forces and won victories by proxy all over the world, but none of this prevented either the dissolution of the USSR or the receding of the international communism of which it saw itself as the standard bearer.

THE NATURE OF STRATEGIC THOUGHT

While tactical and operational thought are personal and tribal, strategic thought is bureaucratic. Strategic thought is bureaucratic in the sense that it is conducted by organizations that meet the criteria for bureaucracies on which sociologists generally agree, in that they are hierarchical, rule-bound, expertise-driven, and permanent or standing. Strategic thought is less tribal than operational thought, because strategy is influenced and conducted by nontribal civilian academics and government officials. Further, it is less personal than tactical thought, because it is conducted over great distances and at a considerable remove from the troops and scenes of conflict. Strategic thought often exhibits the good and bad traits of bureaucracies in general. The term bureaucracy and bureaucrat have devolved into epithets, an evocation of the worst traits of bureaucracies and of organizations in general, particularly those of government. Nevertheless, as the early twentieth-century sociologist Max Weber noted, bureaucracies are in most senses preferable to the kinds of hereditary, ad hoc, and unregulated mechanisms of policy and strategy that came before. While some innovative organizations, mostly in the private sector, have begun to adopt forms of organization that depart from the model laid out by Weber and his successors, for example, by becoming less hierarchical, the organizations dedicated to military strategic planning and execution tend to follow the traditional model. Although strategic thought takes place in a variety of venues, from the war colleges and other service schools, to civilian academic institutions, to a multiplicity of think tanks, actual strategic military planning is focused on the service branch headquarters, the major regional and functional combatant commands, the Joint Chiefs of Staff, and the Office of the Secretary of Defense.

The bureaucratic nature of this military strategic establishment can be an impediment to clear strategic thought. An often read and detailed account of poor strategic thought (which was perhaps intensified by a lack of moral courage) is H. R. McMaster's *Dereliction of Duty: Lyndon Johnson, Robert McNamara, The Joint Chiefs of Staff, and the Lies that Led to Vietnam*. In McMaster's account, service rivalry and careerism contributed to flawed policy and a lack of strategic direction. Strategic direction in Vietnam was guided by complex forces that inhibited clear thinking. In *The Irony of Vietnam: The System Worked*, Leslie Gelb and co-author Richard Betts present a nuanced argument concerning strategic failure. To briefly summarize, they argue that the civil and military bureaucracies of the federal government, realizing victory in Vietnam was probably unlikely, nevertheless fell into line, reluctant to damage their credibility through resistance or half-hearted efforts. The bureaucracies that create strategy have the vices of their virtues, which are efficiency and unity of effort. From the 1940s to the 1960s, the military bureaucracy moved from extreme caution to commitment concerning operations in Vietnam. The Joint Chiefs at first considered the region relatively unimportant, and they warned that effective intervention would likely require a confrontation with China. Nevertheless, once the decision was made that the perils of disengagement outweighed those of commitment, all doubts were suppressed, even in the face of growing evidence that the war was unwinnable. As a prescription, the authors of *The Irony of Vietnam* call for pragmatism over policy and doctrine (and, it might be necessary to add, ideology) in decision-making at the foreign policy and national security level.

OFFICERS AS STRATEGIC THINKERS

The officer functions as strategist in one of three roles: as commander, as staff officer, and as adviser. Most officer-strategists are staff officers. Among commanders, only the very senior, at the three- or four-star level, are usually considered to be functioning as strategists (although junior, tactical leaders require an *understanding* of strategy). The CJCS, the senior American unformed officer, is the president's principal military adviser. Officers' strategic roles may appear to be straightforward and well delineated by statute and table of organization, but like command they are in fact defined by complex personal, cultural, and organizational factors. Strategic thought involves and often demands a multiplicity of voices, of competing concerns and outlooks. This often-discordant chorus can both inform and impede the strategic process. At times strategic thought and direction, overwhelmed by competing demands, has come to a halt, opening a fatal gap in the transmission of policy into military action. This breakdown often leaves operational, and in many instances even tactical, commanders the task of wrestling with strategic issues that should have been worked out for them. In these cases, officers can become strategists by default, the task of strategic direction having been abdicated by those above with whom it was nominally entrusted. Historical examples of this failing are almost too numerous to mention. The example of Vietnam has already been discussed. Korea may offer another. US strategy regarding Korea turned quickly from indifference to commitment to a search for a World War II–style decisive victory. Shaped by the experience of victory in the recent war, it took US planners some time to acknowledge Korea as a different kind of war in which there might be a different kind of victory. Sometimes absent clear strategic guidance, commanders in the field from MacArthur to Van Fleet flirted with and sometimes danced attendance on the idea of decisive victory, reuniting all of Korea at the point of the sword, and punishing or even openly warring with mainland communist China. Aiming sometimes for victory, the United States and its allies achieved stalemate, or status quo antebellum. It might be useful to contrast Korea with Vietnam, a war shaped by the previous experience of Korea, in which aiming at a stalemate produced defeat.

The tendency for American strategic direction to be hazy and ad hoc continues into our own time. In "National-Level Coordination: How System Attributes Trumped Leadership," Christopher Lamb and Megan Franco depict a process for the wars in Iraq and Afghanistan that turns out consensus strategy documents that are largely ignored, leaving real strategy in the minds of a few senior officials, with implementation largely a guessing game by those on the ground.[26] Important questions regarding the nature of the terrorist threat and the priority given to nation-building are left unanswered, to be improvised or intuited by those in the field.

Officers are expected to be the professionals and experts on military strategy, but Georges Clemenceau's statement that war was too important to be left to generals still resonates. It is the means of war that is officers' area of expertise, not the ends, and an incomplete grasp of the ends can limit even their understanding of how the means should be employed. The officer, by her training and experience, will often stop at the military victory, with insufficient thought or preparation to securing the peace. This predilection was arguably played out as the Allies approached victory in World War II, when large sections of Europe were left to Soviet control, in the difficult Civil War Reconstruction, when the freedom of many ex-slaves was rendered almost nominal by a revival of racist policies in the southern states, and most recently following the American-led invasion of Iraq in 2003.

The matching of military strategy to policy presents a paradox. Officers (especially those at the strategic level) are expected to be politically literate and even sophisticated, but neither politically involved nor motivated. In effect, the respect of the civilian leadership for officers as strategists rests on their expectation that officers' expertise and code of honor will ensure that they render well-considered advice that is free of partisan politics and self-interest. Of course, it may be both, as well as simply and honestly wrong, because officers are human, subject to their limitations and sometimes to outside pressure. Interpersonal and interagency relations have a strong influence on the development of strategy, and so may the consensus or laundry-list approach that sometimes seems to be encouraged by doctrine and by the bureaucracy.

The military strategist looks up and down. He implements policy and also creates the conditions for success on the operational and tactical level. Part of the work of the strategist falls within the officer's role as organizer, under training and force planning, but the strategist is chiefly a warfighter. Working at a considerable remove from the fighting, he is also expected to think across a broad area, even the whole of earth, and a long expanse of time. While focusing on the fight, strategists must always consider the position at the end of conflict, of the moment when the fighting ends and the long denouement begins, as the armies return home, reduce in size, change from waging war to keeping peace, as rebuilding begins and the political map is redrawn.

A COMPLEX ENVIRONMENT

Strategy provides an illustration of one of the abiding themes of modern thought, which is that the relationship among things and persons often counts as much or more than the characteristics of the things themselves. From relativity, psychiatry, and existentialism onward, persons, political bodies, ideas, and events have been seen to be defined by how they interact. The challenge of strategic thought may be expressed as the attempt to bring antagonistic elements into agreement. The paradox of military strategy may be expressed by saying that it aims at peace but that its means are violent, inherently unsettling, as likely to inflame antagonism as to extinguish it, or to only temporarily quell antagonisms, leaving the real cause untouched and as ignitable as ever. Not only is strategy dependent on the relationship of opposing forces to one another, of force to the geopolitical landscape and to policy, but the production and execution of strategic thought is also based on many relationships among individuals and organizations, from small departments to nation-states, nonstate actors, and international organizations. The officer-as-strategist must navigate in this complex social and political terrain in which perceptions of commitment and credibility count as much as the inherent merit of plans and ideas. Even the most brilliant plan, lacking necessary support and imaginative and determined execution will fail to be adopted or will simply fail. To accept and execute the best strategy, there will often have to be learning, new ways of thinking, the overcoming of habits and even of allegiances. Strategic thought often involves the overcoming of narrow or parochial loyalties in favor of a broadly national, global, humanitarian outlook, a difficult shift from the merely belligerent to the universal.

The political and pragmatic aspects of strategy must never be confused with moral relativism. It is a challenge for every officer, especially given the sometimes brutal nature of her calling, not to lose sight of the precious things she serves and guards. Whatever role they occupy, the credibility and authority of officers continue to depend on their being persons of honor.

• 7 •

The Visionary

Down these mean streets a man must go.

—Raymond Chandler, "The Simple Art of Murder"

Salesman's got to dream boy; it comes with the territory.

—Arthur Miller, *Death of a Salesman*

$\mathcal{I}$n the pages that follow, I go beyond the officer's immediate obligation to think as an organizer and warfighter to consider the ways in which officers may engage in visionary thought. Military service can be the inspiration for much higher-order thinking. Because of the besetting demands of military service, some of this will have to wait until the officer assumes the identity of a veteran. Like other soldiers and veterans, the officer may find the difficulties of reentry into civilian life insurmountable, and so retreat into silence. The poet Robert Graves said that his service as an infantry officer in World War I was in some ways "incommunicable," and yet his articulate voice was heard on a great variety of topics all his long life, much of his writing inspired by his time in the army. How can the gifts and insights of serving and thinking as an officer be converted to civil and civilizing uses?

Military service is invested with a great deal of importance by nearly all those who experience it. Leaving the service, "taking off the uniform" is nearly always a significant event in a person's life. There is first the overwhelming joy of homecoming, and of having survived, along with perhaps a strange mix of pride and remorse. For both good and ill, military service is very likely the most significant period in the life of a man or woman. The returning officer is usually proud of having served, but few are exempt from the nagging sense that they could have done better, that their service is incomplete.

157

Many ex-officers or returning officers pursue some form of intellectual development. The officer's service has filled her mind with images and impressions that she has barely had time to process, let alone communicate. Many former officers continue their formal education; others pursue writing or the arts. Such undertakings may fuel and enable the desire to continue serving in some way. Some former officers have problems of their own. They may be suffering from the effects of their service, from psychic or physical wounds, from misgivings about the mission they served, about the sacrifices made on its behalf, about their own conduct and that of others. The military veteran may need to heal, but even this, experience has shown, is best served by serving others. The officer or ex-officer might take on the care of wounded or troubled veterans as an extension of her own professional obligation, and the role of healer of course can help the officer to heal herself.

If the greatest possession of an officer is character, and her most important intellectual and moral virtue prudence, for the ex-officer the best which she has to contribute to the larger society is an enlarged sense of the human. Military experience is pursued under conditions of hostility and violence, but closely following the joy and gratitude of homecoming, the veteran often feels an impatience with petty concerns and differences. The comradeship of the military unit has given her a model for the overcoming of difference (maybe especially in a multicultural, multiracial, multigender modern American military) and for working toward a common purpose. Even war (and maybe especially war), the pity of it as well as its leveling effect can strengthen the sense of the essential unity of humankind. The veteran who returns from military service and war may come home with a sense of shared human values, of the kinship of all people. One of the finest depictions of soldiers' homecoming is the feature film *Best Years of Our Lives* about World War II veterans. The three men returning home to the same American town are different in terms of age, social class, service branch, and experience, but all three have been given a standard of conduct by their service and the sacrifices of their comrades. With varying degrees of success, they try to raise the moral bar among their families, friends, and business associates. Fred loses his job rather than put up with the bullying of fellow veteran Homer by an overbearing, reactionary civilian. The grievously wounded Homer makes sure that his fiancé understands the full extent of his disability. Al takes a chance on a bank loan to a veteran, putting his faith in character rather than collateral.

REFLECTION: THINKING ABOUT THE PAST

The military profession is one with a long memory, although perhaps it is never quite long enough. Forgetfulness and selective memory are as much a part of our human condition as are accurate and informative memory. Officers collectively recognize the need for a conversation with the past. The memory of the military profession has even been institutionalized. Military organizations require reports and debriefings on completed exercises and operations. All military branches keep historical archives and files on "lessons learned." In addition to the military history already discussed, there are museums, memorials, and old battlefields that soldiers and others visit to catch an echo of the military past. The insistence on the memory of past military conflicts has even struck some as excessive, a fetishization of military symbols and memorials. The sum of efforts at military recall may reflect an understanding for the evanescence of military acts, for the lives cut short, and for the welcome gaps between conflicts that can promote a harmful forgetfulness of the grim facts of war, even on the part of soldiers and veterans themselves. As Shakespeare's Henry V puts it, "Old men forget."

In their book, *Thinking in Time: The Uses of History for Decision Makers*, Richard Neustadt and Ernest May advance several ways in which a memory of the past can be valuable.[1] One idea is that of thinking in "time streams," and their leading example is George C. Marshall. The authors suggest that Marshall could see events as they were happening in a historical perspective. Marshall was a man of wide reading, but more than this he thought of history as a living, continuing process. This may have been inspired by an experience he had in World War I as a staff officer in France. Taking a book on Roman history from the shelf in the French house in which he was billeted, Marshall realized that he was in the same part of France once a scene of operations for Caesar's legions. Marshall's ability to think from a historical perspective allowed him to formulate, as early as 1943, some of the ideas for what would become the "Marshall Plan" for European recovery. When Marshall began thinking of postwar recovery, the outcome and duration of the war were in question. Marshall and the rest of the Army faced enormous problems of manpower and material. Many strategic questions still needed to be answered. Still, Marshall spared a part of his busy mind for the problems of the peace that all were working toward but that few could visualize. The failures of the peace following World War I and the conflicts of ancient Rome were part of the context within which he saw his own unfolding times so clearly.

Paul Fussell's classic work, *The Great War and Modern Memory*, shows the depth and persistence of the memory of military events. Fussell argues that World War I helped to make war a constant metaphor in much European and American writing, one which the frequency of armed conflict in the past century (Fussell was an infantry officer in World War II) has helped to keep alive. In other writings, Fussell has also attributed his own often skeptical, contrarian, and combative persona to his being thrust into fierce combat in Western Europe in 1944. The memory of war is not limited to officers, but officers have a special responsibility to be the repository of historical knowledge of armed conflict, both as part of their professional function within the armed forces, and in their role in the larger society. Officers must cultivate an institutional memory of the nature of armed conflict that they can make available and express to their fellow citizens, and perhaps most importantly to the civil leadership in times of crisis. Military force is a very direct and dramatic form of power that can be intoxicating. To someone with only a shallow understanding of armed force, it can seem an all-too-easy solution to a variety of problems, a panacea satisfying both in its employment and in its effects. But military force as an instrument of policy is inherently flawed, a tool of ill omen. The officer understands this through study, training, and experience. It is her role to lay out clearly, not just the technical aspects of the military options, but their frankly unpredictable long-term consequences, maybe especially those of historical dimensions, beyond the range of conventional or "effects-based" planning. The temptation to use this flawed military instrument has led to too many dubious decisions, some of recent memory, but many more remote in time and too easily forgotten. Wars begun in error, and conducted with increasing blindness and vengefulness have shaped much of the current state of affairs around the globe. In planning the wars of the future, the consequences of inaction must also be considered, but despite the long Western tradition of just war, which calls on belligerents to weigh the chances of victory and the proportionality of gains and losses, these factors are very difficult to predict or control, and even more bewildering are the long-term *postbellum* consequences. This should add up to a deep reluctance to use armed force unless absolutely necessary and with clear objectives. Unfortunately, perception can also influence the occasions when force appears to be indicated. The demonstrated willingness to use force might deter adversaries when the mere possession of military might does not.

For all its usefulness, history itself is a flawed guide. Michael Howard notes that some official histories glorify the past, leaving a modern soldier "dangerously unprepared for cowardice and muddle and horror when he actually encounters them."[2] Those who forget history may be condemned to repeat it, but those who remember history may fall into a similar trap. Unless we are content to repeat the mistakes of our ancestors, the work in progress must depart from the model. In considering the past, officers must be able to distinguish the admirable from the dubious, the exemplary from the cautionary. Like other arenas of thought, this requires imagination as much as clarity. It has become a cliché that we "fight the last war," but we may also do the opposite, and learn insufficiently from the last conflict, or from history in general. History cannot be a sure guide to the future. If it were, we would make far fewer mistakes, but neither should it be passed over, or forgotten, as it too often is.

It may be undeniable that only the dead have seen the end of war. Efforts to control war and to mitigate its savagery have met with mixed results. Still, the lesson of history is not to cease efforts to control war, but for these efforts to be a prime objective for officers and others. The officer looks to the past for the best and what that it has to offer: for moral lessons and exemplars, for cautionary tales, heroes and inspiration. At their best, soldiers have upheld the values of civilization under the direst conditions, they have contributed to the collective memory of humanity in the form of art, idea, and narrative, they have sometimes, to quote A. E. Housman, "saved the sum of things for pay." Howard, citing historian Jakob Burkhardt, reminds us that the study of history is not just to make people "clever for the next time; it is to make them wise for all time."[3] To this end, an officer must be a student of history, and a careful observer and recorder of her personal past, of the history she sees being played out during her career of service and throughout her lifetime.

IMAGINING: THINKING ABOUT THE FUTURE

He's a good soldier. He believes in the future.

—*The Crying Game*

In *Surfing Uncertainty: Prediction, Action, and the Embodied Mind* cognitive neuroscientist Andy Clark argues that our core mental states are predictions.[4] What the brain does is to make predictions and then revise them as necessary. Not all experts in the field of cognitive science would agree that this is the brain's principal function, but this theory would seem to shed some light on how human beings think, at least some of the time. Officers often must make predictions about the future: about enemy actions, the effects of their own actions and orders, about tragic matters like rates of casualties and mundane but important questions about how quickly supplies will be consumed or equipment wear out. Beyond this, they will and must ask themselves about future conflicts, their location, manner, and intensity, taking in the impact of new technology, and not neglecting the state of the peace to follow. The business of prediction on a grand scale is sometimes entered upon too blithely by those calling themselves "Futurists," who by the nature of their profession may be not sufficiently respectful of the past, and forgetful or neglectful of history. The "Revolution in Military Affairs" touted in the 1990s may be an example of officers and others rushing out too readily to embrace a future that had not yet arrived. Advanced technology certainly has had an impact on warfare, but the idea that the fog of war would be dispersed by a reliance on technology was likely oversold, and it may have contributed to the hubris with which America entered some millennial conflicts. Other fads and intellectual fashions may have had a distracting effect on officers, drawing them away from their experience and the essentials to dubious and untried methods.

Still, efforts to anticipate the future can be fruitful. Change and innovation have been accurately forecast and inspired by efforts to speculate about the future. Despite the relatively recent advent of professional futurists like Alvin Toffler, the most sustained effort at speculation and prediction concerning the future is in the genre of science fiction.[5] In film especially, this genre includes a gallery of science fiction skippers who often represent an effort to imagine the demands to be placed on officers in the future. Officers are often depicted in partnerships with scientists and in their "supporting roles" as psychologists and anthropologists. Their concerns are often "cosmic" and even metaphysical. An excellent example is the classic series *Star Trek*, which spawned many sequels, successors, and imitators that reflected the core concerns of the original. James Kirk, the captain of the starship *Enterprise* in the original series, was often seen defusing a planetary struggle, leveraging culture (and sometimes the threat of force) to attain peace and stability among different races, warring tribes, gamesters, and gangsters. In the episode, "A Taste of Armageddon" (Season 1, Episode 23), he dismantles the apparatus of a cyberwar that has dragged on inconclusively but at great cost of life. He forces the combatants to confront both the half-forgotten causes of the conflict and the prospect of a messy clash of arms. (They decide to make peace.) In the *Star Wars* series, the Jedi Knights may also be seen as a version of the future officer and warfighter, one whose combative skills, moral virtues, and cognitive abilities are dedicated to "peace and justice."[6]

THESE ARE THE DAMNED

These Are the Damned is a 1963 film made by Hammer Studios. With its grim predictions and its tragic end, it is unusual, even among others of its apocalyptic genre. It presents a morally complex picture too, raising difficult questions. How do we prepare for the possibility of nuclear war, or for some other existential crisis affecting the planet and the whole of civilization? Do our efforts center on prevention, or do we also prepare for the worst, adopting a bomb-shelter mentality, setting aside, like Aeneas fleeing the burning city of Troy, what we feel to be most worth saving in a civilization that is coming to an end? *These Are the Damned* seems to address these issues and the role of the military officer in preserving civilized values when a civilization falls, or in other times of great change.

The movie begins with an American tourist docking his boat at an English seaside resort town. A young woman lures him to a back street where he is beaten and robbed by her brother and his gang of thugs. Later, the tourist is helped by some people at a restaurant. One of the people, a government official of obscure function, observes that England is seeing more random violence of this kind. He seems to take a very dim view of the modern world and the future. Two of the other people in the group are army officers in mufti, and another is an artist. It turns out that the officers and government official are engaged in a project involving mutated children who can survive nuclear fallout. The children are themselves radioactive, so that exposure to them is fatal to ordinary people, and their own health can be precarious. They are being carefully schooled in the Western tradition of art, history, and culture so that they can preserve these things after the nuclear war that the people responsible for the project believe is inevitable.

The government official is the true believer in this. The artist is his mistress, but she doesn't really know what is going on in the project. She makes sculptures that evoke the corpses after Pompei or Dresden and that also seem to warn of a nuclear war. Her modern, allusive, admonitory sculptures are arguably more in keeping with and even preservative of the values of civilization than is the rather dismal activity of stuffing facts into lethal, sickly children in a remote-controlled classroom. The two officers are very different from each other. The older one seems overly willing to resort to violence, and the younger officer strongly implies that his senior is merely a bully capable of commanding obedience but not loyalty. The younger officer is more humane and even intellectually curious. He views the artist's sculptures appreciatively, saying that he hopes that looking at them will improve his mind. One of the other characters observes that the young officer is the type that made the empire. Perhaps it is also true that his combination of civility and open-mindedness is closer to the real values of civilization than the pedantry, subterfuge, and manipulation that characterize the government project. By being assigned to this deathly and doubtful project, both officers have been placed in an ethically untenable position, and even the younger officer seems to see no alternative to soldiering on in a bad cause. The movie clearly calls into question the T. S. Eliot–like nostalgia and pessimism that is behind the project. There are still some decent people left: the young officer, the artist, the American, and even the young woman. (She and the American become somewhat unlikely lovers, and they try to rescue the children from their captivity.) Maybe civilization isn't doomed. It can be redeemed, like the young woman, who moves from the role of temptress to that of heroine. The young officer in the film can only play a peripheral role in the preservation of civilized values, but still perhaps an important one.

In partnership with artists and the civil government, the officer, with her tradition of principled leadership, might be an important figure in some future dystopia or post-apocalyptic setting. Threats and new weapons are combining to make the world a highly uncertain and hazardous place, even more than it was in 1963.

There will always be those who spurn present and future, saying *Après moi, le deluge.* The officer must believe in the future, with an emphasis on preventing apocalypse, not on scraping callous survival out of conflicts likely to be terribly destructive to everyone. And if soldiers are ever again required to salvage the wreck of a doomed civilization, we must keep in mind what is really worth saving. If we survive without love, what has been saved?

DEATH AND THE OFFICER

In the long run, we're all dead.

—John Maynard Keynes, *The Tract on Monetary Reform*, 1923

They'll be one child born in this world, to carry on.

—Laura Nyro, "And When I Die"

Like the priest and the physician, the military officer has a professional relationship with death. The two great constants of war may be said to be death and leadership, and the officer is much concerned with both. Military operations may not always be aimed specifically at killing the enemy (although they sometimes may), but they almost always have the least indirect objective of doing some enemy soldiers to death. Soldiers are not the only ones who die in war. Civilian deaths are nearly inevitable, and they are countenanced to varying degrees as "collateral damage" or as the "regrettable" but tacit objective of weakening civilian morale and productive capacity. A military officer requires of her own soldiers that they risk and perhaps even sacrifice their lives. Japanese kamikaze were not completely unique in this. Other soldiers have been ordered into battle with the odds so stacked against them that their deaths were almost assured. Finally, officers must often risk their own lives in the furtherance of the mission. The highest military honors are reserved for those who take the biggest risks, even for those who seem to invite death. Death is, to quote again the Scottish officer Jock Sinclair in *Tunes of Glory*, the soldier's "stock in trade," the coin of military operations which sooner or later some must pay.

How to think about or talk about death in the military community? Most soldiers going to war want to believe in the possibility of their own intact survival. Reasoned reassurances on this point, not empty promises or dismissals, are a valuable part of military communication. Most people have their own (to quote Wordsworth) "intimations of immortality." For many, although not all, these are religious. Immortality does not form an important part of all religions nor of the outlook of all religious people. For some immortality may be children or family, or an idea of infinitude, "the universe," of the survival and slow progress of humanity. For a few, the military unit itself may provide a kind of immortality, in symbols and stories. The officer and historian John Baynes wrote that some soldiers of the early twentieth-century British army of which he wrote, although enlisted out of poverty and to avoid starvation, came to think that if the regiment lived, they would never die. J. Glenn Gray, author of *The Warriors; Reflections on Men in Battle*, who received his World War II induction notice and his Columbia University doctorate in philosophy on the same day, said that comradeship could be a kind of immortality, creating the conditions for self-sacrifice.[7] In my own experience, I recall a conversation with a stocky, much-tattooed platoon sergeant in Iraq. His platoon had just helped to fight the Battle of An Nasiriya, one of the first engagements of the war in Iraq. Nineteen Marines from one company in his battalion had been killed in action in a single day, and it had been a rude awakening for many of the unblooded Marines who were involved. Undaunted, the platoon sergeant feelingly remarked that the Marine Corps had been reborn on that day. He grieved for the deaths, but it may be truthful to say that what mattered to him was the corps, the community, and individual losses less so.

Are officers and other military people better prepared for death when it comes, having been readied, and maybe reconciled, to death as a form of professional obligation? Samuel Johnson said that people accorded a special status to sailors and soldiers because "Mankind reverence those who have got over fear, which is so general a weakness."[8] Is it still true that soldiers have at least accommodated themselves to the fear of death more than have most people? Possibly, if not necessarily. Like the sense of history and tradition that can be part of soldiers' equipment (in fact related to it), the acceptance of death is a matter of individual choice and reflection more than nominal professional membership. Officers perhaps can acquire a greater appreciation of death, but it is not simply theirs by right. It must be the result of experience and reflection. On the other hand, such enhanced understanding need not await seeing people die in battle. Officer and military historian Richard Holmes recounts how his "death" as a company commander in a training exercise led to his reflections on the nature of war and the appeals of writing about war.[9]

One of the most sublimely appealing artistic evocations of the relation between death and the officer is the beautifully photographed feature film *A Matter of Life and Death* (1946), starring David Niven and Kim Hunter. Niven plays a World War II British aviator who is forced to jump from his burning aircraft. Improbably and even miraculously, he survives the jump and wades from the sea to encounter Hunter, an American soldier, on her bicycle at the beach. He later experiences strange symptoms, to include hallucinations. It turns out that a mistake has been made. Niven was supposed to die, and he must justify his survival on earth before a heavenly tribunal. What saves him is Hunter's love and her willingness to die in his place. They both survive, and with the war coming to an end they can look forward to long lives together. A review of the film notes that it may be an allegorical depiction of a combat veteran suffering from a neurological disorder.[10] It also allegorizes the soldier's intimate relationship with death. Combat aviator Niven's survival is an escape from death, but so is every return from a combat mission. Having "lain down his life" he has got it back again, for now. Fate and the enemy may have another chance to kill him, but they have missed this opportunity. The experience of the film has an added dimension if the viewer knows that Niven was a Sandhurst graduate who walked away from a promising film career in 1939 to rejoin the British Army. *A Matter of Life and Death* was his first postwar film, and his personal and professional reprieve.

The former officer assumes a kind of immortality when he considers the future state of his service, country, and humankind after her own flag-covered coffin and sounding of taps that waits for all. She should take no comfort in the fact that this future does not look terribly bright. There are too many scenes of conflict, throwing shadows that are long and lengthening. The officer may have a mental contribution to make by thinking hard and fearlessly about the future of armed conflict. Other, potentially even greater existential threats may lie in the encroachments on humanity made by the machine, the computer, the omniscient and all-seeing eye of surveillance. Climate change, technological developments in communications and weapons technology, the spread of adversarial, even apocalyptic ideas, and the impoverished, unstable state of much of the globe offer some frightening possibilities. Along with these foreboding signs, there are hopeful indications too: technologies that heal and feed, the spread of knowledge, a rising worldwide standard of living (from which, however, some regions are still excluded), and even the prospect that the hearts of men and women grow wiser and more tolerant, given the chance. If the officer in the field exercising moral leadership is indeed a "mini-philosopher" (as she is described by Reichberg) perhaps returned home she becomes a metaphysician, an ontologist laying out the boundaries of human selfhood because her experience has given her an insight into the nature of humanity sometimes pared down to the bare essentials, and also of people at their most selfless and willing to merge their identity with that of a community of souls. Like J. Glenn Gray, we may think that war and military service have not changed us enough, but properly understood they may change us for the better. At the conclusion of his important philosophical work, *War and Existence*, Michael Gelven has this to say,

> [O]ften it is in our darkest and most wretched ways that we find what is most precious, like the jewel in the mud: things like truth for its own sake and esteem for who we are, regardless of how grim the truth and how frail our efforts. Perhaps Plato is right: the lovers of truth must be selected only from those who first manifest the sacrificial spirit of the warrior.

Significant changes are probably called for in civilization and in the armies that defend it and embody some of its highest values. Change is coming, whether we will it or not, but whether these changes will be for the continued betterment and enlightenment of humankind, or amount to a decline in humanity and what it means to be human may still be within the ability of our minds to conceive and direct. In neither the reform of civil society nor that of the military can officers be the sole or even principal actors, but since their forte is leadership, perhaps this is the ingredient that officers can provide. The challenge of a more human civilization obviously concerns everyone, and even meaningful military reform usually involves an entire society. Military officers can draw on a history of helping to marshal, organize, and direct people with a diversity of skills and intellectual capital. Their own profession requires them to think across a spectrum of disciplines and intellectual virtues. Hard experience has taught them not to expect too much. Progress in war takes place slowly and painfully. The enemy is unpredictable and intractable. He will not fight as expected, and his motives, although finally human and recognizable, may be clouded over by cultural difference and manipulated out of shape by those with an interest in struggle or a twisted desire to control others and have someone else do their fighting. These wicked motives may not be absent on our own side, even within ourselves.

THE ETHICAL TURN

> Our whole dignity consists in thought. Let us endeavor, then, to think well: this is the principle of ethics.
>
> —Blaise Pascal, *Pensées*, *II*, 1670

For the individual, military service and its civil afterlife often involve a turn toward ethics. The services today place considerable stress in the ethical aspects of military service, through instruction in leadership, military ethics, and the various sets of branch "core values." Very often, of course, the reality falls far short of the ideal, but the language of ethics, the aspiration, and the challenges remain, so that many veterans feel a yearning for the moral purpose that at least seemed to be latent in military life. This is illustrated in the life and work of philosopher Ludwig Wittgenstein, an officer in the Austrian army in World War I and one of the most brilliant thinkers of the twentieth century. Prior to his military service, Wittgenstein had been primarily interested in questions of logic. In *Ludwig Wittgenstein: The Duty of Genius*, biographer Ray Monk identifies a change in Wittgenstein's thinking at the point when his unit took heavy casualties under a Russian assault.[11] This incident drew from Wittgenstein the beginnings of his famous *Tractatus-Logico Philosophicus*. Wittgenstein obviously did not surrender his involvement in logic, but his wartime service led him outward to a greater interest in the world of real things and people. Logic itself acquired for Wittgenstein an ethical basis, as it became clear to him that the accuracy of statements reflecting the conditions of the world was not only a logical but an ethical imperative. The army put the somewhat sheltered young man into contact with a broad cross-section of humanity, and as an NCO and officer he was responsible for the men in his charge. He found that service on the front lines, with its dangers, lack of rest, and harsh living conditions, was actually more productive of his philosophical thought than the safer, more comfortable and leisurely service in the rear. The nearness of danger and the high-stakes environment lent a seriousness to one's thinking that was often absent in ordinary times. The universe as described in the "Tractatus" consists not of objects but of facts, since objects only attain meaning when they are organized as facts. Similarly, language is composed not of words but of "propositions." Universe and language as described by Wittgenstein are therefore durable in the sense that they can adapt to the loss of things and to changes in words. It is logic that holds both universe and language together, maintaining meaning even in the midst of disorder.

After the war, Wittgenstein taught school for a time in a poor district of Austria. Along with the "Tractatus," another postwar product, was his famous and enigmatic "Lecture on Ethics." In it, he describes two states of mind he sees as ethically desirable: that of wonder at the world's existence and of feeling completely safe. We can see how these ideas might be inspired by wartime, which sometimes seems to grant glimpses of eternity through the smoke and fire; feelings of invulnerability, of essential safety even in danger; and wonder along with fear.

Wittgenstein continued to think of his military service as formative. In World War II, he responded critically to a reference to the "boredom" of military service in a letter by a young American protege in the Navy. Wittgenstein wrote that his young friend could learn "an enormous lot . . . about human beings in this war—*if* you keep your eyes open."[12] Wittgenstein left Cambridge during the war to serve as a hospital orderly. Although he had little medical training, he was responsible for beneficial changes in treatment and procedure. Wittgenstein also turned to literature to express his interest in a language that would accurately reflect the logical and ethical structure of the world. A particular favorite was Tolstoy, another officer-writer and war veteran, whose highly structured short stories like "How Much Land Does a Man Need?" are moral parables. Tolstoy, like Wittgenstein, went through periods of committed social activism, building a school for peasant children and raising money for religious emigres hoping for a better life in the new world.

For today's veteran, different directions for ethical thought and action present themselves. With so many problems to be solved, the list may be almost endless. Many officers have been involved in technological change, and the future of technology is certainly an area to consider, although an even greater challenge may be that of the impact of technology on people's lives rather than technology itself. The advent of autonomous robots has military, ethical, and even more broadly ontological implications. The development of low-cost weapons of mass destruction, even without the phenomenon of terrorism, seems both inevitable and frightening. Such weaponry might even be transmitted electronically, given the development of three-dimensional copying and the enhanced capabilities of the internet. How can societies prepare and protect themselves from this? What effective security or deterrence is possible and permissible?

These developments raise further questions about the nature and efficacy of conventional armed forces. We may be entering a period in which the ability of conventional armed forces, no matter how formidable, to protect a country or its people from outside threats is very limited. This perhaps leaves them with a purely aggressive, or retaliatory function. It may also press them toward a greater role in internal security. Some of the clues to this future may lie in the past. The fragility of order in medieval times meant that not only was every man's home legally his castle, it also had to serve as such. Individual cities and towns had massive walls, and even dwellings might have to serve as strong points in a hostile world in which the rule of law was tenuous. In such a society, not only was every dwelling a potential defensive position, but every man a soldier-in-waiting, an archer or pikeman, even if his pike was a farm implement pressed into service like the man who carried it. Cyberspace will almost surely be a future battlefield. We are already seeing this, but the cyber conflicts of today are likely just the first skirmishes in what may become all-out war, and many computers and their users may be needed in the fight. Or society might decide that the price of connectivity is too great, ending the internet's brief reign in the name of security, closing off one vulnerable gap in a society's all-around defense.

The changing nature of armed conflict raises questions about the future tenure of civil-military relations. If potential threats slip through the fingers of conventional armed forces, what will be the reaction of soldiers themselves and of the civil population that pays them for protection? Some officers after 9/11 experienced a feeling of helplessness, seeing their strength and knowledge rendered irrelevant by a new kind of threat. This feeling may become all too familiar in the future.

THE OFFICER AND POLITICS

The matter of officers and former officers becoming involved in politics is complex and controversial. American military officers inherited a European and specifically British tradition of remaining apart from politics. This tradition is to a degree upheld by regulations forbidding public political activity in uniform and requiring that the officers' respect some appointed and elected officials who are in effect their military superiors. As citizens, officers can vote and express political opinions, but not on the job and certainly neither suggesting that they are expressing the views of the service nor imposing their views on other military members. On the other hand, there have been times when the ability to think like an officer has been a valuable attainment in the political world. Most US presidents have seen some military service as officers, and military service is generally considered an asset in a public or elected official. This preference is partly based on the officer's demonstrated character and willingness to serve, but it is also due to the benefits of an officer's service: the experience of leadership, the organizational ability and exposure to strategic thought, the prudence and humility that may come of lowly service and exposure to danger, like the Guardians of Plato's ideal republic. Washington set the pattern for former officers holding public office. He declined to use his military rank and authority to seize power after the revolution, as some of his subordinates would have liked him to do. He entered office not as a man on horseback but as an elected official who had lain aside his uniform, but not the wisdom of his years as a commander in chief who often had to answer to elected officials and to gauge the mood and capacities of the nation. Two centuries later, George C. Marshall set a very high standard for remaining apolitical, never voting in an election, refusing to be influenced by political agendas or pressure, and avoiding any sign of partisanship. Still, Marshall served as a cabinet official and in other public positions after his retirement from the army in 1945. Marshall's statements often demonstrate that he understood the political world, especially as it existed in Washington, that he understood the pressures on elected officials like Franklin Roosevelt and Eisenhower, and that he accepted and upheld civilian control of the military, as a necessity to a democracy and even to meaningful victory.

As Marshall's own career demonstrates, the experience and mindset of former officers can be a tremendous asset to American public and political life. Unsurprisingly, the periods of greatest political involvement on the part of officers tend to follow times of heightened military activity. Following America's Revolution and two of the costliest wars, the Civil War and World War II, the electorate chose the senior wartime field commander to be chief executive. Their examples perhaps show that the acclaim won in uniform does not always last. Washington continues to be revered, but Grant was pilloried by a generation of pro-Southern historians and later by others who had inherited a tradition of anti-Grantism. Eisenhower was also often misunderstood. The reputations of Grant and Eisenhower have benefited greatly from a diverse group of revisionist historians who have cast a cold eye on the detractors and revived the historical record of the two men's accomplishments.[13] Despite some commonly preconceived ideas about former officers in elected office, neither was an autocrat. In fact, in the case of Grant especially, they may have been sometimes misled by an assumption that others were as fair-minded and committed to the greater good as themselves. Grant and Eisenhower steered the nation through postwar periods in which the challenges may have been greater than those of war. Grant's conduct of Reconstruction reflected his belief in the wickedness and stupidity of slavery as a social and economic institution. While he was not entirely successful, he reversed the racism and excessive concessions to former slave owners of the previous Andrew Johnson administration. His efforts to pursue a policy of conciliation toward Native Americans was likewise a mixed success, in part because it also went against many attitudes of the day, and because of an inevitable collision of cultures that was bound to be hurtful. Eisenhower guided the nation and the globe through the most critical years of the Cold War. His strategic sense and understanding of the costs of war, the processes of government, and the nature of top-level command served the nation well at a time when fears for a nuclear war were justified by feelings of enmity on both sides and by a short nuclear response time that left only minutes to respond to a potential attack. As presidents, both Grant and Eisenhower were distinguished by common sense and decency that secured for them two full terms of office. Both were accomplished writers, Eisenhower patterning his *Crusade in Europe* after Grant's classic *Memoirs*. Perhaps even more notably, both were amateur artists. Eisenhower took up painting as a pastime on the recommendation of Winston Churchill. Grant painted as a young cadet and officer, although he does not appear to have continued the practice after the

Civil War. Their styles are telling. Grant, the junior officer, shows an eye for detail, with horses and their equipage a favorite subject, while Eisenhower, the elder statesman, executed impressionistic landscapes, many of his home in Gettysburg.

In the years of Eisenhower's presidency, a generation of young veterans entered Congress and remained serving into the current century. Men like ex-lieutenant Robert Dole had experienced the comradeship, the sense of service, and the practical problem-solving of military life, and they carried that outlook and skill to the legislature, often creating a bipartisan consensus that allowed government to make important changes in American governance and society. The receding of the World War II generation left a gap in military experience in the Congress, although some Vietnam veterans did enter public life, with Defense Secretary Chuck Hagel and Senators John McCain and John Kerry distinguished examples. The wars of the early twenty-first century and a revival in the prestige of the armed forces have seen veterans of all services and both genders attain elected office, including many young former junior officers. Two retired full generals and a serving three-star general were selected for high appointments in the federal government in 2016. (Although all three were out of government service by late 2018.) A diminishing majority of elected veterans are Republicans, and whether the new generation of Congressional and other elected veterans will rebuild the across-the-aisle comradeship and consensus of the World War II generation remains to be seen. On both sides of the party line divide, one now as sharply drawn as in any time in a century and half, the presence of the veterans is at least a positive sign.

DISSENT, RESIGNATION, AND DISOBEDIENCE

In recent times, some of the issues concerning officers' involvement in politics were crystallized by the 2006 "Revolt of the Generals," in which six retired general officers came out publicly in opposition to the plans and policies of the war in Iraq. Their actions drew criticism, but they may have achieved what was likely a desired result: the departure of the then-Defense Secretary Donald Rumsfeld.[14] Do officers have a right, even a responsibility, to question orders from the civil authority which they believe to be mistaken? This question may go to the heart of the nature of officership, officer thought, and military professionalism. In general, those who define the officer's role relatively narrowly, as the "management of violence" or what has also been called the "doctrinal delivery of ordnance," tend to place very restrictive limits on the scope of officer dissent.[15] Those who believe in a broader role for the officer, especially on a national level, give more allowance for dissent. Both sides have their points. Even representatives of the second group sometimes acknowledge that few officers, even those of senior rank, are equipped by education and experience to address the broader implications of the use of military force, its relation to policy and its historic importance. Supporters of the broader view may point to the Constitutional Oath as providing a basis for dissent in the case of national interest, or even in cases of threats to citizens, to include soldiers.[16]

Dissent may take many forms, of course. Even the narrowest interpretation of an officer's responsibilities would probably find private disagreement unobjectionable, whether one-on-one or in a small group. Serving officers usually refrain from public, or published disagreement, and the propriety of even retired officers airing their dissent over policy is subject to debate. A serving officer may resign in protest. The record of this is spotty. Few American officers have made use of this option, and it is hard to say that any have had much of an impact. Retired navy chaplain George Clifford presents the case studies of two general officers.[17] Marine Lieutenant General Gregory Newbold resigned in 2002 over his objections to plans for war in Iraq. Not until 2006, however, did he come out publicly over the reasons for his resignation, perhaps because at that point other generals were also openly expressing their own objections to the war. Army Chief of Staff Harold K. Johnson considered resigning over the lies being told by the administration about the progress and prospects of the war in Vietnam. He did not, having been advised by Omar Bradley that he could do more good remaining at his post. Johnson later said that he would regret this decision, which he described as a failure of moral courage, for the rest of his life. An officer of my acquaintance left the service after persistent efforts to obtain clear guidance on interrogations by military personnel led to his virtual ostracism and may have even threatened his safety. The matter of principled resignation is perhaps a topic that ought to receive greater attention in professional military education. The door is open to resignation, but little or no direction exists as to what might constitute sufficient reason. Even very intelligent officers of long and distinguished service feel out of their depth when faced with the prospect. The resignation of principle might be a part of every career officer's repertoire, if only as a last resort. A tragic form of radical resignation may be represented by some incidences of soldier-suicide. Many suicides by soldiers and veterans are likely due to some private misery that may have nothing to do with military service, but others are undoubtedly brought on by feelings of remorse and estrangement caused by something seen or done in uniform what I have already referred to as moral injury. For these soldiers, the only way to leave the service is to die, perhaps unless someone can convince them that nothing in life lasts forever, not even a soldier's service.

PEACE AND CONFLICT STUDIES

I hate war as only a soldier who has lived it can.[18]

—Eisenhower

Officers spend their professional lives studying and preparing for war. Many will experience armed conflict first hand, and nearly all have the opportunity to understand war in a way denied to most civilians. Soldiers occupy a community in which there is an ancestral and communal knowledge of war, a conversation on war that reaches back to the past through the experience of veterans, ceremonial practices and training methods, written and symbolic memorials. As Marine officer John W. Thomason wrote,

> There is nothing particularly glorious about sweaty fellows, laden with killing tools, going along to fight. And yet—such a column represents a great deal more than 28, 000 individuals mustered into a division. All that is behind those men is in that column, too: the old battles, long forgotten, that secured our nation . . . traditions of things endured and things accomplished, such as regiments hand down forever.[19]

A former officer might switch from military pursuits to peace and conflict studies. She could bring a highly personal, professional perspective to this multidisciplinary field, and herself benefit on different levels from exposure to students and teachers of peace and conflict studies, many of whom combine academic credentials with operational experience. Many UN, Red Cross, and other nongovernmental organization workers have seen more of war than most military professionals!

A senior fellowship with the New York–based Carnegie Council for Ethics in International Affairs and attendance at the 2018 PeaceBuilding conference at the Peace Palace, The Hague, Netherlands, have involved and informed me in the area of peace studies. I've gained an appreciation for the many organizations dedicated to the maintenance of peace. Most of these groups rely heavily on volunteers and budgets that are meager in comparison to the amounts spent every year on defense and weaponry. My background as a military officer has been valuable in my new role as peacemaker, granting to me a sense of history and the sometimes unspoken reasons nations and people go to war: the enduring seductive appeals of conflict.

The ultimate challenge for the officer-as-visionary is the creation of a world at peace, at least intermittently, and perhaps someday perpetually. The officer's understanding of the dynamics of war gives her insight into the creation of peace. Wars do not grow out of nothing. The prelude to war, the continuation and escalation of violence, the preparation for the next war that often seems to begin even before the cessation of the last, these are familiar phenomenon to many military officers. Through experience, they know that war is not merely the absence of peace, that the suppression of the rights of individuals and groups of people is a formula for war, that tyrants must wage war, externally and on their own people, to justify their tyranny and to remain in power.

The long human habit of war, along with various theories about the nature of humanity and society, have tended to reinforce the perception that war is inevitable. One of the few philosophers who have seriously considered lasting peace is Immanuel Kant. Kant's program for peace rests on three "Definitive Articles": republican governments, a federation of free states, and "hospitality" or open immigration. Kant's prescription is characteristically broad and legalistic, although his call for hospitality would seem to aspire to the kind of international amity espoused by Thomas Aquinas. To be sure, the securing of peace perpetual would require more than law. Even more important would be the change to take place in the hearts of women and men.

In her classic *A Strategy for Peace: Human Values and the Threat of War*, philosopher Sissela Bok devotes a chapter to Von Clausewitz, presenting him as a professional soldier who combined skepticism about the possibility of limiting war or ending it forever with realism about the awfulness of armed conflict as he had experienced it.[20] Bok points out that by the time Kant's *Perpetual Peace* appeared in 1795, the fifteen-year-old Clausewitz had seen two years of war with France. His experience and intellect had given him great insight into the nature of war, but at the same time his immersion in that reality, perhaps along with an element of trauma, had limited his ability to see a way out of war. Bok suggests a synthesis of Clausewitz and Kant might yield an approach to peace that is both informed and imaginative. Clausewitzian ideas of friction and the superiority of the defense point out the futility of much armed conflict, an idea borne out by the events of our time, the hollow victories of the American invasions of Iraq and Afghanistan, for example. Bok says that the same boldness and planning that have characterized the operations of the most successful military commanders should be put to the service of peace.

In seeking peace, the officer may be fueled by a mixture of patriotism and an identification with other nations and peoples gained through experience.

She may be inspired by feelings of comradeship that in effect begin with the military unit but do not end there, extending to embrace all people of goodwill. She may be opened to the possibility of fundamental change by training and exposure to the endlessly dynamic nature of war. As an organizer, he has been experienced in marshaling people and resources toward a common goal. As a warfighter, she has learned to restlessly seek solutions in the most daunting of circumstances.

In Ingmar Bergman's film *The Seventh Seal,* the Swedish knight Antonius Block (played by Max Von Sydow) comes home burdened by sadness and guilt over his participation in a crusade. He finds that home is not a secure refuge but is on the point of social collapse due to the plague. He's used to fear, so he can keep his composure, and finally he saves a young couple and their child by distracting death at chess. He can do this because he's a soldier who sees what's coming, who has been trained to think as a tactician, and who values the love he sees holding the family together, giving them a better chance of survival, and maybe more right to survive, than the other travelers who accompany him. His determination to act, to continue the fight even to the moment of his death, shows off what is perhaps the military leader's crowning capability. If peace does come, maybe the officer's skills and unique combination of character and cognition can be bent to other purposes, to space exploration (in the manner of Captain Kirk), for example, or other fields of human adventure and endeavor that can now only be imagined.

AN OFFICER'S DREAMS

> If you can dream, and not make dreams your master,
> If you can think, and not make thoughts your aim.
>
> —Rudyard Kipling, "If"

> Soldiers are dreamers; when the guns begin
> They think of firelit homes, clean beds and wives.
>
> —Siegfried Sassoon

Not all of what goes on inside an officer's brain comes under the heading of conscious thought. He has feelings too, an unconscious mind, and an individual mental backdrop: the continuing, changing chorus of assumptions and conditioning, of anxieties and aspirations. Vasily Grossman says of the Russian Tank Corps commander Novikov on the morning of battle, "He wasn't thinking about any of these things" (to include tanks and artillery, communications, his long-absent lover, and the first day of the war), "but they were all of them inside him." The things we feel and love are sometimes referred to as "dreams," as if they were related to the literal dreams that we all experience asleep, as perhaps they are. As part of the project of self-understanding that was alluded to in the chapter on military incompetence, an officer should understand her dreams, whether literal or figurative, hopeful, fearful, or otherwise instructive. In his original study, *The Innocence of Dreams*, Charles Rycroft departs from the conventional, pathologic understanding of dreams to claim their "innocence," their universality and naivete. For Rycroft, dreams are an expression of the sleeping imagination. His framing of them is literary rather than clinical. For imagery of dreaming, he quotes from the G. M. Hopkins poem, "The Windhover." Like the bird of the title, the dreamer is borne along as if by the wind, on flights of imagination that seem to come from far away, but which he can in effect control, catching the winds to swoop and soar.

It is perhaps particularly good that soldiers dream, or we might have more to bedevil and distract us during the day. Sigmund Freud, perhaps the leading interpreter of dreams, found his original theories challenged when he spoke to veterans of World War I. Freud had thought that dreams expressed hopes and anxieties about the future, but he found that many war veterans dreamed repeatedly of traumatic experiences in war, often the death of comrades or near-escapes from their own deaths. The veterans often woke from these dreams in a state of terror, but during the day they did not experience fear, as if it had been exorcised.[21] Dreams may function as a protective measure, processing feelings at night that a person cannot face in the day.

An officer's dream may replay her service in a strange but recognizable way. Dreams may seem to correct or affirm what has happened. I dream of my military service often. It sometimes seems to me that the dreams are about unfinished business. Sometimes I'm "checking out," saying farewell to old comrades I may have passed over and missed. I may be going through training again, or even to war. One lengthy, detailed, remembered dream was of a nationwide mobilization. Even old retirees like me were being called up and sent into action. I remember a squat, antiquated armored vehicle clanking along, a symbol of my own obsolescence. Then I was talking to another Marine, saying that I expected to move up soon and expected to meet my son in the front lines. Oh no, he said, those guys are coming back. Suddenly my son Devon appeared, and the dream ended with my joy at seeing him safe.

The officer, asleep or awake, may dream a world recognizable but better than the one she inhabits. Our waking dreams may also lead us astray. As T. E. Lawrence wrote in *Seven Pillars of Wisdom*, "The dreamers of the day are dangerous men, for they may act out their dreams with open eyes, to make it possible. This I did." The secret, to paraphrase Kipling, is to dream, but not make dreams your master, to be inspired but not driven by what we dream. It can be an interesting exercise to spend a period trying to recollect and even write down the dreams we have asleep. Such a practice can reveal hidden hopes and anxieties, fueling the self-knowledge that every officer should seek.

A vivid example of officer dreaming in fiction and film is in the novel and motion picture *Fail Safe* (1962, 1964). The book and the movie both begin with a recurring dream, or maybe more properly a nightmare, that has been disturbing the sleep of Air Force Brigadier General "Blackie" Black. General Black is dreaming of a bull in a ring being flayed by a matador, while Black himself sits helpless and horrified in the stands. On a psychological level, the dream is an expression of Black's misgivings over his role in preparation for nuclear war, which appear to him to be rushing toward self-fulfillment. In a sense, Black stands between the somewhat stolid senior generals who view the preparation for war in pragmatic terms, and the civilian intellectuals, typified in the novel and film by Professor Groteschele (a mix of Hermann Kahn and Henry Kissinger), who are remote from the technical details of aviation and ordnance but who seem to enjoy the intellectual challenges of deterrence and the darker pleasure of flirting with doomsday. For narrative purposes, Black's dream is foreshadowing. The movie ends when, on the command of his friend and former classmate the president, Black drops two atom bombs on New York City to atone for bombs just dropped on Moscow and to convince all doubters that the attack on Moscow was accidental. Black's family is in New York, as is the president's wife. Black commits suicide immediately after completing his mission, and his final thoughts are a revelation that he was the bull in the ring in his own dream. Of course, Black is both victim and assailant. He is a tragic figure undone by his own superior insight and ability. The president, knowing him to be both a competent pilot and man of conscience, picks him as a fit sacrifice. The last scene in the novel has him recommending Black for the Medal of Honor.

THE OFFICER OF THE FUTURE

It is probably accurate to say that officer thought has evolved over time. Especially if we trace this development to the recorded origins of armed conflict, the thinking of those exercising leadership in war can be seen to follow several courses of development. Like other forms of evolution, this development has not been a steady curve of improvement, or simply "survival of the fittest." Bad ideas have sometimes prospered while better ones were neglected or ridiculed. Thought on war has reacted to broad societal, cultural, and political change, to the nature of the wars being fought and the character of those who fought them, to scientific developments and even, since life imitates art, to various depictions of the soldier, in writing especially. War and military leadership have variously been cast in religious, political, and literary terms. One form of evolution that has been constant, and accelerating thanks to technology, is the pace and physical scope of military operations. The most technically competent are not necessarily the most enlightened, however. Technical competence and broad enlightenment may be seen to be in competition, to inhabit separate cultures that see themselves at odds. When C. P. Snow gave his lecture on the separate cultures of science and the humanities in 1959, he was critical of the way that the sciences were neglected in education and derided by social elites. We may be in a period now when the opposite is true. This may be a natural, if not an inevitable consequence of the growing power of science and technology, their constant presence and importance in our lives, but the military culture must be one in which the virtues and benefits of the sciences and humanities are fused. Science can provide the tools, but it cannot frame and express issues, merge cultures, move minds and hearts. Science can manage, but it can't lead. Technology also can distract as well as assist. In an address to West Point plebes in 2009 titled, "Solitude and Leadership," William Deresiewicz decried the influence of multitasking, a practice enabled by social media and other applications of computer technology, on the ability of people to concentrate and therefore to think. Original and creative thought requires periods of time free from distractions and dedicated to the working out of difficult problems.

Another challenge for officer cognition into the future concerns the nature of command. Although the concept and practice of command has evolved, it has remained essentially hierarchical. The hierarchical structure is inefficient in capitalizing on the combined talents and ideas of an organization. This continues to be a reason why some of the brightest young officers leave the service, and it is also why armies fail. The best armies have always been those that combined discipline with the ability to tap into the resourcefulness of their members. The challenge of creating forms of command that do this more effectively has been recognized by the US Army. The Army's doctrinal publication *ADP 6-0 Mission Command* details an approach to command that stresses "disciplined initiative" on the part of subordinates and calls on commanders to "empower agile and adaptive leaders." Mission Command is a departure from the traditional, prevailing American approach to command. It draws on the German model developed by the elder Von Moltke in the nineteenth century. Writing of the Army officers who rose to positions of corps command in World War II, Harold Winton writes that these men were taught an approach to command that stressed the intellect and character of the commander. The American Army was fortunate to have senior commanders who possessed the necessary qualities for an approach to command that asked much of the commander. Mission Command, while not relieving the commander of her responsibilities or authority, in effect seeks to make better use of the abilities of subordinates. There is skepticism about the ability of the Army to execute Mission Command. Doctrine aside, does the Army have the culture and organization that will enable Mission Command, or will large staffs, and a bureaucratic, managerial approach to command, impede its exercise?[22] Going beyond Mission Command, a more cooperative and collegial approach to command and to military leadership could be part of an atmosphere of true professionalism, "special trust and confidence" that extends in all directions in a web of command. Only very high professional standards and dedication can make this possible, but the accelerating rate of change and the hazards of the twenty-first century world may make it imperative. Only a full harnessing of the adaptive and innovative resources of a military organization may be enough to meet these challenges.

Technology, the two cultures, and changes in the nature of command are only some of the issues facing the modern officer. Another question already mentioned is that of the relevance of conventional military force. These questions, raised particularly in the new century, concern the ability of conventional military forces to protect or deter against certain threats and to attain meaningful victory. Meaningful national security may have to come from closer partnerships with civil agencies. Such partnerships raise not only practical questions concerning interagency relations, but also legal and ethical issues. Since the start of the century, US forces have developed an impressive counterinsurgency doctrine that places much more emphasis on training and education on counterinsurgent operations. Still, success in two major counter-insurgent campaigns in Iraq and Afghanistan has been elusive. Most recently, war by proxy seems to have gained in favor, with a campaign in Afghanistan being pursued with minimal US ground forces in favor of advisers, communications assets, and fire support. It may be that ground forces are being ushered back to their focus on conventional, high-end combat as their primary role, although the United States has seen before the sorry consequences of neglect of counterinsurgency training and doctrine.

As Rosa Brooks argues in *How Everything Became War and the Military Became Everything: Tales from the Pentagon*, the world seems to be entering a period of nearly perpetual quasi-war, "a 'gray zone' between traditional notions of war and peace."[23] Officers must adjust their thinking to this fact. With armed conflict pervasive, ongoing, and combined with activities of nation and alliance-building, security, and cultural exchange, officers must increase their range of expertise. Context is all. Armed force and the other instruments of policy may be so close that they can only be taken in and understood all at once.[24] Given a long enough historical memory and an eye for some of the neglected corridors of military, social, and diplomatic history, one can see that this is not entirely new. But the scale and seeming permanence of the "gray zone" are likely going to be a central, global fact of life in the twenty-first century, in a manner not seen since the advent of the nation-state in the seventeenth century, and perhaps not in a thousand years.

In different ways, these developments raise and will continue to raise fundamental questions about the relationship of the officer corps and armed forces with the society that they protect. The military profession plays a broad role in society, both historically, and (I maintain) as a vital professional obligation. The officer corps may be said to collectively function as the superego to humankind's enduring id, to the nightmare of force and violence from which we cannot seem to wake. Between these two is the ego, the individual officer with her capabilities, imagination, insecurities, dreams, and desires. In the future, the officer corps more than ever may have to both defend that which is worth preserving in society, while also embodying some important values, that of service perhaps most particularly.

Whatever changes are in store, some constants remain. The officer will be tasked to think in circumstances that impede and even seem to defy clear thought. Despite fatigue and fear, setback, and disillusionment, "dry with rage and extreme toil" (as Shakespeare has Hotspur say), the officer, sometimes the lone officer, will have to keep his head, and the faith, maybe when all about him are losing theirs. Clear, creative, and principled thought under great stress is the officer's forte. The subject of officer thought needs increased attention from educators, mentors, and commanders, although also on the part of individual officers taking charge of their own evolving ability to think as military professionals.

SOME CONCLUSIONS

There may be a danger in overintellectualizing the officer's profession, but there is a greater danger in thinking too little. Thinking, writing, and talking about how we think must be part of the process of improving officer thought. What can be done to improve the thinking of officers? The solutions are both structural and cultural. On the structural level, militaries should consider adopting nonhierarchical organization and becoming less rigid and authoritarian. This may appear anathema to military ideas of discipline and Command and Control, but real discipline is more a matter of compliance than compulsion. The military must do a better job harnessing its own brainpower. The rigidity of military organizations is responsible for some of the so-called brain drain among some of the brighter junior officers and noncommissioned officers.[25] Many see weary years ahead before their ideas can have much impact, and so are seeking occupations not so tied to mere seniority.

The cultural changes are more numerous and important. A military culture stressing brain over brawn would help to create an atmosphere for better strategic thinking. Diminishing the near-fetishization of athletics in some circles might help. We should not reduce physical standards, but we should consider the evaluation and recognition of mental achievement to match. Currently, professional military education seems to be getting poor grades for the development of strategic thinkers. A more rigorous and reflective approach to professional education is part of the solution. The military should also consider sending more officers (and some enlisted members) to graduate school to earn degrees in fields like history and the humanities. These fields can prepare officers to think in the ways required of strategists, to grasp ends as well as means, to consider history and the future as well as the present and immediate effects. Military officers literally invest their lives in the pursuit of victory. They must also invest in the intellectual capital that makes strategic success and victory attainable. The ends, as well as the means, should always be in sight. I hope that the officer will always be able to take heart and draw inspiration from the hope that the violence and sacrifice may add up to a better world, a better peace, and maybe someday to a world at peace.

Conclusion

Thinking Like an Officer for the Civilian

> Only an alert and knowledgeable citizenry can compel the
> proper meshing of the huge industrial and military machinery of
> defense with our peaceful methods and goals, so that security and
> liberty may prosper together.
>
> —President Dwight D. Eisenhower,
> Farewell Address to the Nation, January 17, 1961

$\mathscr{I}$ begin my conclusion with this quotation from Eisenhower's famous
speech because it is an eloquent and historic reminder of one of the reasons
why civilians ought to understand how officers think, and ought to think,
about the means and goals of national defense. It was in this speech that
Eisenhower warned against the "military-industrial complex," the collusion of
corporations engaged in military production with a large peacetime military
establishment. Eisenhower calls for understanding and oversight (he uses the
strong word "compel") on the part of the citizenry over defense matters. The
challenges described by Eisenhower are still with us, although in altered form.
As in his time, America today has recent experience of large-scale conflict, a
public seemingly obsessed with media and entertainment, and a large defense
establishment and industry spending huge sums on entitlements, upkeep, and
the latest technology. In the meantime, a reaction to the anti-military attitudes
of the Vietnam War and perhaps some "civilian guilt" has fed an uncritical acceptance of the military, what it does, and the money that it spends. Seeing the
burdens of deployments and the traumas of military service being carried by a
relative few, by certain social and regional segments of the country, and by the
families that continue to follow a military tradition, too many Americans have
given up the need to understand, let alone "compel" in the area of military and
defense policy. To return to James Fallows's "The Tragedy of American Mili-

tary," the lack of knowledge and oversight of the military on the part of the American people creates an atmosphere of credulousness and cowardice that makes them willing to "outsource" military service and questions of defense to a small, isolated segment of the populace and to place exaggerated faith in military solutions. Fallows quotes former Chairman of the Joint Chiefs Mike Mullen as saying that he would be willing to sacrifice some of the military's impressive professional competence to "make sure that we stay close to the American people." (And he might have said, "get closer.") Civilians may favor military solutions because they are unacquainted with the difficulties involved. Soldiers sometimes prefer them because, despite being aware of the difficulties, it is what they know best. The real key to clear thinking about the means and ends of armed conflict is an attentive partnership between military and civil. And Mullen is surely right to say that this would merit an increased investment in time and effort on both sides. As writer and former Marine officer Phil Klay has pointed out, contrary to what some civilians believe, there is nothing especially incommunicable about military experience or the insight that might be gained from it.[1] Soldiers have no monopoly on feelings of grief, remorse, sadness, fear, of comradeship and friendship, love and victory. To bridge the gap takes an act of empathy and imagination from both sides, but once the bridge is crossed the realization of the elements of a common humanity is a gift that can never be lost.

Whether officer or not, the reader by now has probably drawn some of her own conclusions about the utility of officer thought in civil life. It may be that every profession and vocation owns a distinctive way of thinking which can be enriched by considering the professional vocabularies and schemata of other professions. How does this work in the case of officership? The possession of the intellectual virtues is obviously not the special province of officers. While some of the pitfalls and challenges of thinking like an officer may be unique, properly considered, there is no purely military thought, and a good thing there isn't! Efforts to wall off military thinking from other areas of endeavor, or to insist on an impenetrable particularism in the thinking of officer must fail, as they have, on occasion disastrously and shamefully. Officers must adopt the thought-patterns of other professions, and consider the civil, historical, cultural, and moral aspects of a situation as well as the straightforward "move-shoot-communicate" aspects of the case. One aspect of officer thought discussed in this book is the careful way that officer thought can be cultivated throughout a military career, both formally and informally. The informal methods are most subject to emulation by the non-officer. Although the progressive PME that career officers undertake is open to only a few civilians, anyone may participate in a program of reading, in discussions of professional issues with peers, in mentoring as both mentor and protege.

It may also profit the civilian (going back to my academic colleague at Kings Point whom I mentioned in the introduction) to think as an active member of an organization, that is, not as a passive part, a mere spoke in the wheel, but as a human entity capable of independent action and fluid movement, one that is informed and enabled by knowledge and ownership of the organization which she serves. For the civilian to think as a tactician and strategist may be helpful in both his work and also in his role as citizen. Most important, although the officer's service may be conducive to the role of visionary, others can also benefit, and benefit others, by adopting a visionary approach to their lives and work.

For all that they ought to overlap, the roles of the officer and the civilian also differ. The challenge to civil society is that it be something worth fighting and perhaps dying for. The soldier, led by the officer, will decide from day to day to what degree this is true and will serve her society with the faithfulness she thinks that it deserves. Wealth and power do not make a society worthy of service. This worthiness is secured by liberty and justice for all, at the least by the sincere, working aspiration to treat all men and women as equals and friends.

Finally, to conclude the book entire, I have to say that much more remains to be said on this subject. The poet Paul Valéry once said that a poem is never finished, it is merely abandoned. This is perhaps also true of many books. On the subject of officer thought and more broadly professional thought, I believe there is much more to be said, read, and studied. I have neglected major areas of warfighting, to include intelligence and logistics. Most of this book has been focused on ground combat, and there is more to be said on the other domains of war, maybe especially on the newest realm of cyberspace. I have mentioned such areas as counterinsurgency and peacekeeping only passingly. Even in "visionary" areas like dreams, politics, and psychology to which I have devoted more attention, I feel that the conversation has just begun. The relationship of thought and humor in military life merits separate study, as do the frankly darker recesses of the military mind, the bullying and misogyny that stalk many military units, the mental processes involved in atrocity, and (what may have even more adverse effects) the overuse and misuse of firepower. A greater challenge than the control of the officer's ability to do harm is the maximizing of her potential to do good in the service of her fellow service members and veterans of the armed forces, the rest of the American people and those of the world. To address the subject of officer cognition fully means not neglecting our mundane personal and professional obligations, but sometimes it requires that we raise our aim. To think well, an officer has to love what she does. She has to love the work, the service, at least some of the people, her country and the broad ideals the are represented by oath and uniform. Without this, her thinking will never have the interest and motivation that her role requires. With it, her thoughts have wings, and her service never ends.

Notes

ACKNOWLEDGMENTS

1. Gregory M. Reichberg, Remarks at McCain Conference, Stockdale Center, US Naval Academy, Annapolis, MD, April 2015; "Thomas Aquinas on Military Prudence," *Journal of Military Ethics* 9, no. 3 (2010); *Thomas Aquinas on War and Peace* (Cambridge: Cambridge University Press, 2017).

2. Reed Robert Bonadonna, *Soldiers and Civilization: How the Profession of Arms Fought and Thought the Modern World into Existence* (Annapolis, MD: Naval Institute Press, 2017).

INTRODUCTION

1. General J. Lawton Collins, *Lightning Joe: An Autobiography* [1979] (Novato, CA: Presidio Press, 1994), 51.

2. C. J. Chivers, *The Fighters: Americans in Combat in Afghanistan and Iraq* (New York: Simon & Schuster, 2018).

3. Mike Rennie, "An Officer and a 'Reflective' Problem Solver: Further Development of Problem Solving and Thinking Skills in Officer Cadets at Sandhurst and Beyond," Sandhurst Occasional Papers No. 15. Royal Military Academy Sandhurst: Central Library, 2013.

4. Morton Braender, Marenne Jansen, and René Moelker, "What Sets the Officer Apart?" academia.edu. Accessed September 19, 2018.

5. Stephen Saunders Webb, *Marlborough's America* (New Haven, CT: Yale University Press, 2013), 35.

6. Howard Gardner, *Leading Minds: An Anatomy of Leadership* (New York: Harper-Collins-Basic Books, 1995), 148.

7. "Vietnam Hero Offers Leadership Lessons," *American Profile*, Online, May 24, 2011.

8. Braender et al., "What Sets the Officer Apart?"

9. Jerome Groopman, *How Doctors Think* (Boston: Houghton-Mifflin, 2007).

10. It has been argued that the distinction between training and education is over-played and counterproductive (See Celestine Perez Jr., "What Military Education Forgets: Strategy Is Performance," *War on the Rocks*, Online, September 7, 2018). Training often involves more than rote learning and set procedure; it may include problem-framing and -solving. Military education, on the other hand, is usually not a purely academic exercise. It both depends and builds on habits and responses acquired in training.

11. Philip Caputo, *A Rumor of War* (New York: Holt, Rinehart, and Winston, 1977), 14.

12. Edward M. Coffman, *The Regulars: The American Army 1998–1941* (Cambridge, MA: Belknap Press of Harvard University Press, 2004), 239.

13. James Fallows, "The Tragedy of the American Military," *The Atlantic*, Online, January/February 2015.

14. "Officership," *Oxford English Dictionary*, Attributed to Captain Massey Shaw of London Fire Brigade.

15. Morris Janowitz, *The Professional Soldier: A Social and Political Portrait* (Glencoe, IL: Free Press, 1960); Samuel Huntington, *The Soldier and the State: The Theory and Politics of Civil-Military Relations* (Cambridge, MA: Belknap Press of Harvard University Press, 1957).

16. Pauline Shanks-Kaurin, "Questioning Military Professionalism," *Redefining the Modern Military: The Intersection of Profession and Ethics*, Nathan K. Finney and Tyrell O. Mayfield, eds. (Annapolis, MD: Naval Institute Press, 2018), 13–14.

17. Examples include Rupert Smith's "Brains, Not Bullets," and "After Smart Weapons, Smart Soldiers," *The Economist*, October 2, 2007, 15, 33–36; David Kilcullen's *Blood Year: The Unraveling of Western Counterterrorism* (New York: Oxford, 2016); Daniel Boger's *Why We Lost: A General's Inside Account of the Iraq and Afghanistan Wars* (New York: Houghton Mifflin Harcourt, 2015).

18. See Thomas M. Williams, "Education for Critical Thinking," *Military Review* (January/February 2013), 49–54, for an argument that service schools should reorient away from content and more toward the development of critical and creative thought. A very disturbing trend has been the decline in intelligence in the US officer corps. This dumbing-down has been attributed to the increased size of the pool of college graduates and the lower average intelligence of this group compared to the smaller pool of college graduates of decades past. Some aspects of military culture, of recruiting and training may also be contributing. For a discussion, see Matthew F. Cancian, "Officers Are Less Intelligent: What Does It Mean?" *Joint Force Quarterly* 81, 2nd Quarter (2016).

19. George Orwell, "Looking Back on the Spanish War," 1943. *A Collection of Essays by George Orwell* (Garden City, NY: Doubleday-Anchor, 1954), 194.

20. See Huntington, *The Soldier and the State*.

21. See, however, George C. Marshall, *Memoirs of My Services in the World War 1917–1918* (Boston: Houghton Mifflin, 1976). This work was published only post-

humously, and apparently it was not intended for publication. (In fact Marshall had asked that it be destroyed.)

22. For the role of the emotions in ethical life, see, for example, Martha Nussbaum's *Love's Knowledge, Essays on Philosophy and Literature* (New York: Oxford University Press, 1990).

23. Richard Choquette, "Bridging the Gap," *Marine Corps Gazette*, 2008 Online, 92, no. 7.

PART I

1. "Neurologist Oliver Sacks," Interview with Terry Gross, *Fresh Air*, October 1, 1987. Printed in *Oliver Sacks: The Last Interview and Other Conversations* (Brooklyn, NY: Melville House), 11.

2. Roger Shattuck, *Forbidden Knowledge: From Prometheus to Pornography* (New York: St. Martin's Press, 1996).

3. Gordon Rattray Taylor, *A Natural History of the Mind.* 1979 (Harmondsworth, Middlesex, UK: Penguin, 1981).

4. Aldous Huxley, *Ape and Essence.* 1948 (Chicago: Ivan Dee, 1992), 14–15.

CHAPTER 1

1. See Stephen Taafe, YouTube video (Lexington, VA: George C. Marshall Foundation, July 28, 2017).

2. See Thomas E. Ricks, *The Generals: American Military Command from World War II to Today* (New York: Penguin, 2012); and Timothy L. Challans, *Awakening Warrior: Revolution in the Ethics of Warfare.* SUNY Series, Ethics and the Military Profession, George R. Lucas Jr., ed. (Albany: State University of New York Press, 2007).

3. Larry I. Bland, ed., *George C. Marshall Interviews and Reminiscences for Forrest C. Pogue* (Lexington, VA: George C. Marshall Research Foundation, 1991), 545.

4. Collins, *Lightning Joe*, 6.

5. Edward Cox, *Grey Eminence: Fox Conner and the Art of Mentorship* (Stillwater, OK: New Forums Press, 2011), 69.

6. Cox, *Grey Eminence*, 70, 71.

7. Cox, *Grey Eminence*, 77.

8. Cox, *Grey Eminence*, 89.

9. Joseph T. Glatthaar, *Partners in Command: The Relationship between Leaders in the Civil War* (New York: The Free Press-Macmillan, 1994), 135–62.

10. Joel Kupperman, *Character* (New York: Oxford University Press), 13.

11. *The Armed Forces Officer* (Washington, DC: Department of Defense, 1950), 12.

12. Lord Moran, *The Anatomy of Courage.* 1945 (Garden City, NY: Avery, 1978), 10.

13. Mame Warren, "The Whole Man," *Marshall* (Fall 2015): 23.

14. Rose Page Wilson, *General Marshall Remembered* (Englewood Cliffs, NJ: Prentice-Hall, 1968), 98–99.

15. S. H. Butcher, trans., "Aristotle's Poetics," *Aristotle's Theory of Poetry and Fine Art* (1911; New York: Dover, 1951), 29.

16. American Shakespeare Center Leadership Programs. The author participated in two ASC leadership programs, one on-site at Blackfriars Playhouse, Staunton, Virginia (Spring 2015), and one at the US Merchant Marine Academy, Kings Point, New York (Fall 2016). Both involved midshipmen and Academy faculty and staff. They were great examples of the efficacy of Shakespeare and of performance in developing the ability to think on one's feet and to reflect on one's own character.

17. Fussell writes admiringly of Eisenhower in several of his works. See, for example, *Doing Battle: The Making of a Skeptic* (Boston: Little, Brown, 1996), 220.

18. Constantin Stanislavski, *Building a Character*, trans. Elizabeth Reynolds Hapgood (1950; London: Methuen, 1968), 250.

19. Kelly Grovier, "Rime without Reason." Review of *Mariner: A Voyage with Samuel Taylor Coleridge* (Hodder and Stoughton), *Times Literary Supplement*, April 28, 2017, 29.

CHAPTER 2

1. Damon Young, *The Art of Reading* (Melborne: Scribe, 2017).

2. See David Masson, *The Collected Writings of Thomas DeQuincey, New and Enlarged Edition*, vol. 13, *Tales and Prose Fantasies* (Edinburgh: Adam and Charles Black, 1890), 340–49.

3. James Stavridis and R. Manning Ancell, *The Leader's Bookshelf* (Annapolis, MD: Naval Institute Press, 2017); Paul K. Van Riper, "The Importance of History to the Military Profession: An American Marine's View," in *The Past as Prologue: The Importance of History to the Military Profession*, Williamson Murray and Richard Hart Sinnreich, eds. (Cambridge: Cambridge University Press, 2006). Van Riper recommends reading in three areas: general humanities, military history, and communications. Van Riper cautions against looking for answers in reading, saying that readers must "absorb . . . the material into their whole being" (pages 46, 53). James Mattis has also written about the importance to the officer of nonmilitary works.

4. Rupert Smith, Printed transcript of interview with Joanne Myers on his book *The Utility of Force: The Art of War in the Modern World* (London: Penguin-Allen Lane, 2005), Carnegie Council for Ethics in International Affairs, New York City, January 24, 2007.

5. Anthony Hartle, *Moral Issues in Military Decision Making* (Lawrence: University Press of Kansas, 1989), 43–44.

6. Hartle, *Moral Issues in Military Decision Making*, 43–44.

7. George Santayana, *The Life of Reason; or The Phases of Human Progress* (New York: Charles Scribner's Sons, 1905), 60–87.

8. See Roger H. Nye, *The Patton Mind: The Professional Development of an Extraordinary Leader* (Garden City, NY: Avery, 1993). The author is an obvious admirer of Patton, although he notes instances of Patton's "insensitivity" and "anti-intellectualism"

(strange in so avid a reader). Patton, with his poetic and aesthetic sense, likely had the capacity for greater sympathies and maturity. One senses a highly intelligent and sensitive person who was perhaps overconscious of his aristocratic social origins and his elite status as an officer, and who is deliberately, if mistakenly, steeling and de-sensitizing himself to the demands of leadership in war.

9. See Olivia Garard, "*Modelez-vous*: Deriving Frameworks from History," *The Strategy Bridge* website, June 6, 2017.

10. Michael Howard, "The Use and Abuse of Military History," Reprint. *Parameters* 11, no. 1 (2008): 10. 2008.

11. Howard, "The Use and Abuse of Military History," 14.

12. See, for example, Douglas Porch, *The Path to Victory: The Mediterranean Theater in World War II* (Old Saybrook, CT: Konecky & Konecky, 2004), 236–39, 292–96.

13. Corelli Barnett, *The Desert Generals*. 1960 (New York: Viking-Ballantine, 1972), ix.

14. Sam E. A. Cates, "Why Was General Richard O'Connor's Command in Northwest Europe Less Effective Than Expected?" (Fort Leavenworth, KS: School of Advanced Warfighting, US Army Command and General Staff College, 2011), 63.

15. Richard Holmes, *The Little Field Marshall: A Life of Sir John French* (London: Weidenfeld and Nicolson, 2004), 359–61.

16. See Adam N. McKeown, *English Mercuries: Soldier-Poets in the Age of Shakespeare* (Nashville, TN: Vanderbilt University Press, 2009).

17. Ulysses S. Grant, *Personal Memoirs of U.S. Grant* (1885–1886; New York: Library of America, 1990).

18. Jean Edward Smith, *Eisenhower in War and Peace* (New York: Random House, 2012), 468.

19. Ronald C. White, *American Ulysses: A Life of Ulysses S. Grant* (New York: Random House, 2016), 47.

20. Ward Just, "Introduction," in *About Face: The Odyssey of an American Warrior*, David Hackworth and Julie Sherman, eds. (New York: Touchstone-Simon & Schuster, 1989), 13; and Marcel Proust, *Remembrance of Things Past*, trans. C. K. Scott Moncrieff (1924; New York: Random House, 1934), 792–99.

21. Brian Holden Reid, "Commanding Heights," review of *The Lords of War, From Lincoln to Churchill, Supreme Command, 1861–1945* by Correlli Barnett. *Times Literary Supplement* September 27, 2013, 28.

22. Jane Austen, *Pride and Prejudice* (London: Thomas Egerton, 1813).

23. Robert D. Kaplan, "The Humanist in the Foxhole," *New York Times*, Online, June 14, 2011.

24. Josiah Bunting, "The Humanities in the Education of the Military Professional," in *The System for Educating Military Officers in the U.S.*, Lawrence J. Korb (Pittsburgh, PA: International Studies, 1976), 155–58.

25. Jonathan Rose, *The Literary Churchill: Author, Reader, Actor* (New Haven, CT: Yale University Press, 2013), 351.

26. Stanley Cavell, *This New Yet Unapproachable America: Lectures after Emerson after Wittgenstein* (Albuquerque, NM: Living Batch Press, 1989).

27. Terry Eagleton, Review of *On the Origin of Stories: Evolution, Cognition, Fiction* by Brian Boyd in *London Review of Books* 31 (18) (2009): 20, 22. Posted summary on blog *Poiesis and Prolepsis* by Allan Parsons, October 13, 2009.

28. William Meredith, "Reading My Poems from World War II." 1970. Poetry Foundation website. Accessed May 18, 2017.

29. Thomas Moore (1779–1852); written after the Irish Rebellion of 1798.

30. John Limon, *Writing after War: American War Fiction from Realism to Postmodernism* (New York: Oxford University Press, 1994), 3.

31. *Soldiers and Civilization*, 24.

32. See Harold Bloom, *Shakespeare: The Invention of the Human* (New York: Fourth Estate, 2008).

33. Duff Cooper, *Sergeant Shakespeare* (London: Rupert Hart-Davis, 1949).

34. Reed Bonadonna, Review of *English Mercuries: Soldier Poets in the Age of Shakespeare* by Adam N. McKeown, *Journal of Military Ethics*, Routledge-Taylor and Francis Group 11, no. 1 (March 2012).

35. Michael Roberts, "The Military Revolution, 1560–1660," reprinted in Clifford Rogers, *The Military Revolution Debate: Readings in the Military Transformation of Early Modern Europe* (Boulder, CO: Westview Press, 1995), 13–36.

36. Michael Murrin, *History and Warfare in Renaissance Epic* (Chicago: University of Chicago Press, 1994).

37. Huntington, *The Soldier and the State*, 14.

38. Rose, *The Literary Churchill*, 355.

39. *Soldiers and Civilization*, 247.

40. Karl Marlantes, *Matterhorn: A Novel of the Vietnam War* (Berkeley, CA: El Leon Literary Arts-Grove, 2010), 122.

41. Marlantes, *Matterhorn*, 82.

CHAPTER 3

1. Norman Dixon, *On the Psychology of Military Incompetence* (1976; New York: Basic Books, 2016), 7.

2. Dixon, *On the Psychology of Military Incompetence*, Geoffrey Wawro, Foreword, xi.

3. This trend is discussed at length in Thomas Ricks's *The Generals: American Military Command from World War II to Today* (New York: Penguin, 2012). See also "The Crimes of Seal Team 6," by Matthew Cole, *The Intercept,* January 18, 2017, for examples of Navy Special Warfare officers promoted despite their failure to halt or prosecute war crimes that included mutilation of the dead.

4. "Mental Models: The Best Way to Make Intelligent Decisions (113 Models Explained)," *Farnum Street* blog. Accessed February 12, 2018.

5. James R. McDonough, *The Defense of Hill 781: An Allegory of Modern Mechanized Combat* (New York: Presidio-Ballantine, 1988).

6. See Nancy Sherman, *Stoic Warriors: The Ancient Philosophy behind the Military Mind* (Oxford: Oxford University Press, 2005).

7. Anton Myrer, *Once an Eagle* (1968; New York: HarperTorch-HarperCollins, 2001), 306.

8. Leo Murray, *War Games: The Psychology of Combat*; 2013 as *Brain and Bullets* (London: Biteback, 2018), 105. Murray (apparently a pseudonym) refers to this phenomenon as "fussing."

9. There is a considerable literature on "moral injury," which may be considered an aggravated form of post-traumatic stress (PTS) or as a separate phenomenon. See for example Shira Maguen and Brett Litz, "Moral Injury in Veterans of War," *Research Quarterly* 23, no. 1 (2012).

10. Virgil, *The Aeneid*, trans. W. F. Jackson Knight (London: Penguin, 1956), 58.

11. See Robert Kegan and Lisa Laskow Lahey, *Immunity to Change: How to Overcome It and Unlock the Potential in Yourself and Your Organization* (Boston, MA: Harvard Business Review Press, 2009).

CHAPTER 4

1. *The Ethics of Aristotle: The Nicomachean Ethics*, trans. J. A. K. Thomson (1953; London: Penguin, 1976), 87.

2. Erik Lund, *War for the Every Day: Generals, Knowledge, and Warfare in Early Modern Europe, 1680–1740* (New York: Greenwood, 1999), 158.

3. 2015 McCain Conference, US Naval Academy, Annapolis MD. Remarks by Gregory Reichberg, April 16, 2015.

4. Gaston Bouthoul, *War*, trans. Silvia and George Lesson (1953; New York: Walker and Company, 1962), 10.

5. Brett D. Steele and Tamara Dorland, eds. "Introduction." In *The Heirs of Archimedes: Science and the Art of War through the Age of Enlightenment* (Cambridge: Massachusetts Institute of Technology Press, 2005), 3.

6. See Hanson, Victor Davis. *Carnage and Culture: Landmark Battles in the Rise of Western Power* (New York: Random House/Anchor, 2002).

7. Steele and Dorland, "Introduction," 8–12.

8. Lund, *War for the Every Day*, 158.

9. Azar Gat, *A History of Military Thought* (Oxford: Oxford University Press, 2001), 29.

10. Hew Strachan, *European Armies and the Conduct of War* (1983; London: Routledge, 2002), 26.

11. Vanya Eftimova Bellinger, *Marie Von Clausewitz: The Woman behind the Making of* On War (Oxford: Oxford University Press, 2016). Also see Youri Cormier, *War as Paradox: Clausewitz and Hegel on Fighting Doctrines and Ethics* (Kingston, Ontario, Canada: McGill-Queen's University Press, 2016).

12. See Ian T. Brown, "John Boyd on Clausewitz: Don't Fall in Love with Your Mental Model," *The Strategy Bridge* website, March 22, 2018.

13. Ian C. Hope, *A Scientific Way of War: Antebellum Military Science, West Point, and the Origins of American Military Thought* (Lincoln: University of Nebraska Press, 2015).

14. Ardant Du Picq, *Battle Studies: Ancient and Modern Battle*, trans. John Greeley and Robert C. Cotton (1880; New York: Macmillan, 1921), 139.

15. Daniel J. Hughes, ed., *Moltke on the Art of War: Selected Writings* (Novato, CA: Presidio, 1993), 110.

16. Michael Howard, "Men against Fire: The Doctrine of the Offensive in 1914," *Makers of Modern Strategy from Machiavelli to the Nuclear Age*, Peter Paret, ed. (Princeton, NJ: Princeton University Press, 1986), 510–26.

17. P. M. S. Blackett, "Operational Research," *Studies of War* (New York: Hill and Wang, 1962), 169–239.

18. Annie Jacobsen, *The Pentagon's Brain: An Uncensored History of DARPA, America's Top-Secret Military Research Agency* (New York: Little, Brown and Company, 2015), 53–54.

19. Glenn Voelze, "Is Military Science 'Scientific'?" *Joint Force Quarterly* 75 (4th Quarter 2014), 84–90.

20. See "Pied Beauty," *Poems and Prose of Gerard Manley Hopkins*, Selected with Introduction and Notes by W. H. Gardner (1953; Harmondsworth, Middlesex, England: Penguin, 1984), 130. Hopkins does not refer specifically to the soldier's equipment, but to "áll trádes, their gear and tackle and trim."

21. Alan Morehead, *Gallipoli* (New York: Ballantine, 1956), 176.

22. The feature film *The Train* (1964) and the novel and film *Castle Keep* (1965, 1969) depict soldiers destroying, stealing, and protecting European art treasures in World War II. These works depict a complex relationship between art and the officer. The German colonel in *The Train* is a connoisseur and self-professed lover of beauty who is willing to murder hostages to carry out his theft of French art treasures. The American soldiers in *Castle Keep* guard a castle filled with art. One of the two officers is strongly interested in preserving the art, but the castle and its contents are destroyed, and all of the soldiers save one killed when they use the castle as a tactical strong point against Germans advancing into "the Bulge."

23. Larry I. Bland, "George C. Marshall and the Education of Army Leaders," Reprint. *Military Review 68* (October 1988): 27–37.

24. Porch, *The Path to Victory*, 106.

25. Vasily Grossman, *Life and Fate*, trans. Robert Chandler (New York: Review Books, 1985), 48.

26. Grossman, *Life and Fate*, 56.

27. *The Armed Forces Officer*, 190–91.

28. Condoleezza Rice, Paret, Ed. "The Making of Soviet Strategy," in *Makers of Modern Strategy*, 657.

29. Grady Scott Davis, *Warcraft and the Fragility of Virtue* (Moscow: University of Idaho Press, 1992).

30. Damon Young, *How to Think About Exercise*. The School of Life Series (New York: Picador), 33.

31. "Vietnam Hero Offers Leadership Lessons."

32. B. C. W. McClean, "Intuition in Modern Command Philosophy," *Military Review* LXXV, no. 5 (September–October 1995): 96–98.

33. Daniel Kahneman, *Thinking, Fast and Slow* (New York: Farrar, Strauss and Giroux, 2011), 238.

34. See Christian Jennings, *Mouthful of Rocks: Modern Adventures in the French Foreign Legion* (New York: Atlantic Monthly Press, 1989), 83. Jennings describes how his battalion, the *2eme Regiment Etranger de Parachutistes* (2nd REP), arguably one of the most highly trained infantry regiments in the world, was organized into companies with specialties in night operations, mountain warfare, amphibious warfare, and sabotage and destruction.

35. Faris R. Kirkland, "Soldiers and Marines at Chosin Reservoir: Criteria for Assignment to Combat Command," *Armed Forces and Society* (Winter 1995/96): 257–72.

36. Yitszhak Benbaji, Amir Falk, and Yuval Feldman, "Commonsense Morality and the Ethics of Killing in War: An Experimental Survey of the Israeli Population." Israel National Science Foundation Grant (676_/09), web, November 13, 2015.

37. Howard Gardner, "Multiple Intelligences Theory," *Encyclopedia of Human Intelligence*, Robert Sternberg, ed. (New York: Macmillan, 1994), 740–42.

38. Some of my discussion of moral prudence that follows first appeared on the website, *The Strategy Bridge*, on 22 September 2017.

39. Arthur D. Kahn, *The Education of Julius Caesar: A Biography, A Reconstruction* (New York: Schocken, 1986), 228, 233.

40. Friedrich Heer, *Charlemagne and His World* (New York: Macmillan, 1975), 151, 154.

41. Alessandro Barbero, *Charlemagne: Father of a Continent*, trans. Allan Cameron (Berkeley: University of California Press, 2004), 123.

42. David Hackett Fischer, *Washington's Crossing* (Oxford: Oxford University Press, 2004), 341.

43. Michael Glover, *Wellington as Military Commander* (1968; London: Penguin, 2001), 234.

44. Ed Cray, *General of the Army: George C. Marshall, Soldier and Statesman* (New York: Cooper Square Press, 1990), 423.

45. Cray, *General of the Army*, 428.

46. Porch, *The Path to Victory*, 488–91.

47. Harry Brown, *A Walk in the Sun* (1944; New York: Carroll & Graf, 1985), 34.

PART II

1. Andrew Gordon, *The Rules of the Game: Jutland and British Naval Command* (Annapolis, MD: Naval Institute Press, 1996), 3.

CHAPTER 5

1. Wilson Heefner, *Dogface Soldier: The Life of General Lucien K. Truscott, Jr.* (Columbia: University of Missouri Press), 1.

2. F. D. Tredey, "Foreword" by Maurice Baring, *Flying Corps Headquarters, 1914–1918*. 1920 (Edinburgh: William Blackwood and Sons, 1968), xvi–xvii.

3. Norman Maclean, *Young Men and Fire* (Chicago: University of Chicago Press, 1992), 219.

4. Dwight D. Eisenhower, *Crusade in Europe* (Garden City, NY: Doubleday, 1949), 314.

5. Oliver Lyman Spaulding, *Pen and Sword in Greece and Rome*. 1936 (Cranbury, NJ: Scholar's Bookshelf, 2006), 12.

6. Hanson, 245.

7. Antulio J. Echevarria II, *Reconsidering the American Way of War: US Military Practice from the Revolution to Afghanistan* (Washington, DC: Georgetown University Press, 2014), 110.

8. In *Thinking Fast and Slow*, Nobel economist and psychologist Daniel Kahneman recalls his experience of officer selection in the Israeli Defense Forces. As a junior officer assigned to improve officer selection, Kahneman found a system that employed a group problem-solving exercise to support assessment of potential officers. This system was very inaccurate in predicting success in officer training or in combat. Kahneman substituted a system of simple questions asked by a trained interviewer. This less subjective method produced better results.

9. *The Armed Forces Officer*. The need to refrain from overconfident, overhasty conclusions about soldiers' potential is a recurring theme in Marshall's book. It is discussed at length in chapter 27, "Fitting Men to Jobs" (246–54). Marshall also makes this point in his discussion of Pvt. Fred Lang, a seemingly unlikely hero of the defense of Bataan (70–71), and of the nineteenth-century Greeley Expedition to the Arctic, during which the hand-picked expedition surgeon proved to be "Among the most fraction and self-centered" (101).

10. See Robert R. Palmer, Bell I. Wiley, and William R. Keast, *The Procurement and Training of Army Ground Troops* (Washington, DC: Historical Division, Department of the Army, 1948), 325–64.

11. This discussion owes a debt to the author's association with the Service Academy Consortium on Character Assessment (SACCA) during 2012–2016. Despite considerable effort and much interesting data, the "holy grail" of a verifiable and operationalizable measure of the impact and effectiveness of a service academy education remained elusive. Still, I agree with those who maintain that the service academies raise the bar of officer intelligence and competence, in part simply because they are so highly selective, and that they also serve as important institutions in preserving the history and ethos of the military profession in America.

12. *The Armed Forces Officer*, 193.

13. See the literature on "Adaptive Leadership" by Ron Heifetz et al. The seminal work in this area is Heifetz's *Leadership without Easy Answers* (Cambridge, MA: Belknap Press of Harvard University Press, 1994). See also my "Adaptive Leadership and the Warfighter," *The Strategy Bridge*, Online. January 24, 2018.

14. See Christopher D. Miller, "Creating the Force of the Future," interview with Brad R. Carson, Acting Principal Deputy Undersecretary of Defense (Personnel and Readiness), *Journal of Character and Leadership Integration* 3, no. 2 (Winter 2016), Special Edition, *Leading in the Profession of Arms*. Carson laments the small and

diminishing number of senior officers with advanced degrees in areas like literature and military history. See also Lieutenant General Peter Chiarelli and Major Stephen Smith, USA, "Learning from Our Modern Wars: The Imperatives of Preparing for a Dangerous Future," *Military Review*, September/October 2007, 2–15. Chiarelli observes that, despite his numerous "muddy boots" assignments, "the experience that best prepared me for division and corps command in Iraq was the 5 years I spent earning a master's degree and teaching in the Social Sciences Department at the U.S. Military Academy."

15. Braender et al., "What Sets the Officer Apart?"

16. McCain Conference, Annapolis, MD, US Naval Academy, April 21–22, 2016.

17. Matthew B. Ridgway, *Soldier: The Memoirs of Matthew B. Ridgway* (New York: Harper, 1956), 125–26.

18. Dennis Drew and Don Snow, "Military Doctrine," in *Making Strategy: An Introduction to National Security Processes and Problems* (Maxwell Air Force Base, AL: Air University Press, 1988), 163–74.

19. Mark Ethan Grotelueschen, *The AEF Way of War: The American Army in Combat in World War I* (Cambridge: Cambridge University Press, 2007).

20. Charles Carrington, *Soldier from the Wars Returning* (New York: David McKay, 1965), 248.

21. Harold R. Winton, *Corps Commander of the Bulge: Six American Generals and Victory in the Ardennes* (Lawrence: University Press of Kansas, 2007), 88, 92.

22. *The Armed Forces Officer*, 190.

23. Jennings, *Mouthful of Rocks*, 108.

24. See, for example, *Tales of Manhattan* (Boston: Houghton Mifflin, 1964). The short story, "Foster Evans on Lewis Bovee," contains the following passage. "But in 1921, when I started to practice law, it was not so ridiculous for a man to put all his heart as well as his mind into his profession. If the sacrifices were great, the rewards could be sweet. . . . Who knows the bond of partnership who has not labored with peers whom he absolutely trusted? . . . the office and the courtroom were laboratories where we could surrender ourselves wholly to the excitement of intellectual combat" (148–49).

CHAPTER 6

1. "Mental Models," *Farnum Street* blog.

2. Hajo Holborn, Paret, ed. *Makers of Modern Strategy*. "The Prusso-German School: Moltke and the Rise of the General Staff," 291.

3. See, for example, Dale C. Eikmeier, "Center of Gravity Analysis," *Military Review*, July/August 2004, 2–5.

4. *The Armed Forces Officer*, 169.

5. B. A. Friedman, *Tactics: A Theory of Victory in Battle* (Annapolis, MD: Naval Institute Press, 2017).

6. For an illustration of the former, see Ricks, *The Generals*, 347, of the latter, see Murray, *War Games*, 273.

7. "Mental Models," *Farnum Street* blog.

8. Brown, "John Boyd on Clausewitz: Don't Fall in Love with Your Mental Model."

9. See especially S. L. A. Marshall, *Men against Fire: The Problem of Battle Command in Future Wars* (Alexandria, VA: Byrrd Enterprises, 1947).

10. This phrase appears in several sources, and it appears to have been said by Mattis in many addresses to troops in the field. My own sometimes-repeated advice was less belligerent but still helpful, I hope. It was to keep your head on a swivel, wear your protective gear, and remember that some (expletive deleted) on your own side can kill you as dead as can one of the enemy.

11. Porch, *The Path to Victory*, 489–512.

12. See Stephen R. Taafe, *Marshall and His Generals: U.S. Army Commanders in World War II* (Lawrence: University Press of Kansas, 2011).

13. Slim's sergeant major's words are nearly echoed by David Hackworth, a distinguished combat leader in Korea and Vietnam. In *Steel My Soldiers' Hearts: The Hopeless to Hardcore Transformation of 4th Battalion, 39th Infantry, United States Army, Vietnam* (New York: Touchstone-Simon & Schuster, 2003), Hackworth writes, "(T)he bare-bones bottom line to winning battles is simply to sneak up on your opponent and belt the shit out of him from behind as hard and quickly as you can before he figures out you're in the neighborhood—and then beat it the hell out of there" (424).

14. Hackworth, *Steel My Soldiers' Hearts*, 424.

15. Winton, 152–53.

16. Hackworth, *Steel My Soldiers' Hearts*, 374–75.

17. See Kahneman, *Thinking, Fast and Slow*.

18. Porch, *The Path to Victory*, 142.

19. Winton, 338–39.

20. Daniel J. Hughes, ed. *Moltke on the Art of War: Selected Writings* (Novato, CA: Presidio Press, 1993), 125.

21. Carl Von Clausewitz, *On War*, ed. and trans. Michael Howard and Peter Paret (Princeton, NJ: Princeton University Press, 1984), 566–73.

22. Corelli Barnett, *Leadership in War: From Lincoln to Churchill* (Annapolis, MD: Naval Institute Press, 2014), 215.

23. Eisenhower, *Crusade in Europe*, 225.

24. For discussions of the preparation and performance of US Army officers at the corps and higher levels of command, see Taafe and Winton, cited above.

25. Gilles Deleuze and Félix Guattari, *Nomadology: The War Machine*, trans. Brian Massumi (New York: Semiotext(e), 1986).

26. Richard D. Hooker and Joseph J. Collins, eds., *Lessons Encountered: Learning from the Long War* (Washington, DC: National Defense University Press, 2015), 168–69.

CHAPTER 7

1. Richard E. Neustadt and Ernest R. May, *Thinking in Time: The Uses of History for Decision Makers* (New York: Simon & Schuster-Free Press, 1988).

2. Howard, "The Use and Abuse of Military History," 10.

3. Howard, "The Use and Abuse of Military History," 10.

4. Reviewed in *Times Literary Supplement*, October 7, 2016, 10–11.

5. See Mick Ryan and Nathan K. Finney, "Science Fiction and the Strategist: A Reading List," *The Strategy Bridge*. Online, February 6, 2017. The authors list several reasons why officers ought to read science fiction: hope, dire warnings, enhancing the imagination, and appreciating the enduring nature of war among them.

6. Judith Barad, "The Aspiring Jedi's Handbook of Virtue," in *Star Wars and Philosophy: More Powerful Than You Can Possibly Imagine*, Kevin S. Decker and Jason T. Eberl, eds. (Chicago: Open Court, 2005), 57–68.

7. J. Glenn Gray, *The Warriors: Reflections on Men in Battle* (1959; New York: HarperCollins, 1967), 48–49.

8. James Boswell, *Life of Samuel Johnson, LL.D.* vol. 2 (1791; London: J. Davis, 1817), 627.

9. Richard Holmes, *Acts of War: The Behavior of Men in Battle* (1985; New York: Free Press, 1986), 1–6.

10. Colin Grant, "States of Grace, Powell and Pressburger's Transport to Another World," *The Times Literary Supplement*, January 5, 2018, 21.

11. Ray Monk, *Ludwig Wittgenstein: The Duty of Genius* (New York: The Free Press, 1990), 140.

12. Norman Malcolm, *Ludwig Wittgenstein: A Memoir* (London: Oxford University Press, 1958), 41.

13. See Ron Chernow, *Grant* (New York: Penguin, 2017) and Jean Edward Smith.

14. Martin Cook, "The Revolt of the Generals: A Case Study in Professional Ethics," International Society for Military Ethics. Online archives.

15. For the phrase "doctrinal delivery of ordnance," and an argument against the narrow-scope perspective on officership, see Celestino Perez Jr. "Strategic Discontent, Political Literacy and Professional Military Education," *The Strategy Bridge* website, January 14, 2016.

16. This argument has been made by Anthony Hartle, cited earlier, and it may also be found in George M. Clifford III, "Duty at All Costs," *Naval War College Review* 60, no. 1 (Winter 2007): 103–28.

17. Clifford.

18. Jean Edward Smith, ix.

19. John W. Thomason, *Fix Bayonets!* (New York: Scribner's, 1926), xiv.

20. Sissela Bok, *A Strategy for Peace: Human Values and the Threat of War* (New York: Vintage-Random House, 1990), 55–78.

21. "A New Kind of Dream: Freud, Trauma, and WWI. A Look at War and Artistic Creation Through the Theories of Cathy Caruth and Sigmund Freud," *United States World War I Centennial Commission*. Online. October 29, 2018.

22. See Donald Vandergriff and Stephen Webber, *Mission Command: The Who, What, When, Where, and Why. An Anthology* (Columbia, SC: CreateSpace, 2017).

23. Rosa Brooks, *How Everything Became War and the Military Became Everything: Tales from the Pentagon* (New York: Simon & Schuster, 2016), 352. The author is here quoting Nora Bensahel and Lieutenant General David Barno.

24. Jim Golby, "Improving Advice and Earning Autonomy: Building Trust in the Strategic Dialogue," *The Strategy Bridge* website, October 3, 2017.

25. See, for example, Tim Kane, *Bleeding Talent: How the US Military Mismanages Great Leaders and Why It's Time for a Revolution* (New York: Palgrave-Macmillan, 2012).

CONCLUSION

1. Phil Klay, "After War, a Failure of the Imagination," *New York Times*, February 8, 2014.

Bibliography

Aristotle. *The Ethics of Aristotle: The Nicomachean Ethics.* J. A. K. Thomson, trans. 1953. London: Penguin, 1976.

———. "Aristotle's Poetics." *Aristotle's Theory of Poetry and Fine Art.* S. H. Butcher, trans. 1911. New York: Dover, 1951.

Auchincloss, Louis. "Foster Evans on Lewis Bovee." In *Tales of Manhattan.* Boston: Houghton Mifflin, 1964.

Austen, Jane. *Pride and Prejudice.* London: Thomas Egerton, 1813.

Barad, Judith. "The Aspiring Jedi's Handbook of Virtue." In *Star Wars and Philosophy: More Powerful Than You Can Possibly Imagine,* Kevin S. Decker and Jason T. Eberl, eds., 57–68. Chicago: Open Court, 2005.

Barbero, Alessandro. *Charlemagne: Father of a Continent.* Allan Cameron, trans. Berkeley: University of California Press, 2004.

Barnett, Correlli. *The Desert Generals.* 1960. New York: Viking-Ballantine, 1972.

———. *The Leaders of War: From Lincoln to Churchill.* Barnsley, UK; Praetorian-Pen and Sword, 2014. (Published in the US as *Leadership in War: From Lincoln to Churchill.*)

Bellinger, Vanya Eftimova. *Marie Von Clausewitz: The Woman behind the Making of* On War. Oxford: Oxford University Press, 2016.

Benbaji, Yitszhak, Amir Falk, and Yuval Feldman. "Commonsense Morality and the Ethics of Killing in War: An Experimental Survey of the Israeli Population." Israel National Science Foundation Grant (676_/09), Web, November 13, 2015.

Blackett, P. M. S. "Operational Research." In *Studies of War,* 169–239. New York: Hill and Wang, 1962.

Bland, Larry I., ed. *George C. Marshall Interviews and Reminiscences for Forrest C. Pogue.* Lexington, VA: George C. Marshall Research Foundation, 1991.

Bloom, Harold. *Shakespeare: The Invention of the Human.* New York: Fourth Estate, 2008.

Boger, Daniel. *Why We Lost: A General's Inside Account of the Iraq and Afghanistan Wars.* New York: Houghton Mifflin Harcourt, 2015.

Bok, Sissela. *A Strategy for Peace: Human Values and the Threat of War.* New York: Vintage-Random House, 1990.

Bonadonna, Reed Robert. "Adaptive Leadership and the Warfighter." *The Strategy Bridge*, Online. 24 January 2018.

———. "Review of *English Mercuries: Soldier Poets in the Age of Shakespeare* by Adam N. McKeown." *Journal of Military Ethics* 11, no. 1 (March 2012).

———. "How to Think Like an Officer: A Prospectus." *War on the Rocks*, Online, September 11, 2018.

———. "Military Command as Moral Prudence." *The Strategy Bridge*, Online. September 22, 2017.

———. "Military Command as Moral Prudence: Examples from History and Literature." *The Strategy Bridge*, Online. November 28, 2017.

———. *Soldiers and Civilization: How the Profession of Arms Thought and Fought the Modern World into Existence.* Annapolis, MD: Naval Institute Press, 2017.

Boswell, James. *Life of Samuel Johnson, LL.D.* 1791. Vol. 2. London: J. Davis, 1817.

Bouthoul, Gaston. *War.* 1953. Silvia and George Lesson, trans. New York: Walker and Company, 1962.

Braender, Morton, Marenne Jansen, and René Moelker. "What Sets the Officer Apart?" *Academia*, Online. Accessed Sept. 19, 2018.

Brooks, Rosa. *How Everything Became War and the Military Became Everything: Tales from the Pentagon.* New York: Simon & Schuster, 2016.

Brown, Harry. *A Walk in the Sun.* 1944. New York: Carroll & Graf, 1985.

Brown, Ian T. "John Boyd on Clausewitz: Don't Fall in Love with Your Mental Model." *The Strategy Bridge*, online, March 22, 2018.

Bunting, Josiah. "The Humanities in the Education of the Military Professional." In *The System for Educating Military Officers in the U.S.*, Lawrence J. Korb, ed. Pittsburgh, PA: International Studies, 1976.

Cancian, Matthew F. "Officers Are Less Intelligent: What Does It Mean?" *Joint Forces Quarterly 81 (JFQ81)*, (2nd Quarter 2016): 14.

Caputo, Philip. *A Rumor of War.* New York: Holt, Rinehart, and Winston, 1977.

Carrington, Charles. *Soldier from the Wars Returning.* New York: David McKay, 1965.

Caruth, Cathy. "A New Kind of Dream: Freud, Trauma, and WWI. A Look at War and Artistic Creation through the Theories of Cathy Caruth and Sigmund Freud." *United States World War I Centennial Commission.* Online, October 29, 2018.

Cates, Sam E. A. "Why Was General Richard O'Connor's Command in Northwest Europe Less Effective Than Expected?" Fort Leavenworth, KS: School of Advanced Warfighting, US Army Command and General Staff College, 2011.

Cavell, Stanley. *This New Yet Unapproachable America: Lectures after Emerson after Wittgenstein.* Albuquerque, NM: Living Batch Press, 1989.

Challans, Timothy L. *Awakening Warrior: Revolution in the Ethics of Warfare.* SUNY Series, Ethics and the Military Profession, George R. Lucas Jr., ed. Albany: State University of New York Press, 2007.

Chernow, Ron. *Grant.* New York: Penguin, 2017.

Chiarelli, Peter, and Stephen Smith. "Learning from Our Modern Wars: The Imperatives of Preparing for a Dangerous Future." *Military Review* (September–October 2007): 2–15.

Chivers, C. J. *The Fighters: Americans in Combat in Afghanistan and Iraq.* New York: Simon & Schuster, 2018.

Choquette, Richard. "Bridging the Gap." *Marine Corps Gazette* Online. 92, no. 7 (2008).

Clausewitz, Carl Von. *On War.* Edited and translated by Michael Howard and Peter Paret. Princeton, NJ: Princeton University Press, 1984.

Clifford III, George M. "Duty at All Costs." *Naval War College Review* 60, no. 1 (Winter 2007): 103–28.

Coffman, Edward M. *The Regulars: The American Army 1898–1941.* Cambridge, MA: Belknap Press of Harvard University Press, 2004.

Collins, General J. Lawton. *Lightning Joe: An Autobiography.* 1979. Novato, CA: Presidio Press, 1994.

Cook, Martin. "The Revolt of the Generals: A Case Study in Professional Ethics." *International Society for Military Ethics.* Online archives, 2008.

Cooper, Duff. *Sergeant Shakespeare.* London: Rupert Hart-Davis, 1949.

Cormier, Youri. *War as Paradox: Clausewitz and Hegel on Fighting Doctrines and Ethics.* Kingston, Ontario, Canada: McGill-Queen's University Press, 2016.

Cox, Edward. *Grey Eminence: Fox Conner and the Art of Mentorship.* Stillwater, OK: New Forums Press, 2011.

Cray, Ed. *General of the Army: George C. Marshall, Soldier and Statesman.* New York: Cooper Square Press, 1990.

Davis, Grady Scott. *Warcraft and the Fragility of Virtue.* Moscow: University of Idaho Press, 1992.

Deleuze, Gilles, and Félix Guattari. *Nomadology: The War Machine.* Brian Massumi, trans. New York: Semiotext(e), 1986.

Dixon, Norman. *On the Psychology of Military Incompetence.* 1976. New York: Basic Books, 2016.

Drew, Dennis, and Don Snow. "Military Doctrine." In *Making Strategy: An Introduction to National Security Processes and Problems,* 165–74. Maxwell Air Force Base, AL: Air University Press, 1988.

Eagleton, Terry. "Review of *On the Origin of Stories: Evolution, Cognition, Fiction* by Brian Boyd in *London Review of Books,*" 31 (18). Posted summary on blog *Poiesis and Prolepsis* by Allan Parsons, October 13, 2009.

Echevarria II, Antulio J. *Reconsidering the American Way of War: US Military Practice from the Revolution to Afghanistan.* Washington, DC: Georgetown University Press, 2014.

Eikmeier, Dale C. "Center of Gravity Analysis." *Military Review* (July–August 2004): 2–5.

Eisenhower, Dwight D. *Crusade in Europe.* Garden City, NY: Doubleday, 1949.

Fallows, James. "The Tragedy of the American Military." *The Atlantic,* Online (January–February 2015).

Farnum Street. "Mental Models: The Best Way to Make Intelligent Decisions (113 Models Explained)." Accessed online February 12, 2018.

Fischer, David Hackett. *Washington's Crossing.* Oxford: Oxford University Press, 2004.

Friedman, B. A. *Tactics: A Theory of Victory in Battle.* Annapolis, MD: Naval Institute Press, 2017.

Fussell, Paul, *Doing Battle: The Making of a Skeptic.* Boston: Little, Brown, 1996.

Fussell, Paul. *The Great War and Modern Memory*. New York: Oxford University Press, 1975.

Garard, Olivia. "*Modelez-vous*: Deriving Frameworks from History." *The Strategy Bridge*. Online. June 6, 2017.

Gardner, Howard. *Leading Minds: An Anatomy of Leadership*. New York: HarperCollins-Basic Books, 1995.

———. "Multiple Intelligences Theory." In *Encyclopedia of Human Intelligence*, Robert Sternberg, ed., 740–42. New York: Macmillan, 1994.

Gat, Azar. *A History of Military Thought*. Oxford: Oxford University Press, 2001.

Gelb, Leslie and Richard Betts. *The Irony of Vietnam: The System Worked*. Washington, DC: Brookings Institution, 2016.

Glatthaar, Joseph T. *Partners in Command: The Relationship between Leaders in the Civil War*. New York: The Free Press-Macmillan, 1994.

Glover, Michael. *Wellington as Military Commander*. 1968. London: Penguin, 2001.

Golby, Jim. "Improving Advice and Earning Autonomy: Building Trust in the Strategic Dialogue." *The Strategy Bridge*, Online. October 3, 2017.

Gordon, Andrew. *The Rules of the Game: Jutland and British Naval Command*. Annapolis, MD: Naval Institute Press, 1996.

Grant, Colin. "States of Grace, Powell and Pressburger's Transport to Another World." *The Times Literary Supplement* (January 5, 2018): 21.

Grant, Ulysses S. *Personal Memoirs of U. S. Grant*. 1885–86. New York: Library of America, 1990.

Graves, Robert. *Good-bye to All That: An Autobiography*. London: Penguin Books, 2014.

Gray, J. Glenn. *The Warriors: Reflections on Men in Battle*. 1959. New York: Harper-Collins, 1967.

Groopman, Jerome, *How Doctors Think*. Boston: Houghton-Mifflin, 2007.

Grossman, Vasily. *Life and Fate*. Robert Chandler, trans. New York: New York Review Books, 1985.

Grotelueschen, Mark Ethan. *The AEF Way of War: The American Army in Combat in World War I*. Cambridge: Cambridge University Press, 2007.

Grovier, Kelly. "Rime without Reason." Review of *Mariner: A Voyage with Samuel Taylor Coleridge*. (Hodder and Stoughton), *Times Literary Supplement*, April 28, 2017, 29.

Hackworth, David. *About Face: The Odyssey of an American Warrior*. New York: Touchstone-Simon & Schuster, 1989.

———. *Steel My Soldiers' Hearts: The Hopeless to Hardcore Transformation of 4th Battalion, 39th Infantry, United States Army, Vietnam*. New York: Touchstone-Simon & Schuster, 2003.

Hanson, Victor Davis. *Carnage and Culture: Landmark Battles in the Rise of Western Power*. New York: Random House/Anchor, 2002.

Hartle, Anthony. *Moral Issues in Military Decision Making*. Lawrence: University Press of Kansas, 1989.

Heefner, Wilson. *Dogface Soldier: The Life of General Lucien K. Truscott, Jr*. Columbia: University of Missouri Press, 2010.

Heer, Friedrich. *Charlemagne and His World*. New York: Macmillan, 1975.

Heifetz, Ronald A. *Leadership without Easy Answers*. Cambridge, MA: Belknap-Harvard University Press, 1994.

Holborn, Hajo. "The Prusso-German School: Moltke and the Rise of the General Staff." In *Makers of Modern Strategy from Machiavelli to the Nuclear Age*, Peter Paret, ed., 291. Princeton, NJ: Princeton University Press, 1986.

Holmes, Richard. *Acts of War: The Behavior of Men in Battle*. 1985. New York: Free Press-Macmillan, 1986.

———. *The Little Field Marshall: A Life of Sir John French*. London: Weidenfeld and Nicolson, 2004.

Hooker, Richard D., and Joseph J. Collins, eds. *Lessons Encountered: Learning from the Long War*. Washington, DC: National Defense University Press, 2015.

Hope, Ian C. *A Scientific Way of War: Antebellum Military Science, West Point, and the Origins of American Military Thought*. Lincoln: University Nebraska Press, 2015.

Hopkins, Gerard Manley. "Pied Beauty." In *Poems and Prose of Gerard Manley Hopkins*, Selected with Introduction and Notes by W. H. Gardner, 130. 1953. Harmondsworth, Middlesex, UK: Penguin, 1984.

Howard, Michael. "The Use and Abuse of Military History," Reprint. *Parameters* 11, no. 1: 10–14 (2008).

———. "Men against Fire: The Doctrine of the Offensive in 1914." In *Makers of Modern Strategy from Machiavelli to the Nuclear Age*, Peter Paret, ed., 510–26. Princeton, NJ: Princeton University Press, 1986.

Hughes, Daniel J., ed. *Moltke on the Art of War: Selected Writings*. Novato, CA, Presidio Press, 1993.

Huntington, Samuel P. *The Soldier and the State: The Theory and Politics of Civil-Military Relations*. Cambridge, MA: Belknap Press, 1957.

Huxley, Aldous. *Ape and Essence*. 1948. Chicago: Ivan R. Dee, 1992.

Jacobsen, Annie. *The Pentagon's Brain: An Uncensored History of DARPA, America's Top-Secret Military Research Agency*. New York: Little, Brown and Company, 2015.

Janowitz, Morris. *The Professional Soldier: A Social and Political Portrait*. Glencoe, IL: Free Press, 1960.

Jennings, Christian. *Mouthful of Rocks: Modern Adventures in the French Foreign Legion*. New York: Atlantic Monthly Press, 1989.

Just, Ward. "Introduction." In *About Face: The Odyssey of an American Warrior*, David Hackworth and Julie Sherman, eds., 13. New York: Touchstone-Simon & Schuster, 1989.

Kahn, Arthur D. *The Education of Julius Caesar: A Biography, A Reconstruction*. New York: Schocken, 1986.

Kahneman, Daniel. *Thinking Fast and Slow*. New York: Farrar, Strauss, and Giroux, 2011.

Kane, Tim. *Bleeding Talent: How the US Military Mismanages Great Leaders and Why It's Time for a Revolution*. New York: Palgrave-Macmillan, 2012.

Kaplan, Robert D. "The Humanist in the Foxhole." *New York Times*, Online. June 14, 2011.

Kegan, Robert, and Lisa Laskow Lahey. *Immunity to Change: How to Overcome It and Unlock the Potential in Yourself and Your Organization*. Boston, MA: Harvard Business Review Press, 2009.

Kilcullen, David. *Blood Year: The Unraveling of Western Counterterrorism.* New York: Oxford, 2016.

Kirkland, Faris R. "Soldiers and Marines at Chosin Reservoir: Criteria for Assignment to Combat Command." *Armed Forces and Society* (Winter 1995/96): 257–72.

Klay, Phil. "After War, a Failure of the Imagination." *New York Times*, February 8, 2014.

Kupperman, Joel. *Character.* New York: Oxford University Press, 1991.

Limon, John. *Writing after War: American War Fiction from Realism to Postmodernism.* New York: Oxford University Press, 1994.

Lund, Erik. *War for the Every Day: Generals, Knowledge, and Warfare in Early Modern Europe, 1680–1740.* New York: Greenwood, 1999.

Maclean, Norman. *Young Men and Fire.* Chicago: University of Chicago Press, 1992.

Maguen, Shira, and Brett Litz. "Moral Injury in Veterans of War." *Research Quarterly* 23, no. 1 (2012).

Malcolm, Norman. *Ludwig Wittgenstein: A Memoir.* London: Oxford University Press, 1958.

Marlantes, Karl. *Matterhorn: A Novel of the Vietnam War.* Berkeley, CA: El Leon Literary Arts/Grove, 2010.

Marshall, George C. *Memoirs of My Services in the World War 1917–1918.* Boston: Houghton Mifflin, 1976.

Marshall, S. L. A. *The Armed Forces Officer.* Washington, DC: Department of Defense, 1950/1975.

Marshall, S. L. A. *Men against Fire: The Problem of Battle Command in Future Wars.* Alexandria, VA: Byrrd Enterprises, 1947.

Masson, David. *The Collected Writings of Thomas DeQuincey.* New and Enlarged Edition. Vol. 13, *Tales and Prose Fantasies.* Edinburgh: Adam and Charles Black, 1890.

McCain Conference. U.S. Naval Academy, Annapolis, MD. April 21–22, 2016.

McClean, B. C. W. "Intuition in Modern Command Philosophy." *Military Review.* Reprint. September–October 1995.

McDonough, James R. *The Defense of Hill 781: An Allegory of Modern Mechanized Combat.* New York: Presidio-Ballantine, 1988.

McKeown, Adam N. *English Mercuries: Soldier-Poets in the Age of Shakespeare.* Nashville, TN: Vanderbilt University Press, 2009.

McMaster, H. R. *Dereliction of Duty: Lyndon Johnson, Robert McNamara, the Joint Chiefs of Staff, and the Lies that Led to Vietnam.* New York: HarperPerennial, 1997.

Meredith, William. "Reading My Poems from World War II." 1970. Poetry Foundation Online. Accessed May 18, 2017.

Miller, Christopher D. "Creating the Force of the Future." Interview with Brad R. Carson, Acting Principal Deputy Undersecretary of Defense (Personnel and Readiness). *Journal of Character and Leadership Integration* 3, no. 2 (Winter 2016); Special Edition, *Leading in the Profession of Arms.*

Monk, Ray. *Ludwig Wittgenstein: The Duty of Genius.* New York: Macmillan-The Free Press, 1990.

Moore, Hal. "Vietnam Hero Offers Leadership Lessons," *American Profile*, Online, May 24, 2011.

Moore, Thomas. "The Minstrel Boy." circa 1798.

Moran, Lord. *The Anatomy of Courage*. 1945. Garden City, NY: Avery, 1978.

Morehead, Alan. *Gallipoli*. New York: Ballantine, 1956.

Murray, Leo. *War Games: The Psychology of Combat* (2013 as *Brains and Bullets*). London: Biteback, 2018.

Murrin, Michael. *History and Warfare in Renaissance Epic*. Chicago: University of Chicago Press, 1994.

Myrer, Anton. *Once an Eagle*. 1968. New York: HarperTorch-HarperCollins, 2001.

Neustadt, Richard E., and Ernest R. May. *Thinking in Time: The Uses of History for Decision Makers*. New York: Simon & Schuster-Free Press, 1988.

Nussbaum, Martha. *Love's Knowledge, Essays on Philosophy and Literature*. New York: Oxford University Press, 1990.

Nye, Roger H. *The Patton Mind: The Professional Development of an Extraordinary Leader*. Garden City, NY: Avery, 1993.

"Officership." *Oxford English Dictionary*, Online. Attributed to Captain Massey Shaw of London Fire Brigade.

Orwell, George. "Looking Back on the Spanish War," 1943. In *A Collection of Essays by George Orwell*, 194. Garden City, NY: Anchor-Doubleday, 1954.

Palmer, Robert R., Bell I. Wiley, and William R. Keast. *The Procurement and Training of Army Ground Troops*. Washington, DC: Historical Division, Department of the Army, 1948.

Perez, Jr, Celestino. "Strategic Discontent, Political Literacy and Professional Military Education." *The Strategy Bridge*, Online. January 14, 2016.

———. "What Military Education Forgets: Strategy Is Performance," *War on the Rocks*, Online. September 7, 2018.

Picq, Ardant Du. *Battle Studies: Ancient and Modern Battle*. 1880. John Greeley and Robert C. Cotton, trans. New York: Macmillan, 1921, 139.

Pois, Robert and Philip Langer. *Command Failure in War : Psychology and Leadership*. Bloomington: Indiana University Press, 2004.

Porch, Douglas. *The Path to Victory: The Mediterranean Theater in World War II*. Old Saybrook, CT: Konecky and Konecky, 2004.

Proust, Marcel. *Remembrance of Things Past*. 1924, C. K. Scott Moncrieff, trans. New York: Random House, 1934.

Reichberg, Gregory M. "Remarks at McCain Conference." U.S. Naval Academy, Annapolis, MD, April 17, 2015.

———. "Thomas Aquinas on Military Prudence." *Journal of Military Ethics* 9, no. 3 (2010): 262–75.

———. *Thomas Aquinas on War and Peace*. Cambridge: Cambridge University Press, 2017.

Reid, Brian Holden. "Commanding Heights." Review of *The Lords of War, From Lincoln to Churchill, Supreme Command, 1861–1945* by Correlli Barnett. *Times Literary Supplement*, September 27, 2013, 28.

Rennie, Mike. "An Officer and a 'Reflective' Problem Solver: Further Development of Problem Solving and Thinking Skills in Officer Cadets at Sandhurst and Beyond." Sandhurst Occasional Papers No. 15. Royal Military Academy Sandhurst: Central Library, 2013.

Rice, Condoleezza. "The Making of Soviet Strategy." In *Makers of Modern Strategy*, Peter Paret, ed., 657. Princeton, NJ: Princeton University Press, 1986.

Ricks, Thomas E. *The Generals: American Military Command from World War II to Today.* New York: Penguin, 2012.

Riper, Paul K. Van. "The Importance of History to the Military Profession: An American Marine's View." In *The Past as Prologue: The Importance of History to the Military Profession*, Williamson Murray and Richard Hart Sinnreich, eds., 34–54. Cambridge: Cambridge University Press, 2006.

Roberts, Michael. "The Military Revolution, 1560–1660." In *The Military Revolution Debate: Readings in the Military Transformation of Early Modern Europe*, Clifford J. Rogers, ed., 13–36. Boulder, CO: Westview Press, 1995.

Rose, Jonathan. *The Literary Churchill: Author, Reader, Actor.* New Haven, CT: Yale University Press, 2013.

Ryan, Mick, and Nathan K. Finney. "Science Fiction and the Strategist: A Reading List." *The Strategy Bridge.* Online. February 6, 2017.

Sacks, Oliver. "Neurologist Oliver Sacks." Interview with Terry Gross, *Fresh Air*, October 1, 1987. In *Oliver Sacks: The Last Interview and Other Conversations*, 11. Brooklyn, NY: Melville House, 2016.

Santayana, George. *The Life of Reason; or The Phases of Human Progress.* New York: Charles Scribner's Sons, 1905.

Shanks-Kaurin, Pauline. "Questioning Military Professionalism" In *Redefining the Modern Military: The Intersection of Profession and Ethics*, Nathan K. Finney and Tyrell O. Mayfield, eds., 13–14. Annapolis, MD: Naval Institute Press, 2018.

Shattuck, Roger. *Forbidden Knowledge: From Prometheus to Pornography.* New York: St. Martin's Press, 1996.

Sherman, Nancy. *Stoic Warriors: The Ancient Philosophy behind the Military Mind.* Oxford: Oxford University Press, 2005.

Slim, William. *Defeat into Victory: Battling Japan in Burma and India, 1942–1945.* London: Cassell, 1962.

Smith, Jean Edward. *Eisenhower in War and Peace.* New York: Random House, 2012.

Smith, Rupert. "After Smart Weapons, Smart Soldiers." *The Economist*, October 2, 2007.

———. "Brains, Not Bullets." *The Economist*, October 2, 2007.

———. Interview with Joanne Myers on his book *The Utility of Force: The Art of War in the Modern World*. London: Penguin-Allen Lane, 2005. Carnegie Council for Ethics in International Affairs, New York City, January 24, 2007.

Spaulding, Oliver Lyman. *Pen and Sword in Greece and Rome.* 1936. Cranbury, NJ: Scholar's Bookshelf, 2011.

Stanislavski, Constantin. *Building a Character.* Elizabeth Reynolds Hapgood, trans. 1950. London: Methuen, 1968.

Stavridis, James, and R. Manning Ancell. *The Leader's Bookshelf.* Annapolis, MD: Naval Institute Press, 2017.

Steele, Brett D., and Tamara Dorland, eds. "Introduction." In *The Heirs of Archimedes: Science and the Art of War through the Age of Enlightenment*, 1–33. Cambridge: Massachusetts Institute of Technology Press, 2005.

Strachan, Hew. *European Armies and the Conduct of War*. 1983. London: Routledge, 2002.

Taafe, Stephen R. *Marshall and His Generals: U.S. Army Commanders in World War II*. Lawrence: University Press of Kansas, 2011.

———. YouTube video. Lexington, VA: George C. Marshall Foundation, July 28, 2017.

Taylor, Gordon Rattray. *A Natural History of the Mind*. 1979. Harmondsworth, Middlesex, UK: Penguin, 1981.

Thomason, John. W. *Fix Bayonets!* New York: Scribner's, 1926.

US Department of Defense. *The Armed Forces Officer*. Washington, DC: Department of Defense, 1950.

Vandergriff, Donald, and Stephen Webber. *Mission Command: The Who, What, When, Where, and Why. An Anthology*. Columbia, SC: CreateSpace, 2017.

Virgil. *The Aeneid*. W. F. Jackson Knight, trans. London: Penguin, 1956.

Voelze, Glenn. "Is Military Science 'Scientific'?" *Joint Forces Quarterly* 75 (4th Quarter 2014): 84–90.

Warren, Mame. "The Whole Man." *Marshall*, Fall 2015.

Webb, Stephen Saunders. *Marlborough's America*. New Haven, CT: Yale University Press, 2013.

White, Ronald C. *American Ulysses: A Life of Ulysses S. Grant*. New York: Random House, 2016.

Williams, Thomas M. "Education for Critical Thinking." *Military Review* (January–February 2013): 49–54.

Wilson, Rose Page. *General Marshall Remembered*. Englewood Cliffs, NJ: Prentice-Hall, 1968.

Winton, Harold R. *Corps Commander of the Bulge: Six American Generals and Victory in the Ardennes*. Lawrence: University Press of Kansas, 2007.

Young, Damon. *The Art of Reading*. Melbourne: Scribe, 2017.

———. *How to Think about Exercise*. The School of Life Series. New York: Picador, 2015.

Index